THE AXIS ALLIANCE AND
JAPANESE-AMERICAN RELATIONS
1941

This book was originally published under the direction of the American Historical Association from the income of the Albert J. Beveridge Memorial Fund.

For their zeal and beneficence in creating this fund the Association is indebted to many citizens of Indiana who desired to honor in this way the memory of a statesman and a historian.

The Axis Alliance and
Japanese-American Relations
1941

BY PAUL W. SCHROEDER

PUBLISHED FOR THE

American Historical Association

CORNELL UNIVERSITY PRESS

ITHACA AND LONDON

CORNELL UNIVERSITY PRESS

First published 1958
Second printing 1961
Third printing 1963
Fourth printing 1971

International Standard Book Number 0-8014-0371-5
PRINTED IN THE UNITED STATES OF AMERICA

Preface

THIS book is not an attempt to redo the research and writing of such scholars as Herbert Feis, William L. Langer and S. Everett Gleason, and F. C. Jones on the origins of the war in the Pacific. I am in fact deeply indebted to their work. It is rather an attempt to concentrate particularly on one aspect of the Japanese-American negotiations preceding the outbreak of the war—the role played by the Tripartite Alliance between Germany, Japan, and Italy—and, by delineating this, to point to an interpretation of the course of the negotiations somewhat different from the one currently prevailing. It is, therefore, more a work of analysis and interpretation than of narrative.

I have believed it important to show the Tripartite Pact in a broad light, as part of the general diplomatic and political developments of the times. For this reason, it is considered first as it figures in the story of Japanese-American relations; then as it fits into the history of Japanese-German relations from 1936 to 1941; and finally as the Pact was seen by the outside world, especially by the American leaders and public. Since public opinion on the Pact and on Japan in general proved so important in the formulation and development of American policy, I have included a discussion of American public opinion in my interpretation and appraisal of that policy.

Fortunately for scholars, there is now a large body of documentary materials available on the subjects treated. I have depended chiefly on these for my research, with some attention also to the considerable and growing body of literature. Although I have tried to cover the essential sources, I am aware that there is still much that could be done, particularly in the area of manuscript materials, and lay no claim to an exhaustive study.

Permission granted by the following publishers for the use of direct quotations from their works is gratefully acknowledged: Harper and Brothers, for quotations from William L. Langer and S. Everett Gleason, *The Undeclared War, 1940–1941;* Houghton Mifflin Company, for quotations from Joseph C. Grew, *Turbulent Era;* the Oxford University Press, for quotations from F. C. Jones, *Japan's New Order in East Asia: Its Rise and Fall, 1937–1945;* Nation Associates, for quotations from the *Nation;* and New Republic, for quotations from the *New Republic.*

I would like to express my thanks to all those who have helped and encouraged me in this project and to acknowledge especially the help of the following individuals and institutions: the Committee on the Albert J. Beveridge Award of the American Historical Association, Professor Ralph W. Hidy, then Chairman, for its favorable consideration of this manuscript in the 1956 competition; Professor Arthur S. Link of Northwestern University, for invaluable editorial work and proposing numerous important revisions and improvements in the manuscript; Professor George F. Kennan of the Institute for Advanced Study, for reading the completed manuscript and making helpful suggestions and criticisms; Professors J. Harry Bennett and William H. Braisted of the University of Texas and Professor W. C. Nunn of Texas Christian University, for having read all or part of the work in various stages of completion and having given valuable criticism and encouragement; Professor R. W. Leopold of Northwestern University, for making useful comments and suggestions on sources; the libraries of the University of Texas and the University of California at Berkeley and the Library of Congress for their assistance in making available the materials for research. Needless to say, all responsibility for mistakes or shortcomings in the work remains entirely my own.

PAUL W. SCHROEDER

Austin, Texas
September 1957

Contents

I

Prelude: A Decade of Hostility

1931-1941

THE YEAR 1931 is often given as the year in which World War II really began. According to this view, Japan's successful invasion and conquest of Manchuria set the stage and established the pattern for all the tragic events to come—the failure of the League of Nations, the collapse of collective security, the successive disasters of appeasement, and finally the full onslaught of Nazi aggression. Whether these sweeping generalizations are true or not, it is certainly safe to say that 1931 marks the beginning of a very important historical phenomenon—the rise of serious Japanese-American conflict in the Pacific.

One can easily point, of course, to incidents of tension and rivalry between Japan and America before this time. Nevertheless, Japan was generally regarded by the United States during the 1920's as a good neighbor, and, indeed, as the best hope for democracy and parliamentary government in the Far East. With the Manchurian Incident, relations took a serious downward turn. From this time on, the United States was to grow steadily more suspicious and hostile, until she finally stood militantly opposed to Japan's aggressive expansion.

In this study, there can be given no more than a very brief survey of the events and developments in the decade between 1931 and 1941. Two facts stand out as paramount. First, by a ten-year course of militant expansion, chiefly at the expense of China, the Japanese accrued for themselves an enormous reservoir of ill will in the United States and provoked America into a program of limited economic and political sanctions against them. Second, the United States did not seriously consider stopping the Japanese advance by force of arms, or consider Japan as an actual enemy, until the Far Eastern war had become clearly linked with the far greater (and, to the United States, more important) war in Europe. This link between the two wars was welded when Japan, thinking to take advantage of the apparent German victory in Europe to promote her own Asiatic empire, entered into the Tripartite Pact of September 27, 1940, with the European Axis powers.

Japanese expansion in the twentieth century, to quote Herbert Feis, was rooted in "poverty and pride." [1] Behind it were grim economic problems—an ever-growing population confined to a few crowded islands; a world-wide depression which created for Japan a serious problem of unemployment; and the raising of trade barriers everywhere, which meant great hardship because Japan depended heavily upon imports of raw materials and exports of finished goods in order to live. The domestic problems created a situation of crisis for the Imperial government, encouraging the rise of activists and militarists on the right and militant Communists on the left. [2] In addition, Japan felt the gnawing sense of insecurity that stemmed from dependence upon sources beyond her control for all important raw materials; she knew, besides, the fears of the national state which finds itself

[1] Herbert Feis, *The Road to Pearl Harbor* (Princeton: Princeton University Press, 1950), 1.

[2] For a discussion of the activity of Communists in Japan in the late 1920's and early 1930's and of their systematic suppression by the Japanese government, see Rodger Swearingen and Paul Langer, *Red Flag over Japan* (Cambridge, Mass.: Harvard University Press, 1952), 27–59.

isolated and surrounded on all sides by historic enemies and potential rivals.

Hence it is not surprising that Japan, the most Westernized of Asiatic nations, sought a typically Western solution to her problems—imperialism. Before her lay an alluring prospect of economic and territorial expansion. In Manchuria, which she considered a semideveloped frontier area, she could expand her industrial base, develop a safe source of food and other important raw materials, and, as she hoped, provide an outlet for her surplus population. A Manchuria safely within the Japanese orbit would not only help protect Korea and the Japanese islands against Japan's northern rival, Russia, but, more important still, would constitute a major step toward the establishment of a solid economic bloc consisting of Japan, Manchuria, and China. Once achieved, this goal could lead to even greater things. To an Asia now oppressed by Western exploitation, distracted by inner weakness, and endangered by communism, Japan could give a new economic and political order. In this new order, because of her culture, her industrial progress, and her national unity, Japan would be the natural leader.

All this was the Japanese dream. How much of it was idealism and how much simple aggrandizement is hard to say. Equally difficult to decide is whether the Japanese military move into Manchuria in 1931 represented deliberate national policy or whether it was an act of adventurism by leaders of the Kwantung Army determined to take matters into their own hands and to present the nation with a *fait accompli*. The immediate causes of the conflict between Japan and China over Manchuria are likewise complicated. The Japanese claimed violations of Japanese treaty rights and legitimate interests through outbreaks of Chinese nationalism; the Chinese claimed infringement of their sovereignty.[3] All these are questions too complex to be investigated here. Suffice it to say that, after hostilities broke out be-

[3] Paul H. Clyde, *The Far East* (2d ed.; New York: Prentice-Hall, 1952), 576–584.

tween Japanese and Chinese forces at Mukden on September 18, 1931, the Japanese troops proceeded on a swift and concerted conquest of the country. By January 2, 1932, with the fall of Chinchow, the Kwantung Army was in control, with only mopping-up operations remaining.

At first, the American diplomatic reaction to this move was extremely circumspect. Secretary of State Henry L. Stimson was reluctant to take any action which might embarrass the moderates in the Japanese government, especially Foreign Minister Baron Kijuro Shidehara, in their attempts to regain control of the situation from the military. With the bombing of Chinchow on October 8, 1931, however, the American attitude began to stiffen. Stimson threw his moral support behind the deliberations of the League of Nations on the Manchurian crisis. After the League's efforts came to nothing, the Secretary resorted to a declaration sent to both combatants on January 7, 1932, announcing that the United States would not recognize alterations of the *status quo* by force and would continue to uphold the Open Door and to honor the administrative and territorial integrity of China.[4]

Stimson had made this move alone. The British, whose support he had hoped to receive, considered China's territorial and administrative integrity too much of a chimera to be worth the price of antagonizing Japan. When Japanese-Chinese hostilities spilled over into China proper with the outbreak of fighting near Shanghai on January 28, 1932, however, the menace to British commercial interests induced the Foreign Office to be more ready to follow the American lead. Eventually, through the good offices of neutral powers, peace terms were reached and Japanese troops were evacuated from Shanghai in May. Stimson

[4] A. Whitney Griswold, *The Far Eastern Policy of the United States* (New York: Harcourt, Brace, 1938), 412–426; U.S. Department of State, *Papers Relating to the Foreign Relations of the United States, Japan: 1931–1941* (Washington: Government Printing Office, 1943), I, 1–157; Henry L. Stimson and McGeorge Bundy, *On Active Service in Peace and War* (New York: Harper, 1948), 226–239.

interpreted this as a triumph for joint American and British protests. There is no doubt, however, that practical considerations, such as the determined Chinese resistance, had something to do with the Japanese withdrawal.[5]

Nonetheless, the Japanese conquest of Manchuria remained an accomplished fact. Manchuria, in fact, had been proclaimed as the independent state of Manchoukuo on February 18, 1932. Japan had apparently successfully defied the League of Nations and had violated both the Nine-Power Treaty of 1922 (which bound its signatories to preserve the Open Door in China and to respect Chinese territorial integrity) and the Pact of Paris of 1928 (by which the signatories renounced the use of war to achieve national policy). Casting about for some means of expressing the American reaction to these treaty violations, Stimson hit upon the device of an open letter, which he sent to Senator William Borah of Idaho on February 22, 1932. The heart of the letter was a warning to Japan that if she chose to ignore essential parts of treaties to which she was a signatory (i.e., if she impaired Chinese integrity contrary to the Nine-Power Treaty), the United States would feel free to ignore sections of other related treaties (i.e., America would no longer feel bound by the limitations on battleships agreed on at the same Washington Conference which had produced the Nine-Power Treaty).[6] As Stimson himself admitted, the letter was part statement of principle and part bluff—the United States was in no mood in 1932 to start a naval armaments race. Nevertheless, the letter was Stimson's boldest action in his attempt to invoke moral sanctions upon aggressors. Without economic sanctions, which President Hoover would not permit, this was as far as he could go.[7]

The Japanese conquest of Manchuria and the American attempts to stop it through diplomacy served to create a mutual

---

[5] Stimson and Bundy, *On Active Service*, 239–242; Griswold, *Far Eastern Policy*, 434.

[6] Stimson and Bundy, *On Active Service*, 249–254; Griswold, *Far Eastern Policy*, 432–433.

[7] Stimson and Bundy, *On Active Service*, 244–245.

tension that was slow to subside and easy to reawaken. At the same time these acts revealed the true nature and extent of the conflict between the United States and Japan. Stimson had firmly committed his government to its traditional Far Eastern principles and policies—the sanctity of treaties, the Open Door, the territorial and administrative integrity of China, the non-recognition doctrine—all of which would lead America to continue to oppose Japan's course of militant expansion. The action of the American government during the Manchurian affair revealed, however, that it would not go beyond moral sanctions in enforcing its principles. Hoover's belief that the enforcement of treaties was a moral obligation to be carried out by moral, and not economic, measures had carried the day. Moreover, as Stimson conceded, "In taking this position Mr. Hoover was squarely in line with the whole tradition of American foreign policy in the Far East. Even Theodore Roosevelt had always insisted that American interests in the Orient were not worth a war." [8] Unless this traditional American conviction were reversed, a Japanese-American war, which Stimson already in 1932 believed was inevitable, would not be likely to occur.[9]

There was no indication in the early years of the Roosevelt administration that this conviction would be abandoned. If anything, isolationism in regard to the Far East was strengthened in the mid-1930's. Early in 1934 Secretary of State Cordell Hull expressed the belief that there was no issue between the United States and Japan not capable of friendly adjustment. Japan's consolidation and expansion of her control in Manchoukuo went almost unnoticed by the American people, while the State Department contented itself with calm statements of its own allegiance to international law and the sanctity of treaties.[10] An issue of some importance was raised by the Japanese campaign for naval parity with the United States and Great Britain, which

[8] Ibid., 244.
[9] Ibid., 255, 262.
[10] Griswold, Far Eastern Policy, 443-445.

resulted finally in the breakdown of the London Naval Conference of 1935–1936 and the end to the program of naval limitations.[11] Since the Japanese stand spurred on all three powers in naval expansion programs, its major practical effect was to increase American suspicion of Japan and to convince the Japanese that it was the United States and Great Britain that stood in the way of her ambitions, rather than to change substantially the three nations' relative positions of naval strength.[12]

Another development, hardly dangerous in itself, but portentous of things to come, was the conclusion of an Anti-Comintern Pact between Japan and Germany in November 1936. Though it was ostensibly a limited agreement for exchange of information and consultation concerning Communist subversion, it served to give a tangible basis for the belief that Nazi Germany and Imperial Japan were very much alike and linked together.

Only after the beginning of the China Affair in July 1937, however, did relations between the United States and Japan decisively take a turn for the worse. In many respects the story of the outbreak of war with China is that of the Manchurian Incident repeated, with, however, still less justification in this

[11] *Foreign Relations, Japan,* I, 249–309, contains a large selection of documents dealing with the naval limitations question. Japan insisted on a principle of equality of armaments, the United States on "equality of security." According to the American argument, such factors as length of coast line, size of land and air forces, and distance from other powers compelled the United States to maintain a relatively larger navy. "Certain nations," it was said, "are so situated as to be endowed by nature with a superior power of defense. If . . . a nation so situated should possess naval armaments equal to those of powers not so favored, then that nation would have a very marked naval superiority far more than sufficient for its defensive needs." Strangely enough, then, the American argument was that Japan, a state surrounded on all sides by historic enemies and powerful rivals, had a superior natural situation for defense, while the United States, in the midst of two oceans without a powerful enemy on two continents, had defensively an inferior natural endowment (memo, Norman Davis to Hull, London, Jan. 15, 1936, *ibid.*, 295).

[12] Griswold, *Far Eastern Policy,* 446–448.

case for Japan. Manchuria had been overrun partly to create for Japan a buffer state against Russia. By 1937, the Japanese Army was determined to create a series of autonomous buffer states in Inner Mongolia and North China as a protection for Manchoukuo.[13] Once again there was the clash between Japanese "interests" in China and the rising tide of Chinese nationalism. The Japanese were convinced that for her own good China must be compelled to co-operate economically and politically with Japan; that what was, in Japanese eyes, the wicked folly of anti-Japanism in China, with its economic boycotts, agitation, and violence, must come to an end; and that China must accept Japanese help in her fight against communism. To such demands as these, amounting to Japanese domination of China, almost all Chinese, no matter how much they disagreed among themselves, were united in opposition.[14] When the undeclared war broke out in 1937, it was not so much a case of deliberate aggression as of mutually incompatible national policies. Japan, to be sure, was the aggressor in the sense that she was exerting pressure to enforce her will on China. As F. C. Jones puts it, "Neither Tokyo nor Nanking was looking for war in the summer of 1937, but both Governments were being impelled towards it by forces which neither could adequately control." [15]

At first, after the outbreak of fighting near the Marco Polo bridge on July 7, 1937, it seemed that the incident could be settled without widespread conflagration. The Japanese extended peace offers in August and early September, calling for Chinese recognition of Manchoukuo, a demilitarized zone in North China, and suppression of anti-Japanese activities.[16] The exten-

[13] F. C. Jones, *Japan's New Order in East Asia, 1937–1945* (London: Oxford University Press, 1954), 19–20, 28.
[14] Werner Levi, *Modern China's Foreign Policy* (Minneapolis: University of Minnesota Press, 1953), 207–210.
[15] Jones, *Japan's New Order*, 29.
[16] *Ibid.*, 43; Ambassador Joseph C. Grew to Hull, Tokyo, Sept. 1, 1937, *Foreign Relations, Japan*, I, 359–360.

sion of the fighting to the Shanghai area in mid-August, however, greatly dimmed any prospects which might have existed for settlement. By early September, Japanese spokesmen announced Japan's firm intention to crush the resistance of the Chinese armies.[17] Although peace terms and feelers continued to be extended by Japan through the good offices of Germany, the Japanese government finally withdrew all terms on January 16, 1938, and announced its determination not to deal with the regime of Chiang Kai-shek, but to create a new government in China.[18] The campaign in China, meanwhile, proceeded at a rapid pace through 1937 and 1938, until by the end of the latter year Japan had occupied the richest and most populous sections of China, including its major cities, great areas in northern and central China, and strategic ports and cities on the southeast coast. Japan still seemed, however, to be as far as ever from crushing resistance in China, both that of the Communists in the northwestern provinces and that of the Nationalists with their capital at Chungking.[19]

Japan's next peace offensive reflected her successes and expanding aims. In November 1938 Premier Prince Fumimaro Konoye proclaimed Japan's intention to create a Greater East Asia Co-Prosperity Sphere. The Co-Prosperity Sphere would bring a new order to East Asia, based on Konoye's principles of close co-operation between China, Manchoukuo, and Japan, anti-Bolshevism, and economic and cultural co-ordination. Translated into concrete realities, the Japanese peace terms of November 1938 would have made China a semivassal state. Japanese troops,

[17] Reports of speeches before the Imperial Diet by Foreign Minister Koki Hirota and Premier Prince Fumimaro Konoye, Tokyo, Sept. 3 and 5, 1937, *Foreign Relations, Japan*, I, 364–369.

[18] Grew to Hull, Tokyo, Jan. 10, 1938, statement by the Japanese government, Jan. 16, 1938, *ibid.*, 437–438; Jones, *Japan's New Order*, 68–69.

[19] Harley Farnsworth MacNair and Donald F. Lach, *Modern Far Eastern International Relations* (New York: D. Van Nostrand, 1950), 491–495.

according to the proposal, would be stationed in Inner Mongolia and North China. Moreover, Japanese officials would supervise Chinese land and water communications, military and police organizations, raw materials for defense, and currency, tariff, and maritime customs administration.[20] Chiang Kai-shek, leader of the Nationalist Chinese, whose government would probably have fallen had he accepted these terms, immediately rejected them. Already in 1938 he was counting on help from the West.[21]

For some time, however, Chiang was to look in vain for concrete aid from the United States. The American government had reacted to the outbreak of hostilities in the Far East in a way that reflected its traditional policies. It wanted to see treaties honored and peaceful means employed among nations; it wished to protect American nationals, rights, and interests in the Far East; but it had no desire to become entangled in a foreign conflict. Hence, the initial American reaction was that of a correct neutrality. Hull informed the Japanese Ambassador that both Japan and China would be held "equally responsible" for the spread of hostilities to Shanghai if this occurred.[22] When the fighting did spread, the State Department, primarily concerned with the safety of American nationals, announced a policy of steering clear both of "extreme internationalism" with its entangling political commitments and of isolationism and withdrawal. Once again, the State Department made no attempt to assess the blame for the conflict, but urged both sides to use peaceful means according to the Pact of Paris.[23] This neutral attitude was altered somewhat when the Washington government announced itself in agreement with the League of Nations

[20] Statement by Japanese government and radio speech by Konoye, Nov. 3, 1938, *Foreign Relations, Japan*, I, 477–481; Jones, *Japan's New Order*, 79.

[21] Jones, *Japan's New Order*, 80–81; Levi, *Modern China's Foreign Policy*, 226–227.

[22] Memo by Hull, Aug. 13, 1937, *Foreign Relations, Japan*, I, 342.

[23] Press releases, Department of State, Washington, Aug. 17 and 23, 1937, *ibid.*, 349–353, 355–357.

reports blaming Japan for the conflict.[24] American sympathies were further indicated when the United States took an active part in the abortive Brussels Conference of 1938, called to seek ways of implementing the League reports. The Japanese, believing the United States to have taken the lead in the conference, charged the Washington government with having abandoned its impartiality. The conference broke up, however, without having achieved anything except to raise among the Chinese false hopes of Western intervention.[25] In spite of these evidences of official American disapproval, Japan remained well enough satisfied with the American attitude. Foreign Minister Koki Hirota, perhaps overoptimistically, could report to the Imperial Diet in January 1938 that relations with the United States were still good and that the American attitude had been fair and impartial throughout.[26]

It was already obvious by this time that the most serious rift in Japanese-American relations would come not simply from Japanese aggression against China, but from the fact that Japan flouted American rights and interests, destroyed American property, and endangered American lives in the course of the war. Protection of American interests in China was to be the major aim of American diplomacy toward Japan until the outbreak of the European war, and probably well into 1940. During these years literally hundreds of protests were lodged with Japan concerning bombings of civilian populations, damage to American property, and injury and insult to American citizens. The most sensational incident of this nature was the deliberate sinking of the American gunboat *Panay* in the Yangtze River by Japanese aircraft on December 12, 1937. The Japanese government reacted to American wrath by prompt acknowledgment of respon-

[24] Two reports, League of Nations Assembly, Geneva, Oct. 6, 1937, *ibid.*, 384–396; press release, Department of State, Washington, Oct. 6, 1937, *ibid.*, 396–397.

[25] Grew to Hull, Tokyo, Nov. 16, 1937, *ibid.*, 413–415; Jones, *Japan's New Order*, 54–56.

[26] *Foreign Relations, Japan*, I, 443–444.

sibility and the payment of full indemnities, and the incident was officially closed.[27] Other incidents of a less serious nature continued to occur, however, until by December 1939 even the Japanese had admitted a total of 144 bombings and seventy-three cases of destruction of property against which the United States had lodged protests.[28] The Japanese answers to these protests were various. Sometimes Japan acknowledged fault and made reparation. Sometimes she protested that such incidents were unavoidable in a large-scale conflict or were caused by the Chinese, who located military installations near American embassies, hospitals, or schools. Often she insisted that the incidents were under investigation or rejected the protests as unfounded.[29]

Equally serious, though not as spectacular, was the strain in relations caused by economic measures taken by Japan in China, measures which the United States considered discriminatory. American diplomats made repeated representations against import and exchange restrictions, currency manipulations, tariff revisions, monopolistic controls, anti-American propaganda, terrorism, illegal seizures and searches, and other violations of American property and rights. The Japanese replied that many of the reports were exaggerated or were the products of false rumors, that the economic measures were taken to restore the stability of currency and trade, not to discriminate against Americans, and that terrorism, especially that of the anti-Japanese elements, was a problem long antedating the Japanese occupation.[30]

The American reaction to these incidents, understandably enough, was a cumulative resentment. Hull had already promised

[27] *Panay* documents, *ibid.*, 517–563.
[28] Grew to Hull, Tokyo, Nov. 4, 1939, *ibid.*, II, 31–34; Embassy Counselor Eugene Dooman to Hull, Tokyo, Dec. 6, 1939, *ibid.*, 43–46.
[29] *Aide-mémoires*, Foreign Minister Hachiro Arita to Grew, Tokyo, Dec. 18, 1939, June 18, 1940, *ibid.*, II, 48–51, I, 694–695.
[30] Memos, Grew to Foreign Minister Yosuke Matsuoka, Tokyo, Sept. 18, Oct. 11, 1940, *ibid.*, I, 872–876, 883–884; memo, Japanese Embassy to Department of State, Washington, Aug. 23, 1940, *ibid.*, 866–871.

that the United States "did not intend to abandon our nationals and our interests in China" and that it would uphold its interests everywhere in the world.[31] Soon American diplomats began to express the belief that the incidents were part of a deliberate campaign on the part of Japan to drive all foreigners out of China.[32] Already in September 1938 Hull confided to the Hungarian Ambassador his conviction, so portentous of American fears in days to come, that Japan was seeking to dominate one-half of the world and Hitler the other.[33] By the end of 1939, even the normally sanguine Ambassador Joseph C. Grew felt constrained to warn Japan, in a speech before the America-Japan Society, that America was firm in its stand for the Open Door. He declared that the United States believed Japan was seeking to dominate large areas of Asia, to impose there a closed economy, and to keep American interests out.[34]

In all this, however, there was no suggestion that the United States was now coming to the conviction that its principles and interests in the Far East were important enough to be supported to the point of war, much less that she was ready to use force in behalf of the embattled Chinese. Both the aims and the methods of American policy were in line with tradition. The American government dealt with diplomatic and military incidents by diplomatic protests. It met economic discrimination with economic countermeasures, in particular the denunciation in July 1939 of the Japanese-American Commercial and Navigation Treaty of 1911.[35] It answered moral outrages, such as the bombing of civilian populations, with moral embargoes, implemented by license control, on shipments of planes, bombs, or materials

[31] Speech by Hull to the National Press Club, Washington, March 17, 1938, *ibid.*, 455.
[32] Grew to Hull, Tokyo, March 30, 1939, *ibid.*, 642–643.
[33] Memo by Hull, Washington, Sept. 21, 1938, *ibid.*, 475–476.
[34] Joseph C. Grew, *Turbulent Era* (Boston: Houghton Mifflin, 1952), II, 1215–1221.
[35] Hull to Grew, Washington, Dec. 18, 1939, *Foreign Relations, Japan*, II, 190–192.

used in their manufacture.[36] For the Chinese, this lukewarm American policy was a great disappointment.[37]

The year 1940, however, marks a profoundly significant change in Japanese-American relations. Before 1940, American complaints had chiefly been concerned with invasion of American rights and interests. From mid-1940 on, the United States became seriously worried about the whole problem of Japanese aggression and of Japan's ambitions for a new order in East Asia. America began to take action commensurate with her concern. Japan in turn began to lodge heated complaints about American aid to Chiang, American economic pressure, and the encirclement of Japan.

The reason for this change was obviously the course of the war in Europe. When the European war began in September 1939, there were indeed many who believed that the Asiatic and European wars were really parts of one global conflict. It would have been difficult, however, to demonstrate that this was true, except insofar as one saw an ideological link between the aggressors and an affinity in the methods they used. The ties between Germany and Japan in the Anti-Comintern Pact were actually quite loose. Germany, as will be seen later, had certainly not favored Japan's move into China, nor had Japan approved the German-Soviet nonaggression pact which set the stage for European hostilities. Throughout the first eight months of the European conflict, Japan maintained an independent attitude toward it. But as the war in Europe progressed and the spring of 1940 brought a series of disasters to the Allied cause, it quickly became apparent that the conflicts in Europe and Asia were definitely linked, if not by design, at least by their effect upon one another. The fall of France and Holland, and the apparently imminent defeat of Great Britain, created for Japan, it seemed, a heaven-sent opportunity to turn from China, where she was bogged down in a stalemated, semicolonial war, into southeast

[36] Relevant documents, *ibid.*, 201–204.
[37] Levi, *Modern China's Foreign Policy*, 227.

Asia. There, in the rice fields of Indo-China, the rubber planta-
tions of the Malayan States, and the oil fields of the Netherlands
East Indies, she might obtain the resources she sorely needed
for her security. Moreover, her great national ambition for a
Japanese-led Greater East Asia Co-Prosperity Sphere, which,
as William L. Langer and S. Everett Gleason point out, had long
"represented an ideal and little more," [38] now seemed capable of
realization. Germany, on her part, would probably not object to
a move southward. The fall of Singapore might be just the blow
sufficient to bring an already battered England to her knees.

If the German victories of May and June 1940 had an important effect upon Japan, they had a still profounder effect upon
the United States. Although the Japanese were encouraged toward a course of southward expansion and of *rapprochement*
with Germany, they still continued to hesitate, temporize, and
proceed with caution. The United States, however, in this same
period turned definitely and irrevocably away from isolation and
toward intervention in the European war. A vast majority of the
American people, it is true, doubtless still wanted to stay out of
the actual fighting, as the presidential campaigns of both parties
in the election of 1940 show. But a majority of the people at the
same time were in favor of all possible aid to Britain short of war
and were determined that Germany should not win. It was this
attitude of opposition to Hitler which began to condition American policy in the Far East more than any other factor. Because
of it, the United States came to regard any closer Japanese approach to Germany and any Japanese move toward the south
with far graver concern than it had hitherto viewed Japanese
expansion and aggression.

Meanwhile, ominous developments were not long in coming
in Japan. As usual, one of the first indications of trouble was a
cabinet upheaval. Already in June 1940 Ambassador Grew had
noted signs of tension within the government headed by Prime

[38] William L. Langer and S. Everett Gleason, *The Undeclared War,
1940–1941* (New York: Harper, 1953), 52.

Minister Mitsumasa Yonai and Foreign Minister Hachiro Arita, both of whom were resisting strong pressure from militarists and activists for a closer approach to the totalitarian powers and a hard policy toward China.[39] On July 16, the cabinet fell, the victim of the German victories in Europe.[40]

Prince Konoye headed the new government, with Yosuke Matsuoka, a diplomat as rash and direct as the Prime Minister was vacillating, in charge of the Foreign Office. The program announced by the new government called for ending the China incident (a plank in the platform of every Japanese cabinet since 1937) and solving Japan's problem of southward expansion without war by a firm attitude toward the United States, a readjustment of relations with Russia, and an enforced understanding with the Netherlands East Indies. Domestically, Japan's strength was to be built up by a planned economy with strong emphasis on self-sufficiency and the development of heavy industry.[41] Politically, Japan took long strides in the direction of fascism. All political parties were amalgamated into one official government party headed by Prince Konoye, called the Imperial Rule Assistance Association.[42] Altogether, the new program seemed to mean more authoritarianism at home and expansionism abroad.

The first major step toward implementing this program came with the "peaceful" Japanese advance into northern Indo-China. Japan had long had her eye on this area and already, in June 1940, had secured acquiescence to her demands that the French close the northern Indo-China border to trade with China. The

[39] Grew to Hull, Tokyo, June 10, 1940, *Foreign Relations, Japan*, II, 69.

[40] Jones, *Japan's New Order*, 191; Feis, *Road to Pearl Harbor*, 76–80.

[41] Feis, *Road to Pearl Harbor*, 85–86; statement, Japanese government, Aug. 1, 1940, *Foreign Relations, Japan*, II, 108–111; Decision of the Liaison Conference, July 27, 1940, *International Military Tribunal for the Far East* (hereinafter cited as *IMTFE*), Document no. 2137E.

[42] Clyde, *Far East*, 663–664, 720. For a reaction from the British Ambassador on the scene, see Sir Robert L. Craigie, *Behind the Japanese Mask* (London: Hutchinson, 1946), 102–104.

Chinese bitterly condemned this move as a treaty violation, which, they claimed, held up more than one hundred thousand tons of Chinese supplies.[43] But this concession was not all the Japanese wanted. For a variety of reasons—to cut off aid to China and to secure bases for the war in China, to secure food supplies, to prepare for a southward advance, and to advance the Co-Prosperity Sphere—Japan determined to occupy northern Indo-China.[44] Negotiations were begun on August 1, 1940, with local French officials and the Vichy government for what the Japanese termed "joint defense" of the area. Unexpectedly, the negotiations were protracted till September 22, with the Japanese encountering repeated resistance from the French as the real Japanese aims became clear and as the French continued to hope in vain for armed assistance from the United States. When Japan finally did secure complete compliance with her demands, it was not due to German help, as many Americans supposed at the time, for Germany had given none. It was rather due to the ultimatums of Japan and the hopeless position of the Vichy government.[45]

This done, Japan turned her attention more exclusively to the question of the Netherlands East Indies. Already in April 1940 Foreign Minister Arita had suggested that Japan would be especially concerned with any development in the European war that would affect the East Indies.[46] This was the prelude to a yearlong diplomatic campaign, from May 1940 to June 1941, in which Japan attempted to draw the Netherlands East Indies into her orbit.[47] Ultimately, Japan's diplomatic efforts failed; but

[43] *New York Times*, June 24, 1940.

[44] Langer and Gleason, *Undeclared War*, 9–15.

[45] *Ibid.*; Jones, *Japan's New Order*, 226–231; various documents on the Indo-China negotiations, *Foreign Relations, Japan*, II, 290–297.

[46] Press release, Japanese Embassy, Washington, April 15, 1940, *Foreign Relations, Japan*, II, 281.

[47] Grew to Hull, Tokyo, June 29, 1940, *ibid.*, 289; Jones, *Japan's New Order*, 239–246; Hubertus J. Van Mook, *The Netherlands Indies and Japan* (New York: W. W. Norton, 1944).

she did secure limited gains by an agreement reached in November 1940, guaranteeing Japan an annual export of 1,800,000 tons of all grades of petroleum.[48]

In the face of these and similar Japanese moves, the United States did not remain passive. It reacted to each move, and anticipated others, not only with diplomatic protests but also with action considerably more positive than it had taken previously. To declarations in Tokyo that Japan would be concerned with any change in the position of the Netherlands East Indies, Hull replied that the United States was especially concerned with the maintenance of the *status quo* throughout the Pacific.[49] More important, the United States was able to begin applying economic pressure on Japan in a way that would eventually hurt. Under the National Defense Act of July 2, 1940, the President had authority to put important materials and products on the defense list, subjecting them to license for export. Already, by July, the possibility of a complete embargo on oil and scrap iron was being sharply debated in the cabinet, as it had long been debated in public discussion and in Congress. Only the top grades of scrap iron and of petroleum, including aviation gasoline, were at first embargoed on July 26 and 31. After news of the final Japanese ultimatum on Indo-China became known, however, a total embargo on scrap was proclaimed on September 26, 1940.[50] Japanese protests against these actions as discriminatory and not dictated solely by considerations of national defense were bluntly rejected,[51] and the steady tightening of export restrictions continued.

[48] Press release, Department of State, Washington, Nov. 14, 1940, *Foreign Relations, Japan*, II, 297–298.

[49] Press release, Department of State, Washington, April 17, 1940, *ibid.*, 281–282.

[50] *Foreign Relations, Japan*, II, 211–218, 222–223; Feis, *Road to Pearl Harbor*, 88–94, 102–106.

[51] Japanese Embassy to Department of State, Washington, Aug. 3, Oct. 7, 1940, *Foreign Relations, Japan*, II, 218–219, 223–224; memo by Hull, Washington, Oct. 8, 1940, *ibid.*, 225–228; Langer and Gleason, *Undeclared War*, 36–37.

The action that contributed more than anything else to the deterioration of Japanese-American relations during this critical year of 1940, however, was the conclusion of the Tripartite Pact between Germany, Italy, and Japan on September 27. On its face, the Tripartite Pact was a straightforward document combining a mutual recognition of spheres of leadership with a defensive military alliance. In Articles I and II, Japan recognized the leadership of Germany and Italy in establishing a new order in Europe, and Germany and Italy reciprocated for Japan in Greater East Asia. Article III represented the heart of the Pact:

Japan, Germany, and Italy agree to cooperate in their efforts on aforesaid lines. They further undertake to assist one another with all political, economic and military means if one of the three Contracting Powers is attacked by a Power at present not involved in the European War or in the Chinese-Japanese conflict.

Article IV called for the appointing of joint technical commissions to carry out the terms of the treaty, while Article V, as if to make abundantly clear against whom the Pact was directed, stipulated that its provisions would not affect relations between the three powers and Soviet Russia. There was, of course, only one other major power not then involved in world conflict—the United States.[52] At first glance, it was difficult to see just what Japan expected to gain by a treaty implying a bold and direct challenge to the United States. As Ambassador Grew commented shortly after the signing of the Pact, the value of the alliance to the Axis was obvious, but it would not be worth much to Japan unless secret agreements were attached.[53] Hitler, of course, stood to gain enormously. If the Pact succeeded in halting or even slowing down the United States in its professed intention of giving all-out aid to Great Britain short of war (an intention already launched into action by the deal granting Great Britain fifty overage destroyers

---

[52] *Foreign Relations, Japan*, II, 165–166.
[53] Grew to Hull, Tokyo, Sept. 29, 1940, *ibid.*, 169–171.

in exchange for bases), Germany would gain a strategic advantage which might well prove decisive in the outcome of the war. Even if the Pact did not deter the United States, it would certainly force her to pay more attention to her Pacific positions. Moreover, should the United States and Japan come to blows, it would be a war in which Germany and Italy could hardly be expected to give Japan much military assistance. Granting to the Japanese hegemony in the Far East was no great concession for the European Axis partners, for neither of them was in a position to exert great influence there, just as Japan was unable to do so in Europe. Germany, it seemed on the surface, had secured a great diplomatic bargain.

But what had induced Japan to take the fateful step? A full answer to the question would take us into the whole complex question of Japanese-German relations from 1936 to 1940 and in particular into the involved negotiations and discussions by which the Pact was concluded and ratified.[54] Briefly, however, Japan had her reasons, which were always far more matters of opportunistic self-interest than matters of ideology or common purpose with her Axis partners. The first reason was the changed military situation in Europe. The Yonai cabinet had bet on the wrong horse in refusing to back the Axis. To the activists now in the ascendancy in Japan, it seemed highly urgent that they come to terms with the apparent winners in Europe. This was especially important from Japan's point of view because of the effect of the European war on Japan's Co-Prosperity Sphere. With Holland overrun, France crushed, and Great Britain likely to fall, it seemed that the whole of the Far East could be brought under Japanese hegemony almost by forfeit. The Japanese concept of Japan's required sphere of living, which always expanded and contracted with the military situation, had in this moment of opportunity reached its widest and most ambitious extent.[55] To make sure of her vast claims, however, Japan would do well to co-operate with the European conqueror of the co-

---

[54] See below, Chapter V.   [55] Feis, *Road to Pearl Harbor*, 114.

lonial powers. Thus the Tripartite Pact represented in part an attempt on the part of Japan to pave the way for southward expansion.

This was not, however, the only reason for the conclusion of the Tripartite Pact, nor, indeed, in the minds of many Japanese who agreed to it, was it the most important one. For some, including Foreign Minister Matsuoka, the Pact represented the best positive way of dealing with the United States and keeping her from interfering both in Europe and in Asia. Whether Matsuoka himself really conceived of the Pact as an instrument of peace is a moot question; in the opinion of the writer, he actually did.[56] In any case, he certainly was convinced, understandably enough, that relations between the United States and Japan were so bad that they could not become much worse and could only be remedied by bold and direct action. Moreover, he seems really to have believed that he could persuade the United States to accept the Pact as a peaceful and defensive measure and to dissuade and coerce her from her unneutral actions in behalf of Great Britain and China, thereby preventing an extension of the war. The arguments which carried the most weight with the moderates in the Japanese government, however, were, first, that the Pact would help Japan settle the China Incident by discouraging the Western powers from aiding Chiang and, second, that it would pave the way for an adjustment of relations with Russia. In fact, the Soviet Union might very well join the Axis partnership. As for the danger of war arising from treaty obligations, those with fears on this score received many assurances that Japan had retained the right to decide independently whether the Pact was to be invoked and what measures would be taken—as indeed she had.[57]

It need hardly be said that every one of the Japanese expecta-

---

[56] For evidence on this question, see below, Chapter V, pp. 122–125.

[57] Langer and Gleason, *Undeclared War*, 21–32; Jones, *Japan's New Order*, 197–201; Feis, *Road to Pearl Harbor*, 114–119; Grew to Hull, Tokyo, Oct. 5, 1940, *Foreign Relations, Japan*, II, 171–173.

tions in regard to the Tripartite Pact was destined to be frustrated. Indeed, the whole history of the Pact was one of disillusionment and disaster for Japan. The first of such hopes to be blasted was one entertained by Matsuoka, though not held, to be sure, by many other more realistic Japanese leaders—the belief that the United States could either be cajoled into accepting the Pact's "peaceful" intentions or be warned away from intervention in the European and Asian conflicts by the specter of war with all three Axis powers.

Officially, the State Department's reaction to the Pact was a shrug of the shoulders. The alliance, said Secretary Hull, had long been expected and anticipated in the formulation of American policy and merely formalized an already existing situation.[58] Actually, American reaction both within the administration and in public opinion was very sharp. Secretary of War Stimson and some others regarded the Pact as a bluff to be met with strong action, but Hull himself saw it as the prelude to a Japanese southward move which might bring war.[59] More important, apart from any strategic and military implications, the Pact caused a profound hardening of American public opinion toward Japan— a once-for-all identification of the Empire with the Axis, with Hitler and the whole program of world conquest and the menace of aggression which America was sure he represented. Even Ambassador Grew, not usually pessimistic, was deeply impressed:

Japan has associated herself with a team or system of predatory Powers, with similar aims and employing similar methods. It will be the better part of wisdom to regard her no longer as an individual nation, with whom our friendship has been traditional, but as part and parcel of that system which, if allowed to develop unchecked, will assuredly destroy everything that America stands for.

[58] Press release, Department of State, Washington, Sept. 27, 1940, *Foreign Relations, Japan*, II, 169.
[59] Langer and Gleason, *Undeclared War*, 34–35.

It was no longer possible to separate the two wars, Grew believed; the Far Eastern problem had now become "an integral part of the world crisis created by Adolf Hitler's bid for world domination." [60]

Grew's reaction was typical of that of the American people—an equating of the Japanese New Order with Hitler's. In fact, such an identification seemed merely to be taking the Pact at its express word. The impact of the Axis Alliance upon public feeling was readily apparent to analysts at the time. As one commented, "Japan's alliance with the Axis has done more than anything else could have done to convince Americans that the war in Europe and the war in Asia are the same war." [61] The net result of the Pact, according to another, was that the average American "has come now to identify Japan as a partner of Germany and Italy, united with them in an effort to destroy the kind of world for which he stands." While it converted many to this belief, it also immeasurably strengthened the hands of those groups and organs—foreign missionaries, collective security groups, women's clubs, prominent newspapers and journals, organized labor, and others—who had long proclaimed the ideological identity of Japan and Hitler and had urged a stronger policy against Japan, particularly a total embargo. [62] So sharp was the American reaction that Japanese spokesmen, writing and speaking for American consumption, were forced to the defense that the United States and Great Britain had driven Japan into the arms of the Axis. Japan had no real ideological ties with Germany and Italy, they argued; she was compelled to make the alliance because of her diplomatic isolation, dating from the expiration of the Anglo-Japanese Alliance in 1921, and because of

[60] Grew, *Turbulent Era*, II, 1231, 1254–1255.

[61] Robert Aura Smith, "The Triple-Axis Pact and American Reactions," *Annals of the American Academy of Political and Social Science*, CCXV (May 1941), 132.

[62] John W. Masland, "American Attitudes toward Japan," *ibid.*, 163–165; Feis, *Road to Pearl Harbor*, 122 (note).

the persistent Anglo-American discrimination against Japan and aid to China.[63]

In the long run, this change in American public opinion was perhaps the most significant result of the Tripartite Pact. More immediately, however, the Pact had important effects upon both the diplomacy and the strategy of the United States. The change in the diplomatic attitude of America, even though it did not become fully apparent until serious conversations were initiated in the spring of 1941, was nevertheless, one feels, a profound one. From the signing of the Tripartite Pact dates a marked hardening of American requirements for peace. No longer were Japanese-American relations a matter capable of any simple *ad hoc* adjustment and agreement. No longer was the United States simply or even chiefly interested in protecting the rights and interests of American citizens in the Far East, while merely protesting against the use of force in international relations. From now on the State Department would increasingly view the situation in global terms and insist that the only possible solution would have to be a sweeping, broad-gauge, radical one covering the entire Pacific area. American principles, such as the Four Points of Hull which were to play such a large role in the 1941 negotiations, were no longer to be simply principles which the United States would uphold and observe, but a program which it would finally have to enforce. Japan would have not merely to arrest her present course in order to adjust relations with the United States; she would have to repent and be converted. The necessary fruits meet for repentance would have to be evidence that the Japanese government, in the words of Hull, was "ready to give up the use of force as an instrument of policy and adopt the principles that my Government has been proclaiming as the foundation on

[63] Toshi Go, "Japanese Attitudes toward America," *Annals of the American Academy of Political and Social Science*, CCXV, (May 1941), 166–170; U.S. Congress, *Hearings of the Joint Committee on the Investigation of the Pearl Harbor Attack* (Washington: Government Printing Office, 1946), II, 674–675.

which all relations between nations should properly rest." [64]

This adherence to rigid doctrine and a deep distrust of the Japanese—both of which were greatly strengthened, if not produced, by the Tripartite Pact—were accompanied by a profound pessimism as to the possibilities for a peaceful settlement. According to his later testimony, Hull estimated the chances for success from the outset as being one in twenty, in fifty, or even in a hundred. Entering into conversations with the Japanese, though it was done in good faith, was chiefly a matter of gaining time. [65] The reasons in the Secretary's mind were that the Japanese were allies of Hitler, signatories to a Pact aimed at America, ruthless aggressors determined to subjugate half of the peoples of the world, and militarists whose expansion would in time surely menace the security of the United States. [66]

Accompanying the change in diplomatic attitude went developments in strategy as well—developments not always to be perfectly in harmony with the American diplomatic efforts. In diplomacy, there was to be no compromise, no sacrifice of principle. Strategically, however, the United States intended to carry on a delaying action. The policy was to exert enough economic pressure on Japan to deter her from new adventures, yet not so much as would send her on a plunge into the Netherlands East Indies. The United States would try to keep Japan embroiled on the Asiatic mainland by judicious aid to China; at the same time, America's main concern would have to be support of Great Britain, first of all in the Atlantic and secondly in the South Seas. For a short time in October 1940, President Roosevelt considered the possibility of bolder military action—an embargo of Japan in which the United States Fleet would stop all trade between Japan and the Americas by patrols in the western Pacific ranging from Singapore to Siam and from Pearl Harbor to the Philippines. Convinced by Admiral J. O. Richardson,

[64] Cordell Hull, *Memoirs* (New York: Macmillan, 1948), II, 994.
[65] Statement by Hull, Nov. 23, 1945, *Pearl Harbor Attack*, II, 417.
[66] Hull, *Memoirs*, II, 982–983.

Commander in Chief of the Fleet, that the plan was impractical,[67] Roosevelt returned to the global strategy of holding the line and supporting Great Britain in southeast Asia while seeking an eventual decision in Europe.[68]

To be sure, the British pressed hard for firmer American commitments for action in the South Seas than they were actually able to obtain from the Washington government. They wanted, if possible, a definite promise that the United States would go to war if British or Dutch Far Eastern possessions were attacked, and they desired American reinforcements for Manila and/or Singapore.[69] But while the American leaders would not give such binding commitments for military aid, they did engage in co-operation and association tantamount almost to alliance. Informal Anglo-American naval conversations had been going on in Washington since the autumn of 1940. These were now expanded by military conferences beginning in March 1941 among American, British, and Dutch officers, who drew up joint plans for possible Far Eastern defense, but went no farther. The degree to which American support stiffened British policy in the Far East may be seen not only in the reopening of the Burma Road in 1941 (which had been closed the year before under Japanese pressure), but in the British reaction to Japanese mediation of a Siamese–Indo-Chinese border dispute in early 1941 and the war scare which attended it. Under strong British pressure, the Japanese disavowed any but peaceful aims and in fact secured no naval bases in Siam in payment for their mediation, as had been widely feared.[70]

It was not, however, the growing evidence of an American-

----

[67] Richardson to Commander in Chief of the Asiatic Fleet, Oct. 16, 1940, *Pearl Harbor Attack*, XIV, 1006.

[68] Roosevelt to Grew, Washington, Jan. 21, 1941, *ibid.*, XX, 4261–4263.

[69] Two telegrams, British Foreign Office to British Embassy at Washington, Feb. 11, 1941, *ibid.*, XIX, 3447–3451.

[70] Feis, *Road to Pearl Harbor*, 169–170; Langer and Gleason, *Undeclared War*, 46–48, 319–331; Joseph C. Grew, *Ten Years in Japan* (New York: Simon and Schuster, 1944), 369–370.

British-Dutch entente which was to Japan the most baleful result of the conclusion of the Tripartite Pact. It was, rather, the prospect of ever-increasing American support for China and, in fact, an altered American attitude toward the Chinese conflict itself. Up to September 25, 1940, the United States had lent a total of $44 million to China through the Reconstruction Finance Corporation and the Export-Import Bank. In response to Japan's move into Indo-China and reports of her approach to the Axis, the Washington government authorized another loan to China of $25 million on September 25, and a further loan of $50 million on November 30, with the announcement that it was considering a $50 million fund to stabilize the Chinese currency.[71] To be sure, this aid was limited and modest in scale, but it was growing, and in its moral effect, in the opinion of two recent scholars, it "no doubt helped save China from the demoralization and collapse that threatened in October, 1940." [72]

Even more disturbing to Japan than the amount of aid given to China were the reasons advanced by American spokesmen for it and for economic pressure on Japan. One of Japan's most important reasons for entering the Tripartite Pact, as has already been noted, was her desire to prevent American intervention in the China Incident. Until the summer of 1940, the United States had reacted to the war in China as something to be deplored but not essentially America's concern, except insofar as American rights and interests were involved. Japan's great hope in her relations with the United States had been, as it would continue to be, that the other problems in the Pacific could be adjusted without reference to China. Now there came clear indications that, because of Japan's renewed course of expansion and her aggressive alliance, this would not be possible. The United States would insist upon supporting China not simply for the sake of principle

---

[71] Press release, Federal Loan Agency, Washington, Sept. 25, 1940, *Foreign Relations, Japan*, II, 222; memo, Department of State, Washington, May 19, 1942, *ibid.*, 326.

[72] Langer and Gleason, *Undeclared War*, 305.

and of a permanent Far Eastern settlement, but also for the sake of self-defense and national security. In discussing with Ambassador Kensuke Horinouchi the rumored imminent Japanese occupation of northern Indo-China, Undersecretary Sumner Welles warned that the United States would now have to help China just as it was helping Great Britain.[73] When the Japanese protested the American embargo on scrap iron, Secretary Hull rejected the protest bluntly with the argument that Japan and Germany were setting out on a scheme of world conquest, each to subjugate half the world.[74] Japanese complaint about the loan to China in November as an unfriendly act against Japan brought from Hull the angry reply: "If to act in self-defense is an unfriendly act—then we are proposing to do something that is unfriendly." [75]

Thus the lines of antagonism by the beginning of 1941 were clearly drawn. Japan was identified with Germany as America's enemy; China with Great Britain as America's friend, one of the embattled democracies, and a virtual ally. America's rights of self-defense and national security extended not only across the Atlantic, but across the Pacific and to the mainland of Asia as well. The two nations glared at each other, the one with a hostility born of long frustration and growing anxiety, the other with a righteous anger born of hatred for fascist aggression. It was in this poisoned and tense atmosphere that the crucial negotiations leading to peace or war would take place.

[73] Memo by Welles, Washington, Sept. 20, 1940, *Foreign Relations, Japan*, I, 877–881.
[74] Memo by Hull, Washington, Oct. 8, 1940, *ibid.*, II, 225–228.
[75] Quoted in Langer and Gleason, *Undeclared War*, 301.

II

The Negotiations, Initial Phase:

The Pact in Prominence

THE task assigned by the Japanese government to Ambassador Kichisaburo Nomura early in 1941, that of patching up relations between Japan and the United States, seemed at the outset a well-nigh impossible one. Cordell Hull, who estimated the chances for settlement at odds of one hundred to one,[1] could find good grounds for his pessimism in the diametrically opposed stands of the two powers. Japan's alliance with the Axis, her war on China, and her designs on the southwest Pacific as a part of her Greater East Asia Co-Prosperity Sphere could not possibly, it seemed, be reconciled with the American policy of support of Great Britain, aid to China, and the preservation of the *status quo* in southeast Asia.

All, however, was not darkness and gloom. There were some factors at work to make the situation not quite hopeless. For one thing, as will be shown, the Tripartite Pact was not nearly so strong a bond between Japan and Germany as it seemed. In fact, there was enough evidence at hand of discontent over the Pact in high Japanese circles to justify the hope that judicious Amer-

[1] Hull, *Memoirs*, II, 985.

ican diplomacy or a favorable turn in the war might lead to a split or a serious weakening of the Axis.

More important still was the fact that the controversy between Japan and the United States was rather one of principle than of immediate strategic interests. However great a gulf might be fixed between America and Japan in moral principle and ideological conviction, there was no such irreconcilable conflict between them in their basic strategic aims. America's attention was focused chiefly on Europe, Japan's exclusively on Asia. Japan had a primary and overriding interest in concluding the China Affair and in implementing her long-standing plan for an inner Co-Prosperity Sphere consisting of China, Manchoukuo, and Japan. To this were added a secondary concern over southeastern Asia and the southwest Pacific and a very tertiary interest in the outcome of the European war. In this war, in fact, she took an interest only insofar as it affected her own Asiatic plans. To the United States, on the other hand, a British victory in the European war was the primary consideration. Next to this in importance, and in large measure derived from it, was America's concern to preserve the *status quo* in the southwest Pacific, in order to maintain Britain's Far Eastern life line. As for China, America's strategic interest in her was distinctly subordinate. There was a great deal of sympathy for China in America, it is true, a feeling based both on sentiment and on principle. It was because of American sympathy for the embattled underdog and the conviction that Japan was a ruthless aggressor that American diplomats and spokesmen contended so strongly in principle for the liberation of China through the evacuation of Japanese troops. But the strategic interests of the United States and the purpose of her aid to China lay in quite a different direction. The purpose of American aid was to keep China fighting, since her strategic value lay in tying down large numbers of Japanese troops.

The significance of this lies in the fact that there was no immediate clash in basic American and Japanese strategic aims bound to lead the two nations to war. Theoretically, it would be possible for each to concentrate on his basic spheres of interest and make some concessions in the other areas. If the Japanese would retreat on the issues of the Tripartite Pact and of southward expansion and if the United States would at least compromise on China, war could probably be avoided and relations might even be distinctly improved. Whether either nation or both would be willing to follow this course depended in turn on a number of other factors. The vital considerations would be the course of the war in Europe, the influence of domestic politics in each nation, and especially the question of whose policy would prevail in the respective governments—whether expansionists or moderates would hold the reins in Tokyo and whether moral principles or strategic interests would govern policy in Washington. The answers to these questions constitute very largely the story of the Japanese-American negotiations in 1941.

The Japanese-American talks began as informal and preliminary conversations (a stage they never passed) in Washington in February 1941. Ambassador Nomura represented Japan, along with several assistants—Colonel Hideo Iwakuro of the Japanese Army, Tadao Wikawa, a Japanese bank official, Kaname Wakasugi, Japanese Minister-Counselor, and Katsuzo Okumura, Second Secretary of the Japanese Embassy.[2] Cordell Hull personally took charge of the negotiations for the United States, assisted by Joseph W. Ballantine, Max W. Schmidt, and Maxwell M. Hamilton of the State Department. President Roosevelt occasionally met with Hull and Nomura but gave almost complete charge of the day-to-day conversations to his Secretary of State, while Undersecretary Sumner Welles participated chiefly as Acting Secretary during Hull's illness in July. While the Washington discussions were proceeding, subsidiary talks were held from time to time in Tokyo, usually by Japanese request. Participants in these conversations were ordinarily the Japanese Foreign Minister and Vice-Foreign Minister, at this time Matsuoka and

[2] *Foreign Relations, Japan,* II, 427 (note), but see also 455 (note).

Chuichi Ohashi respectively, and, on the American side, Ambassador Grew and Counselor of the Embassy Eugene H. Dooman. The diplomatic conversations continued from March through the middle of July without interruption. It would be pointless to review the course of the individual conferences, for they all covered the same ground over and over with endless repetition. The only really significant products of the negotiations in this period were six draft proposals, three submitted by each side—the Japanese proposals of April 9, May 12, and June 15 and the American drafts on May 16, May 31, and June 21. For various reasons, none of these proposals can be taken as the last word on each nation's position. The first and the last of the Japanese proposals were only semiofficial in nature, the first being produced in the course of informal talks between private American and Japanese individuals and the last being tendered informally by the associates of Nomura.[3] Even the Japanese proposal of May 12, which was official and was approved by the cabinet of Japan, must be read with some caution, because it gives evidence of the inordinate pressure exerted on that occasion within the government by Foreign Minister Matsuoka. As for the American proposals, Hull was anxious that the United States should not be pinned down. For this reason, all the American drafts were labeled with care, "Informal and Unofficial," "Draft Suggestion," or "Unofficial, Exploratory, and without Commitment."[4] However, the differences between the various documents on each side were relatively slight, and all of the drafts show the Japanese and American positions and differences clearly enough.

There were three major points over which the two nations were at odds: first, the interpretation of the Tripartite Pact; second, the settlement to be made of the China Incident; and, third, the nature and extent of Japanese commercial activities and

3 "Proposal Presented to the State Department," April 9, 1941, *ibid.*, 398–402; Langer and Gleason, *Undeclared War*, 314.

4 See, for example, the American proposal of May 31, 1941, *Foreign Relations, Japan*, II, 451.

economic expansion in China and the southwest Pacific. On the first, the matter of the Tripartite Pact, the Japanese were willing to declare that the Pact was defensive and designed to keep the European war from spreading.[5] They balked, however, at committing themselves to any formula which would actually nullify the Pact while theoretically leaving it in force. They were unwilling to give an advance endorsement to any and all actions the United States might take against Germany, as the Americans seemed to wish. The Japanese aim was rather to persuade the United States to accept the alliance as a peaceful measure and even to try to get assurance that the United States would maintain a neutral attitude toward the European war.[6]

These hopes were, of course, diametrically opposed to the policy of the United States. Hull's objective was to nullify the Axis Alliance. American diplomats at this time were not particularly concerned about how this result might be attained. They did not ask for the impossible from Japan, that is, an outright denunciation of the Axis agreement. They tried instead, by means of devices such as supplements, annexes, or exchanges of letters, to secure Japanese agreement to the American interpretation of "self-defense" and of Article III of the Pact. According to the American formula, anything the United States did to help Great Britain or to injure Germany should automatically be considered "self-defense." Under this interpretation, the United States could feel free to extend all possible aid to Great Britain in the Atlantic without the fear that the Tripartite agreement

[5] Draft Document, June 15, 1941, *ibid.*, 475.

[6] Draft Proposal, May 12, 1941, *ibid.*, 421. A dispatch from Nomura to Konoye on April 18 shows that even in his more conciliatory unofficial proposal of April 9 Nomura wanted to make clear that a Japanese-American understanding would not affect Japan's obligations to the Axis and that he desired "to restrain the United States to the utmost from entering into the European War, and to make full use of the spirit of Article 3 of the Tripartite Pact," without, of course, breaking relations with the United States (*IMTFE*, Record, 25687). Nomura had, in fact, been especially warned about faithfulness to the Pact in his original instructions from Matsuoka, Jan. 22, 1941 (*ibid.*, Doc. no. 1383B).

might be invoked by Germany and honored by Japan.[7] On this point, Hull and his associates were not successful. The Japanese were unwilling to concede to the United States any such "blank check" on self-defense. After June 21, as F. C. Jones says, "There was thus a deadlock over the critical question of the interpretation of Article 3 of the Tripartite Pact."[8]

This was not, unfortunately, the only obstacle. An equally hopeless impasse had been reached in regard to the China Affair. The Japanese were ready, indeed eager, to come to a settlement of the stalemated war in China, but they wanted a settlement that would preserve some of their gains. The chief obstacle to a favorable settlement, Japan believed, was American aid to China. Japan's fundamental aim, therefore, was to persuade the United States to forego aid to China and to leave Japan to deal as much as possible with the Chinese alone. Of course, the Japanese never expected to gain this end completely. They were willing to submit the proposed terms on which they would negotiate with China to the United States and to phrase them as innocuously as possible. Japan proposed as a basis for peace the long-standing three principles of Prince Konoye: "1. Neighborly friendship; 2. Joint defense against communism; 3. Economic cooperation —by which Japan does not intend to exercise economic monopoly in China nor to demand of China a limitation in the interests of Third Powers."[9] Translated into specific terms, the principles included:

1. Neighborly friendship.
2. Cooperative defense against communistic activities—including the stationing of Japanese troops in the Inner Mongolia and certain areas of the [sic] North China.
3. Economic cooperation.

[7] See, for example, Annex 3 of the Draft Proposal of June 21, 1941, *Foreign Relations, Japan*, II, 490–491.

[8] Jones, *Japan's New Order*, 276.

[9] Oral Explanation to Draft Proposal, May 12, 1941, *Foreign Relations, Japan*, II, 423.

4. Mutual respect of sovereignty and territories.
5. Mutual respect for the inherent characteristics of each nation cooperating as good neighbors and forming an Eastern Asia nucleus contributing to world peace.
6. Withdrawal of Japanese troops from Chinese territory in accordance with agreement between Japan and China.
7. No annexations.
8. No indemnities.
9. Recognition of "Manchoukuo." [10]

To several of these fair-sounding terms, the United States had no objections. Others, however, seemed to afford Japan a cloak for continued domination of China. The phrase "economic cooperation," for example, might well mean the continuation of monopolistic and discriminatory economic practices by Japan in China. "Cooperative defense against communistic activities" could well be the excuse for an indefinite military occupation of large areas of China. These possibilities or probabilities ran counter to all American hopes for a settlement in China. American policy held that Japan should simply evacuate China, that China's administrative and territorial integrity (such as it was in that chaotic era) should be restored to her whole and entire, and that the Open Door should prevail in Asia, with free economic opportunity for all.

Hence, without rejecting the Japanese proposals on China outright, the American replies amended them in a direction quite opposite to their original intent, so that they ended by conceding Japan little or nothing. The Japanese proposal for "cooperative defense against injurious communistic activities —including the stationing of Japanese troops in Chinese territory" was made "subject to further discussion." The American drafts sanctioned economic co-operation between Japan and China only if such co-operation were safeguarded against Japanese economic imperialism. On the crucial issue of Japanese military occupation of parts of China, the Americans insisted that

[10] Memo by Ballantine, Washington, June 4, 1941, *ibid.*, 460–461.

Japanese troops be withdrawn "as promptly as possible" in accordance with a Sino-Japanese agreement to be concluded. While the Japanese had asked for recognition of Manchoukuo, the United States would offer only "amicable negotiation." [11] In addition, the United States demanded some specific assurances on the course of future Japanese economic policy in China. Hull asked pointedly whether Japan would abandon all commercial monopolies and preferences, how soon and how fully she would withdraw restrictions on the Open Door, and whether she would immediately stop currency manipulations. Without satisfactory answers on these and similar embarrassing questions, he indicated, there was small chance of agreement.[12]

The third major area of dispute concerned the threat of Japanese expansion into the southwest Pacific. Again, Japan was ready to declare emphatically and at length that her expansion into this area was to be commercial and economic only, not military. She shied away from pledging herself to use only peaceful means, however. Further, she wanted America to promise to co-operate in securing for Japan the resources of the southwest Pacific in return for the simple statement that the Japanese expansion was to be peaceful.[13] The United States, on the other hand, wanted specific pledges against territorial expansion of any kind. In return for this she was willing to go no further than to promise Japan co-operation in securing "non-discriminatory access" for both countries to the supplies of raw material which both needed.[14]

Finally, both sides were gravely concerned about the question of military bases in the southwest Pacific, an issue discussed in the conversations but not specifically dealt with in the draft documents. American representatives refused the Japanese re-

[11] Draft Proposal, June 21, 1941, *ibid.*, 488–490.
[12] *Ibid.*, 491–492.   [13] Draft Proposal, May 12, 1941, *ibid.*, 422.
[14] Draft Proposal, June 21, 1941, *ibid.*, 489. It is interesting to note that Nomura's associates in their draft of June 15 accepted the wording desired by America on this point (*ibid.*, 475).

quest for a pledge that the United States would acquire no new bases, citing in justification Japanese moves in Thailand, Hainan, and Indo-China. Japan in turn was afraid of American intentions in regard to Singapore and, after the German attack on Russia, in regard to Siberia.[15] Thus the differences between the two powers ran much deeper than the verbal formulations indicated. Neither side, with good reason, trusted the other not to increase its power in the southwest Pacific area.

The negotiations from March to July showed clearly that no comprehensive settlement was possible at this time. More important, the conversations revealed that the two sides were at complete variance in spirit. The American diplomats, led by Hull, were insistent upon a comprehensive agreement which, in their opinion, alone could form the basis for a lasting peace in the Pacific area. Hull would settle for nothing less than a complete Japanese conversion to the principles of international peace, order, and justice, as he conceived them. As the *sine qua non* for agreement, he insisted upon a sincere and wholehearted subscription by Japan to his Four Points, which read:

1. Respect for the territorial integrity and sovereignty of each and all nations.
2. Support of the principle of non-interference in the internal affairs of other countries.
3. Support of the principle of equality, including equality of commercial opportunity.
4. Non-disturbance of the *status quo* in the Pacific, except as the *status quo* may be altered by peaceful means.[16]

Time and again Hull would complain that the Japanese were avoiding these principles and their application. They did not, he insisted, seem to want a comprehensive settlement based on them. Instead, they were trying to make reservations, and endeavoring, in the Secretary's words,

[15] Memo by Schmidt, Washington, July 17, 1941, *ibid.*, 482–483; memo by Ballantine, Washington, July 5, 1941, *ibid.*, 501.
[16] Memo by Hull, Washington, April 16, 1941, *ibid.*, 407.

(1) To stress Japan's alignment with the Axis, (2) to avoid giving a clear indication of an intention to place Japan's relations with China on a basis which in the opinion of the Government of the United States would contribute to a lasting peace . . . and (3) to veer away from clear-cut commitments in regard to policies of peace and of non-discriminatory treatment which are fundamentals of a sound basis for peace in the Pacific area.[17]

The Secretary's complaints about the Japanese tendency to avoid clear-cut commitments were not without foundation. The trouble was that Japanese diplomacy was simply oriented in a completely different direction from that of the United States. If the keynote of American foreign policy was rigid doctrine and principle, that of Japan was realism and expediency. While the United States demanded a sweeping agreement based on clear principles, Japan wanted any kind of agreement, however limited or partial, which would prevent a Japanese-American war and stop further attrition of Japan's resources without entailing too much in the way of sacrifice of her Asiatic plans. The United States was determined to convert Japan to peaceful policies; Japan wanted only to get America to leave her alone in Asia. Hence, where the United States argued principles, Japan argued circumstances. She repeatedly contended that, while the American principles were laudable and while Japan subscribed to them heartily in theory, the realities of the Far Eastern situation prevented their wholesale or immediate application.

The Japanese representatives pleaded, for instance, that Japan really desired and intended to withdraw her troops from China as soon as feasible. However, the requirements of defense against communism, the necessity for maintenance of stability in China, and considerations of Japanese domestic politics compelled her to keep troops in certain areas for some years.[18] Similarly, they insisted that Japan subscribed heartily to the principle of non-

[17] Informal Statement, Hull to Nomura, June 6, 1941, *ibid.*, 468.
[18] Memos by Ballantine, Washington, May 20 and 28, 1941, *ibid.*, 435–436, 441–443.

discrimination in economic affairs—provided only that certain mining interests and other properties lawfully acquired in China and vital to Japanese enterprise should be considered "outside the scope" of the nondiscrimination doctrine.[19] Japan, they claimed, was quite willing to concede the United States right of self-defense. However, to include a specific avowal of that right, especially as it was interpreted by Hull, in the agreement itself would only raise difficult questions for the Japanese government at home and with her Axis partners. Japan could not, it was true, afford to give the United States a blank check on self-defense. However, such a grant was really quite unnecessary, they argued, for American fears of Japan were groundless. The whole question of the Tripartite Pact, in fact, might best be left alone until after an American-Japanese agreement had been reached. Plainly such a settlement would of itself make any invocation of Article III of the Pact extremely unlikely.[20]

The course that Japan followed during these conversations was far from being one of mere duplicity; on the contrary, it was understandable and, from the Japanese point of view, sensible. It was a policy of expediency, of bowing with the wind, of attempting to wriggle by devious diplomacy out of an increasingly intolerable situation. Sensing this intent, Hull reacted to it with righteous indignation. His anger was particularly aroused at Japan's attempt to get away with her crimes unpunished and her search for "a way to get out of China." He resented her intention "to go forward with methods and practices entirely contrary to the principles which would have to underlie a settlement establishing peace, non-discriminatory commerce and fair, friendly relations in the Pacific area."[21] With the two points of view so completely opposed—realism and expediency on the one hand, rigid principle and a stern, almost vengeful justice on

[19] Memo by Ballantine, Washington, June 16, 1941, *ibid.*, 477.
[20] Memo by Ballantine, Washington, June 9, 1941, *ibid.*, 469; memo by Schmidt, June 17, 1941, *ibid.*, 478–479.
[21] Memo by Hull, Washington, June 2, 1941, *ibid.*, 454–455.

the other—the prospects for a meeting of the minds were dim.[22] While theoretically the situation appeared quite hopeless, from a practical point of view there remained a glimmer of hope. Although the American diplomats were in principle uncompromisingly committed to Hull's Four Points, in actual fact there was one question which worried them more than the others. This was the matter of the Tripartite Pact and of Japan's relations to Germany. It was America's concern over the Pact and her hope of separating Japan from Germany which had served to bring the United States into the negotiations in the first place.[23] This grave concern was reflected clearly throughout the course of the early conversations. President Roosevelt and Hull, for example, both thought that Japan's alliance with the Axis, by which she had apparently surrendered her power of independent decision for war or peace, was the most serious threat to Japanese-American relations.[24] To Hull, the existence of the Pact, the continued Japanese adherence to it, and the belligerent statements made by its defenders, notably by Matsuoka, were the strongest evidence possible that the Japanese did not want peace at all. Moreover, in Hull's view, the United States stood in clear danger from the Tripartite Pact. Just as America could not endure control of the high seas by Hitler, so she could not ignore a treaty which might bring Japan into the European war should the United States become involved in it through acts of self-defense.[25] The con-

[22] Even the ever-hopeful Nomura had given up hope for any but a limited agreement in July (memo by Rear Admiral R. K. Turner to Admiral Harold R. Stark, Washington, July 21, 1941, *ibid.*, 517).

[23] Memo, Bishop James Walsh to President Roosevelt, no place, no date, *Pearl Harbor Attack*, XX, 4291–4293; memo by Ballantine, Washington, June 4, 1941, *Foreign Relations, Japan*, II, 456–457.

[24] Memos by Hull, Washington, Feb. 14, March 14, 1941, *Foreign Relations, Japan*, II, 387–388, 396; U.S. Department of State, *Foreign Relations of the United States, Diplomatic Papers: 1941*, vol. IV, *The Far East* (Washington: Government Printing Office, 1956), 40, Feb. 15, 1941.

[25] Memos by Hull, Washington, March 14, June 2, 1941, *Foreign Relations, Japan*, II, 398, 454; memos by Ballantine, May 28, 1941, *ibid.*, 440.

cern of American diplomats over the Tripartite Pact led them to repeated efforts, as has already been noted, to pin the Japanese down to an interpretation of Article III and of the right of self-defense favorable to America. It also led Hull to attempt to undermine the position of those whom he considered to be Nazi sympathizers within the Japanese government. In an Oral Statement accompanying the American proposal of June 21, he challenged the good faith of those leaders, aiming his words unmistakably at Matsuoka:

Unfortunately, accumulating evidence reaches this Government from sources all over the world . . . that some Japanese leaders in influential official positions are definitely committed to a course which calls for support of Nazi Germany and its policies of conquest and that the only kind of understanding with the United States which they would endorse is one that would envisage Japan's fighting on the side of Hitler should the United States become involved in the European hostilities through carrying out its present policy of self-defense. The tenor of recent public statements gratuitously made by spokesmen of the Japanese Government emphasizing Japan's commitments and intentions under the Tripartite Alliance exemplify an attitude which cannot be ignored.[26]

The normally cautious Secretary of State would hardly have made such a brash diplomatic move, which was quickly interpreted by the Japanese as an outrageous interference in their domestic politics, had he not really been worried over the Tripartite Pact and the danger it presented.[27]

In contrast, the issues of Japanese occupation troops in China and of economic discrimination in Asia, while undoubtedly matters involving strong American principles, were hardly issues of vital national interest. To be sure, Hull and his associates were determined on principle that Japan must ultimately withdraw all her troops from China and must be converted to liberal trade and economic policies. Since these were firm objectives, there

[26] *Ibid.*, 485.
[27] Langer and Gleason, *Undeclared War*, 632–634, 638–639.

was never a substantial chance that the United States would re-treat from them. However, from a practical and strategic point of view, they loomed far less important in the American mind than did the Tripartite Pact.[28]

Because these objectives were less important strategically, the type of sanctions contemplated by American leaders to achieve them was quite different from the type considered suitable to achieve American objectives concerning the Axis Alliance and the support of Great Britain in the southwest Pacific. The United States let Japan understand that there would be war if she adhered to and honored the Tripartite Pact or if she co-operated with Hitler in a move to the south against Singapore.[29] No such implication was made, however, in regard to the issues of China and of economic policy. Instead, if Japan failed to agree with the United States on these, the consequences for her would simply be political and economic sanctions—no settlement with the United States, no renewal of the trade treaty, continued economic pressure, and continued aid to China. In fact, the American representatives clearly intimated that the United States was not as directly concerned about the other issues as she was about the question of the Pact. Hull insisted almost daily that the United States was involved in the struggle with Hitler as a matter of life and death and hence was directly and vitally concerned about the Axis Alliance. At the same time, American diplomats frequently disavowed any direct interest in Sino-Japanese relations, maintaining that the United States was interested in the peace terms offered to China only as a matter of

[28] A memo by Ballantine to Hull, Washington, June 18, 1941, named the Tripartite Pact as the first grave issue between Japan and the United States and Japanese troops in China as the second (though one which concerned the United States only as intermediary between Japan and China). It further remarked that on other questions "any difficulties which may remain are not of a serious character" (*Foreign Relations, 1941*, IV, 271).

[29] For example, the conversation between Eugene Dooman and Vice-Foreign Minister Ohashi, Tokyo, Feb. 14, 1941, *Foreign Relations, Japan*, II, 138–143.

principle. The United States was involved, they said, because a settlement in China was an important part of a general world settlement and because the Japanese proposals called for American mediation.[30] Although American strategists, it is true, placed a considerable emphasis on the practical wisdom of maintaining Chinese resistance,[31] this, too, was in large part due to the fact that Japan was already considered a real or potential enemy because of the Tripartite Pact. Maintaining Chinese resistance was thus a part of the war against Hitler. It would help keep Japan bogged down, would help deter her from southward expansion, and might help pry her out of the Axis.

Was the primary concern felt by the United States over the Pact justified? The answer would seem to be at least a qualified yes. Given the fundamental strategic conception that the chief enemy of the United States was Nazi Germany, the American diplomats had every reason to be concerned about a pact which tied Japan to Germany and which, at least on its surface, threatened to bring Japan into the war on Hitler's side. Moreover, while there was no clear indication that the Pact might actually be invoked at any particular time, it showed sufficient signs of life to make it a potential danger. The strong speeches made from time to time in defense of the Pact by prominent Japanese leaders, particularly by Matsuoka, were cause for worry. The Japanese Foreign Minister, for instance, warned in December 1940 that the Pact was the pivot of Japanese foreign policy and would remain so.[32] Even more ominous were his remarks in the Japanese House of Representatives a month later, when he indicated that the Pact would be invoked in almost any case of German-American conflict, except in the event of a direct German attack upon the United States.[33] Of course, the Pact was

[30] Memo by Ballantine, Washington, May 30, 1941, *ibid.*, 445; Oral Statement, Hull to Nomura, June 21, 1941, *ibid.*, 486.

[31] Langer and Gleason, *Undeclared War*, 492–493.

[32] Speech before the America-Japan Society, Tokyo, Dec. 19, 1940, *Foreign Relations, Japan*, II, 126–127.

[33] Grew to Hull, Tokyo, Jan. 27, 1941, *ibid.*, 134.

always characterized even by its proponents as peaceful. It could hardly be reassuring to the United States, however, to hear that Japan's "peaceful" aims were those of keeping America out of the war and preventing her from interfering with the Japanese efforts to advance southward, of ending the China Affair, and of improving Japan's relations with Russia.[34]

Matsuoka's trip to Rome, Berlin, and Moscow in March and April 1941 further increased American anxiety. Hull described Matsuoka as "astride the Axis on his way to Berlin and talking loudly as he goes."[35] From the American Ambassador to the Soviet Union, Laurence A. Steinhardt, Hull learned that the Japanese Foreign Minister while in Moscow had again interpreted the Tripartite Pact as binding Japan to go to war in case of an American attack upon Germany. The Russo-Japanese non-aggression pact concluded April 13, 1941, was represented by the Japanese government as an outgrowth of the Axis Alliance.[36]

Matsuoka's belligerent talk continued after his return from the Axis capitals to Japan. In May he told Ambassador Grew that, if fighting arose between the United States and Germany over American convoying, the Pact would certainly be invoked.[37] This threat could not be dismissed as idle talk, for Matsuoka did not stand alone in his assertion. Frederick L. Moore, American counselor employed by the Japanese Embassy in Washington, believed that the general opinion of the Japanese government was that convoys would lead to war with Japan.[38] And, as has been noted, American negotiators did not succeed nearly as well

[34] *New York Times*, Jan. 30, 1941; Grew to Hull, Tokyo, Feb. 5, 1941, *Foreign Relations, Japan*, II, 135–136.

[35] Memo by Hull, Washington, March 14, 1941, *Foreign Relations, Japan*, II, 398.

[36] Steinhardt to Hull, Moscow, April 11, 1941, *ibid.*, 184–185; Grew to Hull, Tokyo, April 14, 1941, *ibid.*, 186.

[37] Grew to Hull, Tokyo, May 14, 1941, *ibid.*, 145–146.

[38] Frederick L. Moore, *With Japan's Leaders* (New York: Scribner's, 1942), 175–176.

as they had hoped in drawing the Japanese envoys away from their stand on the Pact. In fact, when asked point-blank whether one of the purposes of negotiations was not to create for Japan a way to drift away from the Axis, the Japanese representatives emphatically denied that Japan had any such intention. The problem of adjusting Pacific relations and the matter of the Tripartite Pact and the European war, they contended, were quite separate issues.[39] It is not too surprising, then, that Ambassador Grew feared war with Japan if the United States fired the first shot in a conflict with Germany or even that Hull, whose suspicions were very active, had dread visions of Japanese plans for southward conquest in conjunction with Hitler reaching all the way from the East Indies to the Suez Canal.[40]

Paradoxically, the deep American anxiety and overriding concern over the Axis Alliance was a source of hope for the negotiations. For in spite of belligerent statements and ominous events, the prospects were not really hopeless for a virtual nullification or drastic weakening of the Pact. Japan had done considerable talking about the Pact, but she had made no moves to implement it, and there were influential Americans who believed she never would.[41] More important, the Pact was evidently the focus of a struggle going on within the Japanese government. The moves made by Japan to begin negotiations with the United States were efforts on the part of moderates to escape from the predicament in which Japan found herself involved, partly because of the Pact. While the concessions made by Japan on the issue of her alliance were never satisfactory to the United States, the Japanese diplomats showed a tendency to concede America considerable leeway in self-defense. They hinted broadly, in

[39] Memo by Ballantine, Washington, June 4, 1941, *Foreign Relations, Japan*, II, 456–457.

[40] Grew to Hull, Tokyo, May 13, 1941, *Foreign Relations, 1941*, IV, 187; Hull, *Memoirs*, II, 1017.

[41] Langer and Gleason, *Undeclared War*, 321–322.

addition, that the Tripartite Pact would not stand in the way of an agreement if other matters could be settled.[42] If the Axis Alliance was America's biggest worry, it was also the most expendable part of Japan's policy. The issue was deadlocked at the moment, but there still remained the hope that the United States could in time achieve a split in the Axis if she really wanted to.

Thus, all in all, three months of steady conversations had shown neither marked improvement nor grave deterioration in Japanese-American relations. There was less hope than ever for a sweeping agreement. Little or no chance remained that the United States would abandon her insistence on a withdrawal of Japanese troops from China and Japanese conversion to liberal trade policies or that Japan would give up what she considered her indispensable national goals in China. On the other hand, the issues of the Tripartite Pact and of Japanese southward expansion, which most directly concerned the United States, seemed somewhat less dangerous than they had in the autumn of 1940. Even if there were little hope of real agreement, there remained a chance that some kind of temporary and limited settlement might be reached. In fact, barring some sudden change in the world situation or some new overt act on the part of Japan, the situation might continue to drift as it was, with the two nations, though tense and hostile, not openly at war.

[42] Memo by Schmidt, Washington, June 17, 1941, *Foreign Relations, Japan*, II, 478–479.

III

Middle Phase:
The Pact in Limbo

EVENTS of late June and of July 1941 made further drifting in Japanese-American relations impossible. Without warning his Japanese ally, Hitler launched an all-out attack upon the Soviet Union on June 22, 1941. The repercussions in Tokyo were instant and violent. Not only was this the latest and most blatant in a series of betrayals dealt Japan by Germany,[1] but it also completely shook the foundations of the Tripartite Pact. In signing the Pact, the Japanese had assumed that Germany would quickly conquer Great Britain, that Russia would either be drawn into the Axis camp or else be neutralized between the Axis powers, and that the United States would be isolated and forced to concede Japan a free hand in Asia. Now every one of these expectations was hopelessly ruined. Germany, occupied with a new and formidable foe, would have to give Great Britain a breathing spell. Even if the Axis should finally win in Europe, a prospect which many Japanese now began seriously to doubt, ultimate victory would be a long way off. Russia, with whom Japan had signed a nonaggression treaty just two months before, was at war

[1] See below, pp. 112, 129–130, 143–144.

47

with Japan's chief ally. Worst of all, it was now Japan and not the United States who was effectively isolated, with no possible help to be expected from her European allies. Even Matsuoka was embarrassed by the German betrayal and the precarious position into which it had placed Japan. In a statement to the Soviet Ambassador to Japan in Tokyo, he confessed, "To be frank, Japan finds herself in the most awkward position faced with the war between Germany and Italy, her allies, on one hand, and the U.S.S.R. on the other, with whom she has but recently begun to improve relations." [2]

The period immediately following the German attack, from June into July, was a time of anxious decision for Japan. Three courses of action were open to her: first, an attack on Russia in the Far East, in conjunction with the German assault in the West; second, an advance on her own toward the south; and, third, a renewed attempt at agreement with the Western powers, especially the United States. The first course, although ardently championed by Matsuoka under German pressure, was quickly rejected by a large majority in the Japanese government.[3] Only the last two constituted Japan's real choices. The question, as everyone saw it, was whether Japan, now willy-nilly on her own, should make one last desperate attempt to go forward or whether she should execute a strategic retreat.

Faced with a clear choice between these two alternatives, Japan, as was her custom, chose to do both. She first decided on an aggressive policy. An Imperial Conference of July 2 determined that Japan should adhere to the plans for her Co-Prosperity Sphere and should press forward with a southward move, risking war if necessary with the United States and Great Britain. The conference further decided that Japan would not move against Russia unless conditions were favorable. As for the Tripartite Pact, while Japan would continue to try to keep

[2] Oral Statement, Tokyo, July 2, 1941, *Foreign Relations, Japan*, II, 504.

[3] Jones, *Japan's New Order*, 217-219.

the United States out of the European war through diplomacy, if America entered the war Japan would honor the Pact, deciding independently the time and manner of her action.[4] This menacing program became known to American officials through the breaking of the Japanese code. It was also soon apparent how the program was to be implemented. By the application of heavy diplomatic pressure the Japanese secured permission from the hapless Vichy government to extend the agreement for joint protection of Indo-China to include the southern as well as the northern half of the country. Japanese troops moved in to occupy this section of the French colony on July 24.[5]

The reasons for the choice of this advance at this particular time are open to some dispute. The Japanese themselves of course argued that it was a defensive move, designed to help conclude the Sino-Japanese conflict, to prevent a joint British–De Gaullist *démarche* on Indo-China, and to secure vitally needed foodstuffs for Japan.[6] In actual fact, there was a little of all these reasons involved, and more, Japan's motives being as complex and devious as her diplomacy was wont to be. The move was made partly to secure raw materials and foodstuffs, partly to obtain bases for further southward advances, partly to counteract what the Japanese considered to be growing Anglo-American encirclement in the southwest Pacific, and, finally, partly to appease the military extremists in Tokyo and in the

[4] "Resolutions concerning the Japanese-American Negotiations Adopted through the Conferences in the Imperial Presence," *IMTFE*, Doc. no. 1652.

[5] Jones, *Japan's New Order*, 260–263. The plans for the occupation of southern Indo-China, to be executed by force if necessary, were already approved by a Liaison Conference on June 25 (*IMTFE*, Doc. no. 2137H). The move was in fact a part of the fixed policy of military authorities in Tokyo since early April ("Gist of Imperial Headquarters Army and Navy Department Policy concerning Measures to Be Taken in the South," early April, 1941, *ibid.*, Doc. no. 2137F). See also the deposition of General Hideki Tojo, *ibid.*, Record, 36236–36237.

[6] Memo by Welles, Washington, July 23, 1941, *Foreign Relations, Japan*, II, 522–525.

Canton Army, who were eager to take even more drastic action.[7] Whatever the Japanese reasons were, there could be no doubt as to the implications of the move for the United States and Great Britain. Japanese troops poised in southern Indo-China constituted a grave threat to Siam, the Malayan States, Singapore, and the Netherlands East Indies—in short, the whole of southeast Asia and the southwest Pacific.

The peace offensive that Japan launched at the same time that she occupied southern Indo-China had, therefore, all the appearances of pure duplicity. It was proof, however, less of duplicity and treachery than of Japan's chronic ambivalence in foreign policy and of the deep rift between the Court party and the Army in her internal political structure. Within limits, the peace move was genuine, with powerful Japanese leaders backing it and determined to make a concerted effort to improve Japanese-American relations. The first step they took was one which they believed would surely impress the United States. Foreign Minister Matsuoka, whose political stock had already gone into a steep decline, especially since the outbreak of the Russo-German war, and who had long been the particular object of American distrust, was dropped from his post in a cabinet shuffle in mid-July. In the new, third Konoye cabinet which emerged, the more moderate Admiral Teijiro Toyoda took Matsuoka's place.[8] The cabinet change was accompanied by a sweeping overturn in Foreign Office personnel, much like that which had accompanied Matsuoka's advent to power in the summer of 1940, except that in this case the pro-Axis men were ousted from their positions both in the diplomatic service and in other government posts.[9] In an effort to impress upon the United States the importance of the change, the new cabinet

[7] Langer and Gleason, *Undeclared War,* 631–632; Prince Konoye, "Memoirs," *Pearl Harbor Attack,* XX, 4004. For further interpretation, see below, Chapter VI, pp. 137–138.

[8] Konoye, "Memoirs," *Pearl Harbor Attack,* XX, 3996–3997.

[9] *New York Times,* July 23, 1941.

announced an independent policy based on none other than Japan's own national interests.[10]

The reaction of the United States to the advance into southern Indo-China and the deposing of Matsuoka was what might have been expected. The latter received little or no attention. While Matsuoka's tenure in office had been reason for grave concern in the United States, his departure was apparently no reason for rejoicing. According to the State Department summary of the negotiations written some months after the war began, "Mr. Matsuoka was relieved of office because he had lost the confidence of Prince Konoe and the dominant elements in Japanese political circles." [11] In other words, the cabinet change was purely a matter of internal Japanese politics. If the American diplomats recognized in the fall of Matsuoka an estrangement of Japan from Germany and a weakening of the Axis ties (an indication almost unmistakably clear), they did not admit it.[12]

The American reaction to the Japanese move into southern Indo-China, in contrast, was clear and forceful. Almost unanimously, the move was interpreted as the last step in preparation for a military advance toward the south, and perhaps the actual signal for that advance.[13] All the Japanese arguments as to Anglo-American encirclement, fear of a British–De Gaullist advance,

[10] *Ibid.*, July 19, 1941.

[11] Memo, May 19, 1942, *Foreign Relations, Japan*, II, 343.

[12] A clear hint that Welles knew the effects of the German betrayal and the significance of the cabinet change is given in his conversation with Nomura July 18 (memo by Welles, *ibid.*, 515). Grew also reported and interpreted the change as meaning Japanese-German estrangement (Grew to Hull, Tokyo, July 18, 19, and 23, 1941, *Foreign Relations, 1941*, IV, 326–327, 332, 336–338).

[13] Memo by Welles, Washington, July 23, 1941, *Foreign Relations, Japan*, II, 524–526; Jones, *Japan's New Order*, 263–264. For evidence that the U.S. Army Intelligence Service (G-2) did not consider the Japanese explanation preposterous, see the memo of July 17, 1941, to the Chief of Staff by Brigadier General Sherman Miles, *Pearl Harbor Attack*, XIV, 1342.

and the like were contemptuously swept aside as being too ridiculous for consideration. Japan's promise that Indo-China would not be used as the base for any further advance was taken as equally worthless. Instead, the American leaders viewed the move as part of a design conceived under German pressure for wholesale aggrandizement in the southwest Pacific. Japan was pictured as a diver poised on the edge of the board, ready to take the final plunge.[14]

For these reasons, the Washington government took a long-delayed and decisive step. Acting Secretary of State Welles broke off the negotiations on July 23.[15] Then, after a proposal for the neutralization of Indo-China apparently was ignored by Japan,[16] the President froze all Japanese assets in the United States, thus placing all transactions with Japan under Washington's control.[17] Great Britain and the Netherlands readily followed suit, and governmental control soon became in effect governmental prohibition of all transactions. By the beginning of August, Japan found herself caught in a virtually airtight embargo on all strategic materials.[18]

[14] Memos by Welles, Washington, July 21, 23, and 24, 1941, *Foreign Relations, Japan*, II, 520–530; statement, Toyoda to Grew, Tokyo, July 25, 1941, *ibid.*, 318–319; Department of State press release, July 24, 1941, *ibid.*, 315–317; statement by Hull, Nov. 23, 1945, *Pearl Harbor Attack*, II, 421–422.

[15] Memo by Welles, Washington, July 23, 1941, *Foreign Relations, Japan*, II, 525–526.

[16] Memo by Welles, Washington, July 24, 1941, *ibid.*, 529. Apparently Nomura failed to transmit this proposal to his government until July 27 (memo by Grew, Tokyo, July 27, 1941, *ibid.*, 535; memo by Welles, Washington, July 28, 1941, *ibid.*, 538).

[17] White House press release, Poughkeepsie, New York, July 25, 1941, *ibid.*, 266–267.

[18] Jones, *Japan's New Order*, 265; Feis, *Road to Pearl Harbor*, 247–248. The freezing orders were not, to be sure, intended at the outset to be tantamount to embargo. The State Department contemplated instead a temporary suspension of trade, followed by the resumption of it on a quota basis, which was to include the export of a limited amount of less strategic petroleum products to Japan. As it turned out, however, the

The seriousness of this step and the crisis into which it forced Japan were readily recognized by officials and analysts at the time. Through the freezing orders, Japan was denied access to all the vitally needed supplies outside her own control, in particular her most crucial need, oil. The *New York Times* described the order as the most severe blow to Japan possible short of actual war. London experts believed that it would cripple Japan within six months after an outbreak of conflict.[19] Admiral R. K. Turner, Director of the War Plans Division of the Navy Department, and Admiral Harold R. Stark, Chief of Naval Operations, viewed the psychological and strategic effects of an embargo on Japan as so serious that they advised against it, warning, "An embargo would probably result in a fairly early attack by Japan on Malaya and the Netherlands East Indies, and possibly would involve the United States in early war in the Pacific."[20] Brigadier General Sherman Miles, acting Assistant Chief of Staff of the Army Intelligence Service, on the other hand, urged the application of sanctions, commenting, "The United States today is in a position to wreck completely the economic structure of the Japanese Empire."[21]

Least of all, of course, were these hard facts lost upon the Japanese, to whom the joint freezing orders came as a stunning

---

plan was not put into effect; no new licenses were issued. Trade remained suspended until, in late September, by common consent with the British and Dutch, the licensing system hardened into complete prohibition (relevant documents in *Foreign Relations, 1941*, IV, 828–887. See especially the following memos: by Adviser on Political Relations Stanley K. Hornbeck, Washington, July 16, 1941, 828–832; by Assistant Secretary of State Dean Acheson, July 23, 841–842; by Welles to Roosevelt, July 31, 847–848; by Welles to Grew, Aug. 1, 851; by Acheson to Hull, Sept. 22, 881–884; by Alger Hiss, assistant to Hornbeck, Sept. 26, 886–887).

[19] *New York Times*, July 26, 1941.

[20] Memo, Turner to Stark, Washington, July 19, 1941, *Foreign Relations, 1941*, IV, 837–840.

[21] Memo, Miles to Chief of Staff, July 25, 1941, *Pearl Harbor Attack*, XIV, 1344–1345.

blow. It may be true that the Japanese leaders, who unaccounta-
bly had failed to foresee the American embargo and to prepare
for it, now reacted to it too late and with too little in the way
of concrete concessions. It can hardly be denied, however, that
the embargo altered Japanese diplomacy to a considerable degree. The knowledge that Japan was faced with the prospect
of a steady attrition of her carefully hoarded resources led
Japanese moderates to intensify their efforts to conciliate the
United States. As F. C. Jones says, "After 26 July it was Tokyo
which pressed for a settlement, while Washington held off." [22]
From the beginning of August till late November the Japanese
government bent all its efforts toward securing some kind of
agreement with the United States which would relax the economic pressure now grown intolerable, without sacrificing all of
Japan's gains. The Russo-German war had propelled Japan upon
a policy independent of German desires; the Anglo-American
embargo convinced her that her new policy had better include,
if at all possible, a *rapprochement* with the United States.

The first Japanese efforts at a new settlement did not, to be
sure, seem very promising. In response to President Roosevelt's

[22] Jones, *Japan's New Order*, 280. An indication of the effect of the
freezing orders on the minds of some Japanese leaders is given in the
diary of Marquis Koichi Kido, Lord Privy Seal and closest adviser to
the Emperor (entries of July 31, Aug. 2, and Aug. 7, 1941; *IMTFE*, Doc.
no. 1632W). Kido records that Admiral Nagano, Chief of Naval Staff,
sought audience with the Emperor on July 31 to explain Japan's crucial
situation as a result of the freezing orders. Pointing out that the Navy
had enough oil only for one and one-half years of operations and that
the outcome of a long war was very doubtful, he urged that everything
possible be done to reach a quick settlement with the United States, including scrapping the Tripartite Pact. Although Kido did not favor the
outright nullification of the Pact, he and Konoye were likewise convinced
of the inadvisability of war. Kido even suggested that to avoid it, Japan
might do well to adopt the attitude of 1895 (the year in which, after
victory in the Sino-Japanese War, Japan had had to stand aside and see
the fruits of victory taken away by a three-power European intervention).

neutralization proposal of July 24, the Japanese government countered on August 6 only with the suggestion that it should promise not to advance beyond Indo-China, to respect Philippine neutrality, and to withdraw from Indo-China at the conclusion of the China Incident. In return, the United States was to suspend her military build-up in the southwest Pacific, to relax her economic pressure on Japan, and to "recognize a special status of Japan in French Indo-China even after the withdrawal of Japanese troops from that area."[23] Hull quickly rejected this as being unresponsive to the President's proposal.[24]

At the same time, far more auspicious and important ideas were being discussed behind the scenes in Tokyo. Konoye, long enamored of the idea of a personal meeting with Roosevelt to thrash out Pacific problems, finally secured the consent of his cabinet for what he called a Leaders' Conference. One may argue about Konoye's motives in proposing the conference and the sincerity of his professed desire for peace. It seems quite clear, however, that Konoye really wanted the meeting and that he was ready to negotiate. According to his own account, he was willing in effect to sacrifice the Axis Alliance in exchange for some concessions to Japan in Asia.[25] Once having proposed the meeting, he staked his political life on being able to bring it about. From the beginning of August to mid-October, the

[23] Proposal by the Japanese Government, Nomura to Hull, *Foreign Relations, Japan*, II, 549–550.

[24] Hull to Nomura, Aug. 8, 1941, *ibid.*, 552–553.

[25] Konoye, "Memoirs," *Pearl Harbor Attack*, XX, 3999–4000. See also Jones, *Japan's New Order*, 281–282; Feis, *Road to Pearl Harbor*, 252–254. The difficulties faced by Konoye at home and abroad are pointed out by German Ambassador Eugen Ott in a telegram to the Foreign Office in Berlin on Sept. 4, 1941. Reporting that Konoye was genuinely trying to reach a *modus vivendi* with the United States, he nevertheless predicted that "the negotiations with the United States could possibly drag on for some time, but a compromise, which can be had only by maximum concessions on the part of Japan, would at once result in grave inner convulsions" (*IMTFE*, Doc. no. 4080A).

projected Leaders' Conference, with the Japanese attempts to gain American agreement to it, was the central theme of the negotiations.

The first Japanese feelers for a Konoye-Roosevelt meeting got nowhere in Washington. Hull, ever suspicious and doctrinaire, greeted the invitation proffered by Nomura with obvious coolness.[26] Rebuffed by the Secretary, Nomura tried to interest another American cabinet officer (unnamed, possibly Postmaster General James C. Walker) in the proposal, but was turned down.[27] The return of President Roosevelt from the Atlantic Conference with British Prime Minister Winston Churchill at Argentia, however, brought a gleam of hope. Nomura promptly secured an audience with the President to present him with Japan's invitation to a conference. Roosevelt first read Nomura a message drawn up by Churchill and himself, giving Japan a thinly veiled warning that further advances into the southwest Pacific would bring war with Great Britain and the United States. He followed it, however, with another statement opening the door to a renewal of the conversations broken off in late July.[28] Moreover, the President reacted favorably to the idea of a meeting with Konoye in the Pacific, even suggesting Juneau, Alaska, as a site rather than Honolulu, as the Japanese had proposed.[29] At the same time, Ambassador Grew in Tokyo was impressed by Foreign Minister Toyoda's insistence that Japan was not bound within the confines of her proposal of August 6 and that Premier Konoye's offer to leave the country for a conference with a foreign head of state, an offer unprecedented

[26] Memo by Ballantine, Washington, Aug. 8, 1941, *Foreign Relations, Japan*, II, 550–551.

[27] Nomura to Toyoda, Washington, Aug. 16, 1941, *Pearl Harbor Attack*, XII, 17–18.

[28] Memo by Hull, Oral Statement from Roosevelt to Nomura, and Statement from Roosevelt to Nomura, Washington, Aug. 17, 1941, *Foreign Relations, Japan*, II, 554–559.

[29] Nomura to Toyoda, Washington, Aug. 18, 1941, *Pearl Harbor Attack*, XVII, 2749–2754.

in Japanese politics, was evidence of the sincerity of Japanese desires for peace. Grew urged that the proposal be given profound consideration. "The good," he wrote, "which may flow from a meeting between Prince Konoye and President Roosevelt is incalculable." [30]

Noting these hopeful developments, the Japanese pressed ever harder for a meeting. "We have reached the point," Toyoda wrote to Nomura, "where we will pin our last hopes on an interview between the Premier and the President." [31] In the Japanese campaign to persuade the Americans, many officials took part. Toyoda conferred with Grew, arguing that Japan was in a precarious position because of the Tripartite Pact, the proponents of which might be strengthened in Japan should the conference fail to come to pass. [32] Nomura continued to work at the ungrateful task of trying to influence Hull, [33] while Premier Konoye intervened by writing an urgent and conciliatory letter to President Roosevelt. The President, impressed by the letter, commented again that he was "keenly interested" in the meeting, once more suggesting Juneau as the site. [34] In fact, as Nomura reported, the President's response—"I am looking forward to having approximately three days' talk with Prince Konoye"— amounted to virtual acceptance of the Japanese offer. [35]

The one obstacle that the Japanese were never able to overcome was the deep-seated distrust and suspicion of Secretary Hull. The reasons for Hull's determination to hold off on any such meeting were numerous. Distrust of Konoye, fear of caus-

[30] Memo by Grew, Tokyo, Aug. 17, 1941, and Grew to Hull, Tokyo, Aug. 18, 1941, *Foreign Relations, Japan*, II, 560–565.

[31] Toyoda to Nomura, Tokyo, Aug. 26, 1941, *Pearl Harbor Attack*, XII, 20.

[32] Toyoda to Nomura, Tokyo, Aug. 27, 1941, *ibid.*, 34–35.

[33] Memo by Hull, Washington, Aug. 23, 1941, *Foreign Relations, Japan*, II, 568.

[34] Memo by Hull, Washington, Aug. 28, 1941, *ibid.*, 571–572; text of letter, Aug. 28, 1941, *ibid.*, 572–573.

[35] Nomura to Toyoda, Washington, Aug. 28, 1941, *Pearl Harbor Attack*, XVII, 2794.

ing uneasiness in China, unwillingness to see his own theoretical diplomacy and firm principles laid aside for the personal diplomacy of Roosevelt, and an often-expressed fear of a Far Eastern Munich, resulting in a weakening of the American moral position the world over—all these were factors in Hull's mind.[36] For these reasons, Hull used his considerable influence to throw cold water on the scheme. To Nomura's pleas he turned a deaf ear, commenting, "I made no promises of any kind . . . [as to] when it would be held, if it should be held at all." [37] On the basis of a State Department memorandum of August 28, he urged that no meeting be held until preliminary agreement had been reached through regular channels on all the basic issues under consideration.[38] This policy, of course, would effectively torpedo the conference, since the whole idea behind it, according to the Japanese, was that agreements could be reached and undertakings assumed through a Leaders' Conference which could not be made for political reasons through normal diplomatic channels and in talks held among subordinates.[39] The Secretary, however, succeeded in converting Roosevelt to his point of view. In an Oral Statement delivered to Nomura on September 3, Roosevelt duly informed the Japanese that they would have to agree on Hull's basic Four Points and their implications in the Far East before a meeting could take place.[40] This was clearly the beginning of the end for the proposed Leaders' Conference. The Japanese continued to plead for a speedy meeting; Grew continued to advise acceptance of their offer; and Roosevelt, it would seem, continued to entertain the idea as a possibility. But

[36] Memo of Department of State, May 19, 1942, *Foreign Relations, Japan,* II, 350–352; statement by Hull, Nov. 23, 1945, *Pearl Harbor Attack,* II, 425–426.

[37] Memo by Hull, Washington, Aug. 23, 1941, *Foreign Relations, Japan,* II, 568.

[38] *Pearl Harbor Attack,* XX, 4406–4410.

[39] Memo by Hull, Washington, Sept. 3, 1941, *Foreign Relations, Japan,* II, 589.   [40] *Ibid.,* 589–591.

Hull, never wavering in his convictions, eventually had his way.[41]

Significantly enough, the issue of the Tripartite Pact played no role of any importance in the crucial American decision to refuse the Japanese offer of a Leaders' Conference. The aspect most obvious in the new independent policy of Japan was her shrinking away from her Axis obligations and her resultant estrangement from Germany. By August, the Japanese were convinced that the Pact was an unreal issue and that the only point on which there was any real difference between Japan and the United States was the China Affair.[42] Confronted by this Japanese contention, Hull did not seriously take issue with it. Nomura argued that the Tripartite Pact was no real problem, "as the Japanese people regarded their adherence to the Axis as merely nominal and as he could not conceive of his people being prepared to go to war with the United States for the sake of Germany." To this contention Hull raised only the mild demurrer that since previous Japanese governments had seemed disposed to emphasize the Pact, something needed to be done to convince American public opinion that a change had taken place.[43] The Chinese question plainly was the pivotal one in the mind of the Secretary, with the fear of disillusioning the Chinese one of his main reasons for opposing the Leaders' Conference.[44]

As for Roosevelt, though he had returned from the Atlantic Conference deeply concerned over Japanese expansion to the south and its possible effects on the European war, he was sufficiently impressed with the evidences of Japanese estrange-

[41] Grew to Hull, Tokyo, Sept. 4, 1941, *ibid.*, 594–595; Sept. 5, *ibid.*, 601–603; Sept. 29, *ibid.*, 645–650; memo, Hull to Roosevelt, Sept. 28, 1941, *Pearl Harbor Attack*, XX, 4424–4427.

[42] Grew to Hull, Tokyo, Aug. 18, 1941, *Foreign Relations, Japan*, II, 562.

[43] Memo by Ballantine, Washington, Aug. 28, 1941, *ibid.*, 577.

[44] *Ibid.*, 578–579.

ment from the Axis to look favorably upon the idea of a meeting with Konoye. Moreover, the officials of the Tokyo Embassy, Grew and Dooman, were both convinced that the Japanese proposals meant a definite change in alignment for Japan. Grew argued strongly in letters to Roosevelt and Hull that Konoye was sincerely trying to get out of the Tripartite Pact obligations and to avoid war. As the Ambassador put it:

Germany's action [the attack on Russia] upset the basis for the Tripartite Pact, Japan having joined the Italo-German Axis in order to obtain security against Russia and thereby to avoid the peril of being caught between the Soviet Union and the United States. At the present time Japan is attempting to correct this miscalculation by getting out of an extremely dangerous position.[45]

The Embassy in Tokyo was also convinced that the cabinet change in Japan in July was evidence of this switch in policy. When asked by Tokohiko Ushiba, Prince Konoye's private secretary, how the Embassy had interpreted Matsuoka's fall to the Washington office, Dooman had replied:

We had reported that the Cabinet change was due chiefly to two causes: First, the German attack on Soviet Russia, which upset Japanese expectation, when signing the Alliance, that peace would be maintained between Germany and Russia; and, second, the conflict of interpretations by the Prime Minister and Mr. Matsuoka with regard to the scope and significance of the Triple Alliance. Mr. Ushiba said that we had been entirely correct.[46]

Thus while American distrust of Japan had not abated, especially in the State Department, there was no longer any real need to fear that the Tripartite Pact would at present be invoked against the United States. The Axis Alliance was in fact

[45] Grew to Hull, Tokyo, Sept. 29, 1941, *ibid.*, 646; see also Grew to Roosevelt, Tokyo, Sept. 22, 1941, *Pearl Harbor Attack*, XX, 4214.
[46] Memo by Dooman, Tokyo, Sept. 18, 1941, *Foreign Relations, Japan*, II, 628–629.

rapidly becoming a dead issue. Nothing shows this more plainly than the course of the conversations from September 3 to October 16. By all odds this was one of the most crucial periods of the negotiations and one full of frantic diplomatic activity. The Konoye government, fighting for its political life and bending every effort to secure the Leaders' Conference on which it had pinned its hopes, worked desperately to persuade the American leaders of Japanese sincerity. Formula after formula was presented to meet the American demands, only to be tried and found wanting. Talks were held not only in Washington but also in Tokyo, with officials high and low, from counselors and private secretaries up to Premier Konoye himself, taking part. Yet in all this flurry of diplomatic activity, the Tripartite Pact went almost unnoticed and undiscussed.

The issue of Japan's obligations under the Pact, it should be noted, was ignored by the United States, not by Japan. The Japanese representatives were ready enough to talk about the Pact and to use Japan's new attitude toward it as part of their campaign of conciliation. Having made what they considered important concessions on the point, the Japanese were anxious to impress these on the United States. They cited the difficulties which the concessions would cause for Japan, both in domestic politics and with her Axis partners, as proof of Japan's sincerity and as reasons why the United States should agree to a quick meeting of the leaders. The American spokesmen, on the other hand, were careful to ignore the Pact as much as possible, to make no statements on it, and to concentrate on the other issues, which they considered the real obstacles to a restoration of normal relations.

The concessions which the Japanese would make on the Pact, to be found in Japan's proposals of September 6 and September 25, were substantial. The Imperial government was willing, first, to make the right of self-defense enjoyed by each party entirely mutual. In addition, it declared:

In case the United States should participate in the European War, Japan would decide entirely independently in the matter of interpretation of the Tripartite Pact between Japan, Germany, and Italy, and would likewise determine what actions might be taken by way of fulfilling the obligations in accordance with the said interpretation.[47]

This commitment would largely have met the American requirements as put forward in the spring of 1941. It did not, to be sure, give the United States a complete a priori guarantee on any measure of self-defense she might take; this was the one thing which the Japanese insisted they could not do.[48] But it asserted emphatically Japan's independence of decision, stipulated that the Pact was defensive, and set down in black and white an independent course of action for Japan in case of American participation in the European war. A comparison of this clause with the parallel one of the Japanese proposal of May 12 shows that it was a major step forward.

This step, the Japanese maintained, was as far as Japan could go on the Pact publicly and in writing. However, they insisted that in a meeting of leaders Prince Konoye could give President Roosevelt an assurance, already cleared with the influential members of the Japanese government, which would entirely satisfy him on this issue.[49] Moreover, the very existence of the Pact, according to the Japanese, was the more reason for a speedy conference of leaders. Should Japan's conciliatory offer fail of acceptance, this would strengthen the pro-Axis and extremist elements in Japan.[50] The United States would have nothing to fear from the present cabinet in regard to the Pact, but should it fall because of failure to secure a conference, a new cabinet might interpret Japan's obligations differently.[51] Moreover, the

[47] Proposal submitted to Grew, Sept. 25, 1941, *ibid.*, 638.
[48] Memo by Ballantine, Washington, Aug. 28, 1941, *ibid.*, 577.
[49] Memo by Dooman, Tokyo, Sept. 18, 1941, *ibid.*, 628.
[50] Memo by Grew, Tokyo, Sept. 3, 1941, *ibid.*, 586.
[51] Memo by Welles, Washington, Oct. 13, 1941, *ibid.*, 684.

occurrence of such inflammatory incidents as the fight between the American destroyer *Greer* and a German submarine, for which the Germans might try to invoke the Pact, made a speedy meeting even more desirable.[52] The pressure exerted on the government by pro-Axis elements in Japan, who were focusing attention on the coming anniversary of the Pact on September 27, was another reason for haste.[53] The very fact that the Japanese Premier was willing to sacrifice the good will of his country's allies by proposing such a meeting should prove that Japan was really seeking a settlement.[54]

To all these overtures, the American representatives reacted with cool evasiveness. Ambassador Grew, to be sure, without committing himself on the trustworthiness of Konoye's promise to give satisfactory assurances on the Pact at a Leaders' Conference, did report that Japan's willingness to enter into negotiations with the United States reduced the Pact to nullity.[55] Officially, however, the State Department chose to ignore the Pact issue where possible, and where this was impossible to bring up further objections. American public opinion was a factor which needed to be considered, said Hull, since the Japanese had formerly emphasized the Pact.[56] Without complete guarantees against a Japanese attack, the Secretary said, the Senate Foreign Relations Committee might cause trouble.[57] The fact that the Pact was a military alliance, moreover, was still a troublesome one.[58]

To the specific Japanese proposals, moreover, the Americans gave no answer. Grew's reply (under instructions) to the Japanese proposal of September 6 dwelt almost entirely upon the issues of troops in China and economic nondiscrimination. On

[52] Memo by Grew, Tokyo, Sept. 8, 1941, *ibid.*, 609.
[53] Memo by Grew, Tokyo, Sept. 22, 1941, *ibid.*, 632.
[54] Document, Nomura to Hull, Sept. 29, 1941, *ibid.*, 653.
[55] Grew to Hull, Tokyo, Sept. 29, 1941, *ibid.*, 650.
[56] Memo by Ballantine, Washington, Aug. 28, 1941, *ibid.*, 577.
[57] Memo by Ballantine, Washington, Sept. 4, 1941, *ibid.*, 596.
[58] Memo by Ballantine, Washington, Sept. 10, 1941, *ibid.*, 614.

the clause dealing with the Pact, Grew said merely that, while Japan's suggestion "does not fully meet the requirements of the situation," the point would be further studied by American representatives before essaying another suggestion.[59] Apparently the State Department never got beyond "further study" of the Japanese proposals, for on September 19, in response to Nomura's query as to whether there was any new proposal on the Tripartite Pact, Hull merely replied that there was no answer as yet to the Japanese suggestions.[60]

The American statement of October 2 provides the definitive expression of the noncommittal attitude of the American government toward the Axis Alliance at this stage of the conversations. This statement was of great importance. It gave the quietus to the idea of a Leaders' Conference, interring thereby the most hopeful development since the negotiations began and sealing the doom of the Konoye government. The statement contains an exhaustive catalogue of the American reasons for refusing to agree to a meeting between Roosevelt and Konoye: the United States insistence on fundamental agreement on basic principles prior to a meeting, her disappointment at the "narrow" Japanese proposals, and the conflict over withdrawal of troops from China and economic nondiscrimination. On the issue of the Pact, however, the statement made only this incidental comment:

With reference to the attitude of each country toward the European War, this Government has noted with appreciation the further step taken by the Japanese Government to meet the difficulties inherent in this aspect of the relations between the two countries. It is believed it would be helpful if the Japanese Government could give further study to the question of possible additional clarification of its position.[61]

[59] Statement, Grew to Toyoda, Sept. 10, 1941, *ibid.*, 613.
[60] Memo by Ballantine, Washington, Sept. 19, 1941, *ibid.*, 630.
[61] *Ibid.*, 656–661.

The reaction in Tokyo to this statement was one of despair and frustration. The Americans, the Japanese complained, refused to lay their cards on the table. Why would the United States not say, for example, what undertaking it expected from Japan in regard to the Tripartite Pact? [62] No answer, however, was soon forthcoming. The reply the Japanese regularly received to their question was that the American position on the Pact had long been clearly set forth. If Japan did not now understand it, there was little the United States could do. When Grew was asked what specific actions the United States wanted from Japan, he significantly omitted the Tripartite Pact from his list of the troublesome issues.[63] Sumner Welles, confronted in Washington with a similar question in regard to the Pact from Counselor Wakasugi, chose to evade the question with the reply, "I would have to refer this question to the Secretary of State to determine whether any further clarification was necessary." [64]

The only American official who seems to have given the Japanese any concrete suggestion as to how to meet American requirements on the issue was Counselor Eugene Dooman. In a conversation with Ushiba, Konoye's secretary, Dooman was told that, while prominent Japanese officials had agreed on a virtual abandonment of the Pact, one problem for Japan was how to inform Germany of this development. Dooman agreed that this presented a difficulty. "I remarked," he reported, "that the United States, which was committed to supporting the principle of the sanctity of treaties, could not well request Japan to betray its treaty commitments." His suggested solution to the problem was that Japan should inform Germany that, although the treaty would remain in force, Japan would interpret it conformably with its own policy, which policy was now oriented along American lines. As far as Dooman was concerned, this

---

[62] Memo by Dooman, Tokyo, Oct. 7, 1941, *ibid.*, 662–663.
[63] Memo by Grew, Tokyo, Oct. 8, 1941, *ibid.*, 666–667.
[64] Memo by Welles, Washington, Oct. 13, 1941, *ibid.*, 685.

would not constitute a repudiation of the treaty by Japan, for, he said,

Technically the Alliance is a defensive alliance; and it is clear from the rescript issued by the Emperor at the time of the signing of the Alliance that it was then considered by the Japanese Government as an instrument for peace.[65]

There was nothing new or impractical about this proposed solution to the problem of the Pact. It was in line both with the ends desired by the United States at the outset of the negotiations and with the policy which the Japanese were now following in regard to the European war at this stage of the talks. The Japanese, as will be shown, were in fact ignoring Germany and the Tripartite Pact completely. The United States had originally wanted—or said it wanted—only a reasonable assurance that the Pact would not be invoked. Dooman's suggestion would provide this. It was thus reasonable and practicable. Since, however, it was not backed by any other person higher in authority than he, it is doubtful that he spoke the mind of the State Department. The conspicuous silence of his Washington superiors on the Pact raises the question whether they wanted the issue settled in this manner.

The American attitude at this time is readily explained. There were two plain reasons why the American representatives were content largely to ignore the Alliance for the time being. The first was that there were other knottier issues on which the Japanese were trying to use evasive action and deception. Of these, the principal one was the American demand for evacuation of China. Japan continued to insist on the need for "cooperation between Japan and China for the purposes of preventing communistic and other subversive activities." [66] This meant, she contended, that Japanese troops would have to re-

<hr>

[65] Memo by Dooman, Tokyo, Sept. 18, 1941, *ibid.*, 628.

[66] "Text of Basic Japanese Peace Terms with China," Toyoda to Grew, Sept. 22, 1941, *ibid.*, 633.

main in specified areas of North China for an indefinite period.[67] Over and over the Japanese arguments were repeated. Over and over they were met with steady American refusal on the ground that continued occupation would not be conducive to a lasting peace or in accord with American principles.[68] Time after time Japan tried to get the question of China laid aside, to be settled by Japan and China alone. Repeatedly she was told that the China Affair was a key factor in any settlement with America. The Japanese argued that the China Affair was incidental to Japanese-American relations; the Americans insisted that it was paramount. An exchange between Sumner Welles and Counselor Wakasugi shows the crucial divergence of view:

The Minister [Wakasugi] then asked whether, if it were possible to reach a basis for an understanding with regard to all of the other major principles which this Government regarded as fundamental, the two Governments could not go ahead and leave the China question in abeyance. I said it seemed to me that this question was very much like asking whether the play of "Hamlet" could be given on the stage without the character of Hamlet.[69]

There were also other matters in dispute. Hull, still profoundly distrustful of Japan's intentions, believed that the Japanese were trying to hedge on economic nondiscrimination, were seeking to retain for themselves special privileges in China by virtue of geographical propinquity, and wanted to leave themselves loopholes for southward or northward military expansion, despite the repeated Japanese assurances to the contrary.[70] Still, there is good reason for believing, as did Nomura, that the issue of occupation of China remained the one real obstacle. Aware of this fact, and still determined to insist on a sweeping funda-

---

[67] Oral Statement, Terasaki to Dooman, Sept. 23, 1941, *ibid.*, 640–641.
[68] Oral Statement, Hull to Nomura, Oct. 2, 1941, *ibid.*, 660.
[69] Memo by Welles, Washington, Oct. 13, 1941, *ibid.*, 685.
[70] *Ibid.*, 684; Oral Statement, Hull to Nomura, Oct. 2, 1941, *ibid.*, 659–660.

mental agreement,[71] the State Department chose to concentrate on this issue.

The other reason for the relative lack of American concern over the Pact was, unlike the first, a practical and mundane one. It was the fact that at this time everything was going America's way as far as the Pact was concerned. In the autumn of 1941, the United States extended its naval action in Great Britain's behalf in the Atlantic ever farther and more dangerously. The United States Navy proceeded from convoying to patrols to open, though limited, warfare with German submarines. Yet all this went on without a single significant indication that the Tripartite Pact might be invoked. Indeed, there was every evidence that Japan would simply hear and see no evil in the American naval activities. Until this time, the danger that the Japanese would honor the Pact as the result of such American activity had been the crux of American concern over the Axis Alliance. As Hull puts it in his *Memoirs*, "If incidents then rose [as a result of American convoying] between Germany and ourselves in the Atlantic, Japan was free . . . to decide that we were making an aggressive attack, and to declare war against us." [72] The trends and events of September, October, and November, however, demonstrated in the most concrete fashion that Japan would not in fact so interpret the Pact and that the United States was in no danger from it. These trends and events merit closer examination.

The first clear signs of Japanese "coolness toward the Axis" [73] were already plain when the new cabinet, with its changed personnel and its avowedly independent policy, took office. More specific evidence that the Tripartite Pact was not to be enforced by Japan began to accumulate rapidly. First, because of the tight secrecy imposed by Foreign Minister Toyoda, the Germans

[71] Memo by Schmidt, Washington, Oct. 9, 1941, *ibid.*, 674-675.

[72] Hull, *Memoirs*, II, 992; cf. also Langer and Gleason, *Undeclared War*, 750.

[73] Langer and Gleason, *Undeclared War*, 719.

were unable to find out what was going on in the Japanese-American negotiations.[74] Next, the Japanese witnessed the extension of American patrols all the way to Iceland without a qualm and, when informed by the United States of the move, had no comment to make on it.[75] The Germans tried to use the *Greer* incident to exert pressure on Japan in the hope of getting her to adopt a firmer attitude toward the United States,[76] but met with no success. The anniversary of the Tripartite Pact came and went on September 27 with only the most restrained observances in Japan.[77] Pressed strongly by the Germans for a protest against American naval actions in the Atlantic and a return to the interpretation of the Tripartite Pact held formerly under Matsuoka, the Japanese candidly informed the United States of the German demand, stating that Japan was putting Germany off with a noncommittal statement to be issued to the United States.[78] Having thus drawn the fangs of any "warning" to be issued to America in advance, Japan sent a message which did nothing more than express "deep concern" should American-German relations worsen. The message, harmless though it was, was not even delivered in Washington.[79]

The Konoye government thus gave ample evidence that the Tripartite Pact was to be treated as a dead letter. The government which succeeded it on October 16, however, might well have been expected to take a different stand, led as it was by a military man, General Hideki Tojo, as Premier. This was exactly what Americans expected and feared. Yet (to anticipate the

[74] Memo by Grew, Tokyo, Sept. 6, 1941, *Foreign Relations, Japan*, II, 603–604.

[75] Memo by Ballantine, Washington, Aug. 28, 1941, *ibid.*, 577.

[76] Memo by Grew, Tokyo, Sept. 8, 1941, *ibid.*, 609.

[77] Memo by Grew, Tokyo, Sept. 22, 1941, *ibid.*, 631–633.

[78] Memo by Grew, Tokyo, Oct. 15, 1941, *ibid.*, 686.

[79] Toyoda to Nomura, Tokyo, Oct. 16, 1941, *Pearl Harbor Attack*, XII, 71–72; U.S. Congress, *Report of the Joint Committee on the Investigation of the Pearl Harbor Attack*, Senate Document no. 244, 79th Congress, 2d Session (Washington: Government Printing Office, 1946), 325–326.

narrative somewhat) the first few weeks of the Tojo government's tenure were to show that on the Tripartite Pact, at least, its attitude was no different from that of its predecessor. On October 17 occurred the most serious incident of all between Germany and the United States, an attack, allegedly unprovoked, by a German submarine on the destroyer *U.S.S. Kearny.* Many persons suspected Japanese connivance in the attack and feared joint Axis action under the Tripartite Pact. The British press was quick to link the incident with the Japanese cabinet change as evidence of an Axis squeeze. In the United States, House Democratic Leader John McCormack viewed the attack in a similar light, while Representative Charles Faddis, Democrat of Pennsylvania, urged that if Japan made a move as a result of this "attack," the United States should destroy the Japanese Navy.[80]

Days passed, however, without a word from Japan on the whole matter. Fresh fuel was added to the explosive situation when on October 30 Secretary of the Navy Frank Knox revealed that the *Kearny* had actually been engaged in active combat with the submarine at the time it was hit.[81] The implication was clear. The United States Navy was engaged in belligerent action against Germany in the Atlantic. Still, however, the Japanese maintained a discreet silence. Hitler now proclaimed that the United States had attacked Germany in both the *Kearny* and *Greer* incidents.[82] This proclamation by the German *Fuehrer* was the most direct and severe test to which Article III of the Tripartite Pact had ever been subjected. If Hitler's charge were true, Japan would be required by the terms of the Pact to go to war with the United States. The Japanese, however, paid no attention to Hitler's pronouncement, Japan's Information Board blandly declining to comment on it.[83] Just one day after Hitler's statement, Germany disclaimed any intention of asking

[80] *New York Times,* Oct. 18, 1941.   [81] *Ibid.,* Oct. 30, 1941.
[82] *Ibid.,* Nov. 2, 1941.   [83] *Ibid.*

Japan to honor the Pact at this time,[84] and with this, the whole incident passed over. One reason for this abrupt switch, one may safely conjecture, was that the Germans knew Japan would politely ignore any request Germany might make.

The months from September to November 1941 thus saw the United States move to a status of active belligerency with Germany in the Atlantic, while Japan did nothing to stop her. Winston Churchill, British Prime Minister, could at this time tell his countrymen, "Now a large part of the United States Navy, as Colonel Knox has told us, is constantly in action against the common foe." [85] Admiral Harold R. Stark, American Chief of Naval Operations, was later to testify that this was a period of real though limited war for the United States in the Atlantic.[86] The Japanese, however, far from making any protests against this action, declined to honor the Tripartite Pact against it, and did nothing to discourage the United States from carrying it on. As Langer and Gleason conclude:

It is clear that Tokyo successfully resisted German pressure to warn the United States against attacking German vessels in the Atlantic. The Japanese likewise evaded all Berlin's attempts to invoke the Tripartite Pact pending the outcome of the Washington conversations.[87]

The evasion by Japan of her treaty obligations to the Axis did not, however, help her cause at all with the United States. By October, the two powers were hopelessly deadlocked over one issue, that of troops in China. The Japanese hopes that Japan's conciliatory attitude on the Pact might gain for her

[84] *Ibid.*, Nov. 3, 1941.
[85] Speech at Lord Mayor's Day Luncheon, London, Nov. 10, 1941, in Sir Winston Churchill, *The War Speeches of Winston S. Churchill, 1939–1945,* compiled by Charles Eade (London: Cassell and Co., 1952), II, 102.
[86] Testimony, Jan. 4, 1946, *Pearl Harbor Attack,* V, 2310–2314.
[87] Langer and Gleason, *Undeclared War,* 905.

concessions in regard to China were doomed to disappointment, this being the issue on which the Japanese, from their viewpoint, could not give in and on which the United States would not. As a result of the deadlock, what the Japanese had been predicting all along finally occurred. In mid-October, the Konoye government, unable to secure a Leaders' Conference or to hold out any rational hope of a settlement with the United States, was forced to resign, giving way to a cabinet of ominously military cast, headed by Tojo as Premier, Home Minister, and Minister of War, with Shigenori Togo as Foreign Minister. With the advent of the Tojo government, the negotiations entered their final phase, one filled with frantic diplomatic activity, but barren of any real changes in the deteriorating situation.

IV

Final Phase: The Pact as a Pretext

SOME Americans at first feared the worst from the new Japanese cabinet—a renewed approach to the Axis, a resumption of Japan's southward drive, and even an attack on Russia.[1] Nomura himself was so discouraged over the hopeless state of the negotiations that he tried to resign.[2] The Tojo government, however, had received an Imperial mandate to make a last attempt for peaceful settlement, and the talks went on.[3] The atmosphere, nevertheless, grew steadily more tense and desperate. The Japanese pressed still harder for a quick agreement, urging that the United States recognize the "realities" of the Far Eastern situation and the critical stage which the conversations had reached.[4] American spokesmen, notably Roosevelt and Hull, answered arguments on "realities" with little sermons on moral principles and long-range reforms. They argued that Japan's salvation lay in adopting, like the United States, a good-neighbor policy to-

[1] *New York Times*, Oct. 18, 1941.

[2] Nomura to Togo, Washington, Oct. 22, 1941, *Pearl Harbor Attack*, XII, 81.

[3] Jones, *Japan's New Order*, 293; memo by Grew, Tokyo, Oct. 25, 1941, *Foreign Relations, Japan*, II, 697–698.

[4] Memos by Grew, Tokyo, Oct. 30 and Nov. 10, 1941, *Foreign Relations, Japan*, II, 699, 711–714.

ward nearby countries and reciprocal trade programs to solve
her problems of material shortages.[5] Sharp recriminations were
exchanged over the diplomatic tactics employed by each side.
The Americans complained of Japanese pressure and "ultimatums," [6] while the Japanese protested against the American
use of "strong-arm measures of economic pressure" and accused
the United States of deliberate delaying tactics in the negotiations.[7] The tone of the press in both countries became more
belligerent and provocative. In Japan, for example, the semiofficial *Domei* warned that war was inevitable unless the United
States quickly lifted her economic pressure on Japan.[8] The problem raised by the warlike press in Japan was serious enough to
draw the attention of Nomura, who requested and received the
assurance from the home office that "all utterances which may
tend to excite the United States will be censored." [9] Beneath all
the surface tension was the inescapable fact that Japan's oil reserves were dwindling day by day and therefore that her time
for decision between submission to the American demands and
war was growing ever shorter.[10]

Most of the negotiations at this time, as ever, consisted of
fruitless maneuvering and wrangling which meant little. Nomura
presented Japanese proposals on November 7 (Part "A" of
Japan's last-ditch proposal, to be discussed shortly). They offered nothing new, other than Japan's acceptance of the prin-

[5] Nomura to Togo, Washington, Nov. 10, 1941, *Pearl Harbor Attack*,
XII, 113–116.

[6] Hull, *Memoirs*, II, 1062.

[7] Togo to Nomura, Tokyo, Nov. 10, 1941, *Pearl Harbor Attack*, XII,
109–111; Nomura to Togo, Washington, *ibid.*, 124.

[8] *New York Times*, Nov. 2, 1941.

[9] Nomura to Togo, Washington, Nov. 5 and 6, 1941, *Pearl Harbor
Attack*, XII, 100–101, 103; Togo to Nomura, Tokyo, Nov. 9, 1941, *ibid.*,
107.

[10] Feis, *Road to Pearl Harbor*, 268–269. The Japanese oil reserves
dropped 30 per cent between December 1940 and December 1941, most
of the loss, of course, coming in the last half of 1941 ("General Production and Financial Preparations for War," *IMTFE*, Doc. no. 9030, p. 11).

ciple of economic nondiscrimination in the whole of the Pacific, including China, provided "the principle in question is to be applied uniformly to the rest of the entire world as well." [11] The State Department reply was an exhaustive rehash of the familiar economic principles of Hull, to which Japan was again urged to pledge herself.[12] All of this, it must have seemed painfully clear, was fiddling while Rome burned.

There was, however, to be one more significant development before the diplomatic game played itself out. Japan, determined to make a final attempt to stave off war, launched a last flurry of activity. Crucial conferences within the Japanese government during the first few days of November produced a new set of final Japanese proposals.[13] The Japanese plan was divided into two parts, Part "A" presenting the terms for a general settlement, Part "B" proposing a limited and temporary agreement. If the first were rejected, the second could then be tried as a final resort. Through intercepted messages, the United States was fully informed on both the provisions and the character of these proposals. American officials knew that this was to be Japan's last countermove and that the alternative to its acceptance was war.[14] They were also aware that the crucial issue in Tokyo was still the same—the problem of occupation of China—on which point the Imperial Army refused to give way.[15] The Japanese proposal was therefore tried and found wanting even before it was officially proffered.

Japan, however, did her best to put over her proposition. A special ambassador, Saburo Kurusu, was sent to help Nomura break the deadlock before the November 25 deadline on which Japan had determined. The importance of this final proposal

[11] Nomura to Hull, Nov. 7, 1941, *Foreign Relations, Japan*, II, 710.
[12] Oral Statement and Draft Document, Hull to Nomura, Nov. 15, 1941, *ibid.*, 734–737.
[13] Feis, *Road to Pearl Harbor*, 292–295.
[14] Togo to Nomura, Tokyo, Nov. 4, 1941, *Pearl Harbor Attack*, XII, 92–93.
[15] Langer and Gleason, *Undeclared War*, 729–730.

and the need for haste were repeatedly impressed on the Japanese envoys.[16] There can be little doubt that not only Nomura and Kurusu in Washington, but also Togo and Tojo were earnestly trying to gain acceptance of the Japanese proposition and thus striving, within limits, to reach an agreement with the United States and avert war.

Part "A" of the Japanese proposal was presented by Nomura on November 7, as has been noted. Togo had set considerable store by this proposal for a general settlement. He still entertained the hope that, if the United States received essentially what it wanted on two of the three vital issues, it would give way on the third and allow troops to be stationed in parts of North China, the island of Hainan, and Inner Mongolia for an indefinite period (when pressed for a time limit, the Japanese would specify twenty-five years).[17] The Japanese Foreign Minister was being wildly optimistic, however. Hull rejected Part "A" out of hand. Nomura, seeing its hopelessness, did not even try to revive it. Instead, when Kurusu arrived, he and Nomura proceeded directly to Part "B," the Japanese *modus vivendi* proposal, presenting it in the famous Japanese note of November 20.

Part "B" was short and to the point, its five provisions reading:

1. Both the Governments of Japan and the United States undertake not to make any armed advancement into any of the regions in the Southeastern Asia and the Southern Pacific area excepting the part of French Indo-China where the Japanese troops are stationed at present.

2. The Japanese Government undertakes to withdraw its troops now stationed in French Indo-China upon either the restoration of peace between Japan and China or the establishment of an equitable peace in the Pacific area.

In the meantime the Government of Japan declares that it is prepared to remove its troops now stationed in the southern part of

[16] Togo to Nomura, Tokyo, Nov. 5, 1941, *Pearl Harbor Attack*, XII, 98–99.

[17] Togo to Nomura, Tokyo, Nov. 4, 1941, *ibid.*, 94–95.

French Indo-China to the northern part of the said territory upon the conclusion of the present arrangement which shall later be embodied in the final agreement.

3. The Government of Japan and the United States shall cooperate with a view to securing the acquisition of those goods and commodities which the two countries need in Netherlands East Indies.

4. The Governments of Japan and the United States mutually undertake to restore their commercial relations to those prevailing prior to the freezing of the assets.

The Government of the United States shall supply Japan a required quantity of oil.

5. The Government of the United States undertakes to refrain from such measures and actions as will be prejudicial to the endeavors for restoration of general peace between Japan and China.[18]

Hull read this proposal in its worst possible light. It was, in his eyes, an ultimatum substantially more extreme than any Japan had yet made, whose acceptance by the United States would mean virtual American surrender. The United States would be required to supply Japan with all the oil she wanted, to abandon China, and to stop her own military build-up in the Pacific. Japan in turn would still be free to fight China, to attack the U.S.S.R., and to keep her troops in northern Indo-China. The withdrawal of her troops from southern Indo-China would be meaningless, since they could be very easily moved back again. American agreement to the Japanese proposal would make the United States a condoner of Japanese crimes, a silent partner in Japanese imperialism, a traitor to China and Russia, and an active accessory in building up a threat to America itself.[19]

The importance of the Japanese proposal justifies a closer examination of it and of the Secretary's charges against it. Few, if any, of the latter would appear to stand careful investigation.

[18] Draft Proposal, Nomura to Hull, Nov. 20, 1941, *Foreign Relations, Japan,* II, 755–756.

[19] Memo by Ballantine, Washington, Nov. 22, 1941, *ibid.*, 760; Hull, *Memoirs,* II, 1068–1069.

Some of them seem to be assertions contrary to fact. The proposal was certainly not an ultimatum in any usual sense.[20] Far from being the most extreme of the Japanese proposals, it represented the farthest point she had gone in offering concessions. The Japanese were not demanding an unlimited amount of oil. As Hull knew from intercepted messages, Nomura was instructed to ask for four million tons a year, the average of Japanese imports from the United States in the years 1938–1940. Even this, Togo made plain, was a bargaining figure—Japan would have accepted less.[21]

As for the charge that the agreement left Japan free to fight China, to attack Russia, and to plan further aggression, it would seem to ignore a number of salient considerations. In the first place, Japan's proposal "B" was only intended to be a limited, temporary agreement, of the same nature as the *modus vivendi* proposals which the American leaders were themselves seriously considering at that time. It was not supposed to settle all the problems between Japan and the United States or to provide for all possible contingencies. Its only purpose was to take care of the most immediate and pressing problems—for the United States the danger of a Japanese move to the south, for Japan

[20] Norman L. Hill, in his article "Was There an Ultimatum before Pearl Harbor?" (*American Journal of International Law*, XLII [April 1948], 355–367), argues that neither the Japanese note of Nov. 20 nor the American reply of Nov. 26 was a genuine ultimatum.

[21] Togo to Nomura, Tokyo, Nov. 26, 1941, *Pearl Harbor Attack*, XII, 177. The figure of four million tons requires further comment to be set in its proper proportion. Four million metric tons of oil equals approximately 27,500,000 barrels. The American production in 1941 was 1,486,-518,000 barrels; in 1945, 1,828,539,000 barrels. The "unlimited" Japanese demand at its maximum therefore called for approximately 2 per cent of the production of the United States in 1941, or about one-third the amount of the average annual increase in production during wartime. Had the Japanese been satisfied with a return to the pre-July 26 rate (a not unreasonable assumption), this would have called for about 21,-000,000 barrels annually—about 1.5 per cent of current production. (Figures are derived from *Petroleum Facts and Figures, 1950* [9th ed.; New York: American Petroleum Institute, 1951], 1, 320–332, 464.)

the pressure of the embargo—and thus to avert war at least for the time being. Secondly, Japan had a nonaggression pact with Russia in force which she had scrupulously observed until this time and which she had often promised both the United States and Russia that she would keep. If Hull had wanted a repetition of the Japanese pledge not to attack Russia, he could have had it.[22] Thirdly, the Japanese were "free," as Hull put it, to continue to fight China mainly because the United States, determined that Japan should not have her way in China, was sustaining the Chinese war effort and refusing to approve the Japanese peace terms. The reason for the war's continuance was not simply an obstinate refusal on the part of Japan to stop fighting, but the American insistence on terms which the Japanese considered tantamount to complete surrender, and therefore unacceptable. It is quite possible to contend, of course, that Hull was right in rejecting the Japanese terms for peace in China. Having rejected them, however, it was not then consistent for him to complain because the fighting was still going on. Had the United States desired a truce or cessation of hostilities in China, it could undoubtedly have secured it—at least as far as the Japanese were concerned. The Japanese leaders, pledged, like every other cabinet since 1937, to seek a conclusion of the China Incident, leaped at every hint that the United States might help arrange one.[23] Finally, it is difficult to see how the absence from Part "B" of a general pledge against military expansion left Japan loopholes for further aggression. Paragraphs 1 and 2 cov-

[22] Memo, by Ballantine, Washington, Nov. 19, 1941, *Foreign Relations, Japan*, II, 752; memo by Welles, Oct. 13, 1941, *ibid.*, 684. Such a statement was also included in the resolutions of the Imperial Conference of Sept. 6, "Resolutions concerning the Japanese-American Negotiations Adopted through the Conferences in the Imperial Presence," *IMTFE*, Doc. no. 1652.

[23] Note, for example, the hopes which the Japanese pinned on Roosevelt's suggestion that he might act as "introducer" between Japan and China (Grew to Hull, Tokyo, Nov. 24, 1941, *Foreign Relations, Japan*, II, 762–764).

ered the whole of southeast Asia and the southwest Pacific. Paragraph 5 envisioned (in Japanese eyes) a step toward restoration of peace with China. Russia was covered by the nonaggression pact and the other pledges mentioned above. Japan could have made no move without breaking this agreement or other pledges—which, one supposes, would have been tantamount to declaring war on the United States. Moreover, it is probable that Hull could have obtained a general pledge against military expansion, such as that contained in the Japanese proposal of September 25, had he desired. Nomura was instructed to include other sections of Part "A" in Part "B" (the statements on economic nondiscrimination and the Tripartite Pact) if the Americans demanded it.[24] In all likelihood Hull did not think such a promise from the Japanese to be of much value; but if so, there was no point in complaining because the pledge was not included in Part "B."

As for the contention that the proposed withdrawal of Japanese troops from southern Indo-China was meaningless, it is in flat contradiction to the whole American and British position in regard to southern Indo-China. For months American spokesmen had been insisting that the Japanese troops in southern Indo-China were poised for a drive southward and represented a grave menace to British and American possessions. The Japanese move into south Indo-China had precipitated the freezing orders, the embargo, and the existing crisis. With Japanese occupation of southern Indo-China, as American, British, and Dutch military officers agreed, the danger to Malaya, Singapore, and the whole southwest Pacific would be a very serious one; without Japanese troops there, the danger would be greatly decreased.[25] It is, therefore, to say the least, a sign of inconsistency that when the

[24] Togo to Nomura, Tokyo, Nov. 17, 1941, *Pearl Harbor Attack*, XII, 144.

[25] "Report of the American-British-Dutch Military Conversations," April, 1941, *Pearl Harbor Attack*, XV, 1562–1563. See also Hull's testimony, Nov. 23, 1945, *ibid.*, II, 449, 455.

offer was made to remove the Japanese troops from this most advanced and menacing position, it was dismissed as meaningless by the American Secretary of State.

As a matter of fact, in its first four points the Japanese proposal was not unreasonable. It resembled fairly closely the *modus vivendi* proposal which prominent American spokesmen, including President Roosevelt, were contemplating offering to Japan. The stinger of the plan, as Sir Robert L. Craigie, British Ambassador to Japan, comments, was in the tail, that is, Point 5, which seemed to require the United States immediately to stop aiding Chiang Kai-shek.[26] Again the crux of the problem was China. It is far from certain either that Point 5 actually was a demand for immediate cessation of aid or that the Japanese would have insisted upon this point as *sine qua non* for agreement. Kurusu argued that it meant only that the United States would stop aid once peace negotiations were actually begun between Japan and China, a view supported by Togo.[27] Craigie, moreover, felt that this point was not absolutely crucial, that Tojo would have given in on it had he been able to gain concessions on other points, particularly on oil.[28] But whatever its exact meaning, Point 5 was the real stumbling block. In Herbert Feis's opinion, "Whoever insisted on the last paragraph—Tojo and the Army certainly did—insisted on war." [29]

[26] Craigie, *Behind the Japanese Mask*, 130.

[27] Memo by Ballantine, Washington, Nov. 20, 1941, *Foreign Relations, Japan*, II, 755; Grew to Hull, Tokyo, Nov. 24, 1941, *ibid.*, 763-764. It is interesting to note that, in a *modus vivendi* proposal prepared in the Division of Far Eastern Affairs on Nov. 11, 1941, State Department officials Ballantine and Schmidt proposed that the United States suggest direct peace negotiations between Japan and China, for the sake of which Japan should offer China an armistice. During the period of the armistice and the negotiations, neither Japan nor the United States would send military supplies to China. The proposal, which thus on this point approximated Japan's, was never acted upon (*Foreign Relations, 1941*, IV, 581-582).

[28] Craigie, *Behind the Japanese Mask*, 130.

[29] Feis, *Road to Pearl Harbor*, 309.

Aside from the mooted question of the merits and faults in the Japanese proposal, it is clear that in view of the adverse American reaction there was never any prospect that Japan's *modus vivendi* would be accepted as it stood. Since it purportedly represented Japan's final offer, there seemed now to be no more room for negotiation or compromise. Nevertheless, the Washington government gave strong consideration to the idea of answering Japan with a countercompromise plan of its own, an American *modus vivendi*. American representatives dropped hints, upon which the Japanese seized eagerly, that the United States might be willing to see the China issue displaced from the center of the stage. Hull, for instance, in a conversation early in November, sounded out Nomura as a "private individual" on what the Japanese would do if a representative from China desiring peace were to enter into negotiations with Japan for a settlement of the China Affair. Hull, unfortunately, was expressing no more than a pious wish. The Japanese, however, naturally took this as evidence that the United States was now becoming willing to leave the China Incident up to Japan and China for direct negotiations, a development for which Japan had nothing but overwhelming approval.[30]

The Japanese soon discovered that Hull was merely indulging in conjecture. Still, their hopes of a change in the American attitude were once again revived from an even more authoritative source, the President. In an interview with the two Japanese emissaries, Roosevelt proposed himself as an "introducer" for Japan and China, saying:

With regard to the China problem, I have been advised that Japan finds the withdrawal of troops from China a very difficult undertaking. The United States is not trying to intervene or mediate in the problems of Japan and China. I don't know whether there is

[30] Nomura to Togo, Washington, Nov. 7, 1941, *Pearl Harbor Attack*, XII, 106–108.

such a word in the parlance of diplomats or not, but the United States' only intention is to become an "introducer." [31]

No words could be more welcome to Japanese ears than these. Here was evidence that on the crucial issue of China the United States might reverse its policy of recent months, abandoning its insistence on prompt and complete evacuation of troops. If this were the case, the deadlock between Japan and the United States would be broken. Tokyo responded to Nomura's report of the conversation with hopeful plans on just how the China Affair could be settled in accord with Roosevelt's proposal. With the President as introducer, Chiang would confer with the Japanese and arrange an armistice. With the armistice, American aid to China would cease, after which would follow a permanent cessation of hostilities and a peace treaty.[32] The Japanese were soon to learn that Secretary Hull's ideas on American mediation between Japan and China were far different from theirs, and evidently also from those of the President. Hull rejected the Japanese argument that the United States should cease giving military aid to China once an armistice was reached, in line with American mediation efforts. He contended, "If we promise Japan that we shall cease aiding China, the United States could no longer be considered a fair and neutral party to propose peace between China and Japan." [33] In other words, his argument seemed to run, a nation cannot be neutral in a dispute unless it is aiding one of the parties involved. Hull then quashed the whole idea by commenting that the time was not yet ripe for the President to suggest peace to China. Thus all hints that the United States might let the China issue slide finally proved to be false alarms.

A more solid and hopeful development, nonetheless, was the

[31] Nomura to Togo, Washington, Nov. 17, 1941, *ibid.*, 142.
[32] Togo to Nomura, Tokyo, Nov. 22, 1941, *ibid.*, 166.
[33] Nomura to Togo, Washington, Nov. 22, 1941, *ibid.*, 169.

actual formulation of an American *modus vivendi* counterproposal. Once again the impulse for this move came from Roosevelt. The President first brought up the matter in a cabinet meeting of November 7, in which the imminent prospect of war with Japan was discussed. He suggested some sort of limited temporary agreement as a means of gaining time. Secretary of War Stimson opposed the idea because he felt it would interrupt the American Far Eastern build-up and would critically discourage China.[34] However, the President, still attracted by the idea, drew up shortly thereafter a memorandum containing his proposals for a *modus vivendi*, which read (abbreviations are in the original):

6 Months

1. U.S. to resume economic relations—some oil and rice now—more later.
2. Japan to send no more troops to Indo-China or Manchurian border or any place South (Dutch, Brit., or Siam).
3. Japan to agree not to invoke Tri-Partite Pact if U.S. gets into European war.
4. U.S. to *introduce* Japs to Chinese to talk things over but U.S. to take no part in their conversations.
Later on Pacific agreements.[35]

What the President had in mind in this surprisingly moderate plan was plainly little more than a six months' truce or standstill in the Pacific. In sharp contrast to the American policy of the last few months, he was willing to see the China issue laid aside for a time. He was plainly far more interested in the Tripartite Pact and in halting the Japanese southward advance than he was in the settlement of the China Affair. His plan, moreover, called only for holding the Japanese at bay and did not require them to retreat from any of their more advanced positions.

[34] *Pearl Harbor Report*, 346.
[35] *Pearl Harbor Attack*, XIV, 1109; Langer and Gleason, *Undeclared War*, 872.

By the time this proposal had gone through the hands of the State Department, however, it emerged considerably revised and sharply narrowed. The proposed duration for the *modus vivendi* was cut from six months to three. The Japanese were required to withdraw all troops from southern Indo-China and to maintain no more than twenty-five thousand in northern Indo-China, for which they were to receive only a very limited relaxation of the embargo.[36] Thus drastically revised, the proposal certainly had much poorer chances of acceptance by Japan. Even after State Department approval, however, the proposal still was not ready to be submitted to Japan, for it first had to be approved by the other ABCD powers. Hull sought their approval by submitting the plan to the Australian, British, Dutch, and Chinese ministers in Washington, to be transmitted to their respective governments.

To the Secretary's surprise and dismay, the reaction was far from favorable. Only the Dutch approved the proposal outright, while the British and Australians were lukewarm; the Chinese, sensing a sellout, were violently hostile.[37] In vain Hull argued that the proposal in reality safeguarded and advanced Chinese interests. Hu Shih, the Chinese Ambassador to the United States; Owen Lattimore, the American political adviser to Chiang Kai-shek; T. V. Soong, Chiang's brother-in-law; and Chiang himself—all lodged bitter protests. Even Winston Churchill finally intervened in Chiang's behalf. With this, the Secretary gave up on the *modus vivendi* proposal and, after a consultation with the President, dropped the plan without presenting it to Japan.[38] Once again, and at a crucial juncture, the China issue had shown itself to be decisive. The American *modus vivendi* died a-borning, as Hull was later to testify, because of

[36] *Pearl Harbor Attack*, XIV, 1110–1115, 1124–1131, 1150–1154.
[37] *Ibid.*, 1143–1146, 1160–1183; Langer and Gleason, *Undeclared War*, 887–890.
[38] Langer and Gleason, *Undeclared War*, 890–894; Hull, *Memoirs*, II, 1076–1082.

the violent Chinese opposition and the danger of the collapse of her morale and resistance.[39] There were other reasons behind the decision, no doubt—fear of adverse public opinion and of the charge of "appeasement" among them. The concern over public opinion nevertheless also had to do with the China issue, for had the public known of the *modus vivendi* and had they, as is probable, condemned it as appeasement, they would have done so only on the ground that it betrayed the embattled Chinese.[40]

The abandonment of the *modus vivendi* left the way open for an already-prepared alternate American proposal. This was presented to the Japanese on November 26 and is commonly known as the Ten Points Plan. Originally drafted by Harry Dexter White, assistant to Secretary of the Treasury Henry Morgenthau, the proposal had been submitted by Morgenthau to Roosevelt and then to the State Department. Morgenthau advanced it as a scheme of daring and generous diplomacy which could at one stroke solve all the dangerous and weighty problems of Japanese-American relations. Some of its provisions seem incredibly naïve. For instance, it called upon Japan to sell to the United States three-fourths of her output of war material, to withdraw her troops from Manchuria, to expel all the German officials resident in Japan except diplomats, to evacuate China, and to grant the Chungking government a billion yen loan for reconstruction. On its part, the United States was also to make concessions—a two billion dollar loan to Japan, a favorable trade treaty, withdrawal of the bulk of American naval forces from the Pacific, and a twenty-year nonaggression pact with Japan. The proposal represents at its peak the American belief in sudden conversion. At one stroke, in prospect of American goods and dollars, Japan was to be changed from a hostile

[39] Statement by Hull, Nov. 23, 1945, *Pearl Harbor Attack*, II, 435.
[40] Langer and Gleason, *Undeclared War*, 891; Jones, *Japan's New Order*, 312–313.

expansionist empire, with great pride in its destiny and ambitious plans for its future, to a peaceful, contented nation of merchants subcontracting with the United States to aid America's fight against Hitler.[41]

Nevertheless, purged of some of its more unlikely provisions, the proposal became the basis for the Ten Points Plan. The plan purportedly was intended simply to make the basic American position, as it had always been held and presented, once more perfectly clear. In Hull's words, it represented "an effort to bridge the gap between our draft of June 21, 1941 and the Japanese draft of September 25." [42] Actually, it went far beyond any previous American proposal. After an introductory "Mutual Declaration of Policy," pledging Japan to an observance of Hull's familiar Four Points, with special emphasis on free trade, the proposal got down to its ten specific undertakings. Briefly summarized, these were:

1. Both governments would try to conclude a multilateral nonaggression pact embracing Britain, China, Japan, the Netherlands East Indies, the Soviet Union, Thailand, and the United States.

2. French Indo-China would be neutralized under the protectorate of all the above-named powers except Russia, with no nation to seek or receive preferential treatment.

3. Japan would evacuate China and Indo-China completely and immediately.

4. Neither government would support any but the Chungking government in China.

5. Both governments would give up all extraterritorial rights and concessions in China and would try to persuade other nations to do likewise.

[41] Letter and memo, Morgenthau to Roosevelt, Nov. 18, 1941, *Pearl Harbor Attack*, XIX, 3668–3682; Langer and Gleason, *Undeclared War*, 875–877.

[42] Statement, Hull to Nomura, Nov. 26, 1941, *Foreign Relations, Japan*, II, 767.

6. Both governments would negotiate on a favorable trade treaty.

7. Both governments would remove freezing restrictions.

8. Both governments would jointly set up a fund for stabilization of the dollar-yen rate.

9. Both governments would agree that no existing agreement to which either was a party (i.e., the Tripartite Pact) would be interpreted so as to conflict with the purpose of the new agreement.

10. Both governments would seek to bring other nations into line with the spirit of this agreement.[43]

Hull made a determined defense of the Ten Points Plan subsequent to 1941, describing it as an "honest effort to keep our conversations going," stressing the fact that it provided for what he called "mutual commitments," and insisting that it was a generous plan with which any peace-loving nation would have been delighted.[44]

Once again, it is difficult to follow the Secretary's reasoning, which flies in the face of some facts about the proposal plain beyond dispute. First, the proposal was unprecedented. No doubt Hull and his associates always considered the ten points, or something like them, to be an ideal solution of Asiatic problems. But never before had they been presented as demands to Japan in so bald and sweeping a fashion. It is safe to say that had this been done, the Japanese would have given up on the talks long before they did. Second, the Ten Points Plan was one-sided. While most of the proposals were indeed mutual in form, they were completely unconciliatory and uncompromising in reality. Numbers 1, 2, 3, 4, 5, and 9 demanded what was, in effect, complete surrender by Japan of her contentions and goals in regard to Far Eastern security, the occupation of China and Indo-China, her future commercial policy, and the matter of the Tripartite Pact. There was no proposal which called for an ap-

[43] Text, *ibid.*, 768–770.   [44] Hull, *Memoirs*, II, 1083–1084.

preciable sacrifice on the part of the United States in return. The only concession which America offered to Japan in exchange for the commitments required of her was the prospect of renewed commercial relations. Third, the proposal was not designed to keep the talks going, but was final in character. There was not, and could not have been, any rational hope or expectation that the talks could continue on the basis of this proposal. Whether Japanese acceptance of the American proposal would have brought great blessings to her in the long run, as Hull contended, is a highly debatable question.[45] It is quite certain, however, that presenting such a proposal to Japan meant writing finis to any serious negotiation with her.

As a matter of fact, this was precisely the effect which the proposal produced. When the Japanese emissaries received it, they threw up their hands, contending that they could not even report such a document back to Tokyo. If the United States seriously expected Japan simply to recognize Chungking and apologize to Chiang Kai-shek, it was asking the impossible. The terms demanded, said the Japanese, were tantamount to breaking off the negotiations. In despair, Nomura concluded that the United States was too bound up with Great Britain, China, and the Netherlands ever to come to an agreement with Japan.[46]

The reaction in Tokyo was the same. Although a milder and less uncompromising rejection of Japan's *modus vivendi* plan of November 20 would doubtless have had the same final effect, the nature of the American reply helped further to discourage and discredit the peace party in Tokyo. Even the most moderate and conciliatory Japanese regarded the American terms as completely unacceptable and humiliating.[47] Clearly, the only alterna-

[45] See Feis, *Road to Pearl Harbor*, 327–328, for a criticism (not always too convincing) of Japanese arguments for rejection of the proposal.

[46] Memo by Ballantine, Washington, Nov. 26, 1941, *Foreign Relations, Japan*, II, 764–766; Nomura to Togo, Washington, Nov. 26, 1941, *Pearl Harbor Attack*, XII, 181–185.

[47] Togo's deposition, *IMTFE*, Record, 35706–35712.

tive, if Japan were not weakly to submit or slowly to strangle under the embargo, was to fight. Despite some last-minute opposition from certain naval leaders and senior statesmen, the final decision for war, long delayed and twice postponed in the hope of concessions from the United States, now was formally made in conferences concluded on December 1.[48] The plans for an attack on Pearl Harbor had always from their inception depended for execution upon the breakdown of negotiations with the United States. Now the plans became irrevocable. The fleet, already dispatched, was not called back, as it could have been.[49] To keep up appearances, sporadic diplomatic activity continued on both sides, including a last-minute spectacular appeal direct from President Roosevelt to Emperor Hirohito.[50] Most of the activity, however, including the famous Japanese message delivered by Nomura and Kurusu on December 7, and the angry reply to it made by Hull, consisted of acrimonious name-calling and denunciation which meant nothing.[51]

Dominating the scene in the last phase of negotiations was the issue of troops in China, plainly the real cause of the war. The concessions Japan was ready to make, toward the end, on southward expansion and economic policy indicate that these issues could have been settled, or at least dealt with, short of open conflict. As for the Tripartite Pact, by November it was neither an operative instrument in Japanese policy nor a factor of any importance in the breakdown of Japanese-American relations, nor (as will be argued) a consideration in the final Japanese decision for war. It could be dismissed as of little or no conse-

---

[48] Jones, *Japan's New Order*, 317–319, 457; Kido's Diary, Nov. 29, 1941, *IMTFE*, Doc. no. 1632W; Tojo's deposition, *ibid.*, Record, 36366–36379.

[49] See the report on Japanese data concerning the attack, compiled by General Headquarters, Supreme Command of the Allied Powers in Japan, Nov. 1, 1945, *Pearl Harbor Attack*, I, 235–242.

[50] Dec. 6, 1941, *Foreign Relations, Japan*, II, 784–786.

[51] Memo, Nomura to Hull, Dec. 7, 1941, *ibid.*, 787–792; statement by Hull, Dec. 7, 1941, *ibid.*, 793.

quence were it not for one surprising and perhaps significant fact: This moribund issue of the Pact was revived as a major point of controversy during the very last weeks of negotiations. It was not the Japanese who were responsible for this development; they winced every time the subject of the Pact came up. Instead, the same American representatives who had ignored the Pact in September and October chose in late November to renew the issue on the same terms as it had been argued in April and May. It is worth while to see how this change came about, and why.

Quite clearly the cause was not any change in the Japanese position on the Pact. Americans might have feared a *rapprochement* with Germany on the part of the new cabinet under Tojo, but the new government soon proved to be just as much disposed toward an independent policy centered strictly on Japanese interests as the cabinet of Konoye had been. If anything, it was even more indifferent to the European war. Diplomatically, there was no change. Japan continued to insist that she could not go in writing beyond her declaration of September 25 on the Pact, but that she would be happy to make a joint declaration with the United States on the mutual right of self-defense.[52] Both Tojo and Togo shared the optimistic belief that there was "almost no division" between the United States and Japan on the issue of the Pact.[53] The Japanese emissaries continued their attempts to persuade Americans that the Pact represented no menace. Nomura compared it to the Anglo-Japanese Alliance terminated in 1921, while Wakasugi insisted that it was self-evident that no political agreement such as the Tripartite Pact could possibly obligate its signatories to military action against a third power.[54] Even if the Pact should continue to

[52] Memo by Hull, Washington, Nov. 10, 1941, *ibid.*, 715–716.
[53] Togo to Nomura, Tokyo, Nov. 6, 1941, *Pearl Harbor Attack*, XII, 102; statement by Hull, Nov. 2, 1945, *ibid.*, II, 430.
[54] Nomura to Togo, Washington, Oct. 17, Nov. 12, 1941, *ibid.*, 76–77, 121.

exist, the Japanese argued, an agreement between Japan and the United States would far outshine it.[55]

Moreover, there were Japanese actions which spoke louder than words in making it plain that the Tripartite Pact as an operative instrument meant little to Japan. As has already been noted, it was in late October and early November that the Japanese government studiously ignored the *Kearny* incident, the disclosures following it, and Hitler's charge of American aggression against Germany. All through November, even while Japanese protests against American policy in the Pacific mounted daily, American naval action in the Atlantic continued to go unnoticed. As if this were not sufficiently clear indication of its indifference to the fate of Germany, the Tojo government undertook to bring Great Britain in as a participant in the Japanese-American discussions. Foreign Minister Togo, believing that the British were often more flexible and realistic than the Americans in foreign policy, urged Ambassador Craigie to persuade his government to intercede in the hope of improving Japanese-American relations. He further announced to Ambassador Grew that, as soon as Japan had reached agreement with the United States, she wished simultaneously to conclude the same pact with Great Britain.[56] Obviously, there would not be much left of the Tripartite Alliance were Japan to conclude treaties of friendship with two of Germany's mortal enemies, the United States and Great Britain, while she maintained peace and honored her nonaggression pact with the U.S.S.R., Germany's third foe.

One more action by a Japanese emissary in regard to the Pact deserves mention, not because it had any effect on the outcome of the conversations, but because it represents the farthest extent to which Japan went by way of verbal formulation to conciliate

[55] Memo by Ballantine, Washington, Nov. 18, 1941, *Foreign Relations, Japan*, II, 746.

[56] Togo to Nomura, Tokyo, Nov. 2, 1941, *Pearl Harbor Attack*, XII, 91; memo by Grew, Tokyo, Nov. 10, 1941, *Foreign Relations, Japan*, II, 712–713.

the United States on this issue. Alarmed by renewed American denunciations of the Axis Alliance, Ambassador Kurusu, who had been the Japanese signatory for the Pact in Berlin, proffered an explanatory letter to Hull. It was written in the hope, as he put it, of erasing a "deep-seated misconception" about the Pact. The points he made were familiar, though they were stated in even more sweeping fashion than usual. Emphasizing the Pact's defensive nature and Japan's complete independence of decision, Kurusu said, "My Government would never project the people of Japan into war at the behest of any foreign Power; it will accept warfare only as the ultimate inescapable necessity for the maintenance of its security and the preservation of national life against active injustice." More important than this assurance, perhaps, was something new—an offer by Kurusu to allow his letter to be published whenever an agreement was reached.[57]

Hull dismissed these assurances out of hand as worthless, arguing in familiar fashion that all of Japan's attempts to explain away the Pact were fraudulent.[58] Scholars like Langer and Gleason have found it astonishing that the Japanese should ever have imagined that the sort of assurances they gave on the Pact would satisfy the United States.[59] Knowing Hull and his rigid principles, the Japanese should indeed have realized that nothing short of a public nullification would satisfy him. Viewing the matter realistically as they did, however, one can see very well how they concluded that they were meeting the Americans more than halfway. The original fear on the part of the United States was that the Pact might be invoked and honored and that Japan had surrendered her independence of decision. Here was repeated assurance that Japan considered herself entirely independent in regard to her obligations to the Axis powers, as well as a clear statement that she had no inten-

[57] Draft letter, Kurusu to Hull, Nov. 21, 1941, *Foreign Relations, Japan,* II, 756–757.
[58] Memo by Hull, Washington, Nov. 21, 1941, *ibid.,* 756.
[59] Langer and Gleason, *Undeclared War,* 858.

tion of honoring them. The United States had wanted freedom to act in "self-defense" against Germany in the Atlantic; Japan had not interfered over the course of five months with a very sweeping exercise of that freedom. American representatives, notably Dooman, had suggested that the Pact could remain in existence if Japan reoriented her policy in the direction of the United States; Japan was trying to do precisely this by seeking an agreement with the United States and Great Britain while keeping her Axis partners in the dark and resisting their pressure for action. Earlier in the negotiations Hull had tried to solve the problem of the Pact by using an exchange of letters which would define the Pact as defensive; Kurusu's letter, which assuredly defined the Pact as defensive, was offered for publication. The Japanese, then, can hardly be blamed for supposing that they had substantially met American demands as to the Axis Alliance.

It was, therefore, with a dismay undoubtedly genuine that the Japanese emissaries watched the American leaders revive the Pact as a serious issue and cite it as a fundamental reason for failure to reach an agreement. For some time after the fall of Konoye, to be sure, American strictures on the Pact remained moderate and incidental. Japan was reminded of her evil past and of the machinations of Matsuoka and admonished that she would have to do something concrete to prove her repentance. Hull answered Wakasugi's argument that the Pact was not directed against the United States, for example, with the charge that "for months it was proclaimed as intended principally to keep this country out of war with Germany and that it was a joint movement on the part of Japan and Germany to this end. It was, therefore, no easy matter for us to convince this country that it was a harmless document." [60] Replying to the contention that Japan was now entirely independent in her

[60] Memo by Hull, Washington, Oct. 16 and 17, 1941, *Foreign Relations, Japan*, II, 688.

policies, Sumner Welles conceded that "this might be the case" but reminded the Japanese Counselor that formally, at least, Japan was still tied to the Axis, a fact which bore great weight with the American people.[61] Hull revealed only a very mild concern with the Pact as late as November 12. After again citing the difficulty of explaining the Pact to the American people, the Secretary admitted that the Alliance per se was not a great problem or present danger. His words, "For even though we understand clearly the Ambassador's attitude and that of the present Japanese Cabinet, there must be considered the possibility of another Government coming into power in Japan," indicated that for reasons of future contingencies Hull still considered a break in the Pact desirable. Nevertheless, he concluded, "the matter of the Tripartite Pact relationship ought not to be a problem with Japan if we could work out our proposed agreement in other ways."[62]

However, the issue which Hull thus treated as relatively unimportant quickly and inexplicably took on great new importance. The tenor of American denunciation and demands regarding it suddenly changed. From November 15 on, American condemnation of the Pact rose daily in volume and urgency until, by the end of the month, Hull had returned to the arguments and invective of the previous May and June. It was almost as if nothing had changed since Matsuoka was in power at the Foreign Office. On November 15, the Secretary demanded that "the alliance be automatically abandoned." He insisted that he could never make Great Britain believe in Japan's peaceful intent as long as she adhered to a "fighting alliance" with Hitler, while at home "he might well be lynched" for making an agreement with an Axis partner. The Tripartite Pact would have to "automatically disappear"; indeed, as long as Japan insisted even on wanting to interpret it independently, she could not be pursuing

[61] Memo by Welles, Washington, Oct. 24, 1941, *ibid.*, 696.
[62] Memo by Ballantine, Washington, Nov. 12, 1941, *ibid.*, 723–724.

peaceful purposes. To Wakasugi's query as to whether this was the American reply to Japan's formula, Hull answered, "When we got an answer from the Japanese Government in regard to . . . the Tripartite Pact automatically becoming a dead letter in case we entered into an agreement with Japan we would be better able to make reply." [63]

This strong language was only the beginning. Hull next returned to the old demand that Japan accept the American definition of "self-defense" against Hitler. The Secretary complained of Japanese obtuseness on the matter: "The United States feels the danger [from Hitler] so acutely that she has committed herself to ten, twenty-five, or fifty billions of dollars expenditure for self-defense—but when Japan is asked whether this is self-defense she indicates she has no opinion on the subject." [64] The American people, Hull continued, regarded the Co-Prosperity Sphere as being no better than the Hitler program in Europe. For this reason he and the President would be denounced if any agreement were made while the Pact still stood. [65]

By this time, it was no longer the interpretation but rather the very existence of the Pact which was the crucial point at issue. Hull was now insisting that "countries cannot promote peace so long as they are tied in any way with Hitler." [66] From November 17 on, it was common for conversations to be occupied almost entirely with the Pact, a fact which Nomura reported in bewilderment to his home office. He pointed out that Hull was now emphasizing the Pact more than China, which meant a distinct change from the trend of the past six months. Having reached the stage of desperate improvisation, Nomura suggested that Japan might do well to give the Americans wholesale assurances regarding the Pact, in order to prompt the United States to

[63] Memo by Ballantine, Washington, Nov. 15, 1941, *ibid.*, 732–733.
[64] Hull, *Memoirs*, II, 1064.
[65] Memo by Hull, Washington, Nov. 17, 1941, *Foreign Relations, Japan*, II, 740–742.
[66] Memo by Ballantine, Washington, Nov. 18, 1941, *ibid.*, 747.

become completely involved in the Atlantic war. This, he thought, might relieve the pressure on Japan.[67]

Even had the Ambassador's suggestion been accepted in Tokyo, it would not have helped Japan's cause. For, as Nomura soon learned, Japan, according to Hull, was already inextricably wedded to Hitler and effectively fighting in his cause. Angered by the Japanese proposal in their *modus vivendi* plan of November 20 calling on the United States to cease aid to China, Hull declared, "The American people believed that there was a partnership between Hitler and Japan aimed at enabling Hitler to take charge of one-half of the world and Japan of the other half." Therefore, said the Secretary, "We are helping China for the same reason we are helping Britain; that we are afraid of the military elements led by Hitler." [68]

Thus the American position had come full circle, back to that of September 1940. Despite everything that had happened since that time, Japan was again identified, perhaps more completely than ever before, with Hitler, and China with Great Britain and the democracies. There was only one world, one great fascist conspiracy designed to conquer it and one united democratic effort to meet the threat. Nor was Hull's charge that Japan was already fighting for Hitler intended as metaphor. On the contrary, the Secretary insisted that the Japanese were even now aiding Hitler and hurting the United States simply by keeping large forces among Hitler's enemies tied up in the Far East. If Japan wanted to show her peaceful intent, she might well begin by allowing Russian and British troops to go back to Europe and the United States Navy to concentrate in the Atlantic.[69] The belligerent attitude displayed by Japan in the Tripartite Pact, Hull contended, was a major reason for the impossibility of

[67] Nomura to Togo, Washington, Nov. 17 and 18, 1941, *Pearl Harbor Attack*, XII, 146–148, 151.

[68] Memo by Ballantine, V ashington, Nov. 20, 1941, *Foreign Relations, Japan*, II, 754–755.

[69] Memos by Ballantine, Washington, Nov. 19 and 22, 1941, *ibid.*, 751–752, 760–761.

reaching a *modus vivendi*. Japan was confronting the United States with her troops in Indo-China, armed with the Tripartite Pact in one hand and the Anti-Comintern agreement in the other, and demanding American oil.[70] In this and a similar vein down to the very end of the conversations, Hull continued to sound the tocsin on the terrible menace of the Tripartite Pact.

Why should the American diplomats have revived the once dormant issue of the Pact at the last stage of the negotiations? The answer of the State Department is that all the Japanese assurances in regard to it were worthless and deceitful:

The Ambassador [Nomura] did, however, on several occasions make vague statements to the effect that if an agreement were reached with the United States, the psychological effect in Japan would be such that there would be no possibility of Japan interpreting its obligations under the Tripartite Pact adversely to friendly relations with the United States. This Government of course had to evaluate such statements in the light of developments and deep-seated trends in the field of actual events with which such statements were inconsistent.[71]

Just what these unspecified developments and deep-seated trends were is difficult to imagine. As will be shown in the succeeding chapters, they could hardly be the routine and nominal professions of allegiance to the Axis made by Japan during this period. These were so faint and lukewarm as to be positively damning. Nor could they be evidences of close liaison between Japan and Germany, for there was none. There was, to be sure, a Japanese military build-up going on in southeast Asia which gravely disturbed American leaders,[72] but there was nothing to show that this was the product of Japan's Axis relationship. As American leaders knew, at this time Germany was urging Japan

[70] Nomura to Togo, Washington, Nov. 27, 1941, *Pearl Harbor Attack,* XII, 194.

[71] Memo by Department of State, May 19, 1942, *Foreign Relations, Japan,* II, 361.

[72] Langer and Gleason, *Undeclared War,* 887, 892.

to move in exactly the opposite direction, against Russia, and not toward the south. The military build-up in Indo-China and elsewhere was only clear evidence of what was already obvious: If Japan could not come to terms with the United States and so get relief from economic pressure, she would move into the south Pacific in search of raw materials, especially oil. Both sides, expecting a conflict, were preparing for a war in this area as fast as they could.

Nor does it seem too likely that the American concern over the Pact centered on the possibility that a future Japanese government might honor it, even if the present one did not. Apart from the inherent improbability of such an occurrence, there were far too many immediate reasons for conflict to allow American statesmen to worry much about such remote contingencies.

One can discern in reality three reasons for the last-minute resurgence of the issue of the Pact. The first was the importance of moral principles in American diplomacy. Secretary Hull denounced the Pact because in his eyes it deserved to be denounced. He demanded its abrogation because it deserved to be abrogated. An alliance with Hitler was simply an international crime which the United States could not condone, much less in any way be connected with it. Moreover, as the Ten Points Plan shows, Hull had a strong dislike for compromise and a great penchant for keeping the record clear. Even if the Tripartite Pact were not a pressing issue, as even he surely knew at the end, his sweeping denunciation of it would show where the United States stood on the matter.

Another more powerful factor, however, was that of American public opinion, to which Hull alludes time and again. There is every reason to believe that the Secretary estimated it correctly. The American people identified Japan with Germany and would have denounced any agreement with Japan which would have allowed the Tripartite Pact to remain in existence. Whether the public, with its meager background and still more meager information, could have been expected to understand the fundamental issue is another question. That treaties may continue to exist long after they have lost any practical validity, and that they often do so, is one of the most obvious lessons in the history of international relations. In those days of extreme tension, however, it would have been a difficult lesson for the American people to learn and an embarrassing one for the administration to be required to teach.

There is, however, a third possible reason. The Tripartite Pact was revived as an issue by the American diplomats because it was expected to be useful in selling the anticipated war with Japan to the American people. At the beginning of November, the American cabinet, like the Japanese, faced a crucial decision. The American leaders knew, through intercepted Japanese messages, that Japan had no intention of retreating further on the China issue.[73] For this reason, there was every likelihood that the talks would break down soon and that, following this breakdown, Japan would move. Since the prevailing opinion was that she would launch a drive southward, American leaders now had to decide whether, as the Atlantic Conference decisions had indicated, the United States would meet this move by a declaration of war. On November 5 the Joint Board of the Army and Navy recommended war if Japan invaded any one of a large number of specified territories to the south.[74] In a meeting of November 7, the cabinet accepted the Joint Board's recommendation.[75] Every informed official could now assume that war was imminent and all but certain. A serious problem remained, however—the question of how a declaration of war made under such circumstances would be received by the American people. Would they agree that an attack on non-American soil—on Thailand, Malaya, Singapore, or the Netherlands East Indies—constituted an attack on the United States? Would they unite behind a

[73] Togo to Nomura, Tokyo, Nov. 4, 1941, *Pearl Harbor Attack*, XII, 96.
[74] Langer and Gleason, *Undeclared War*, 844–847.
[75] *Ibid.*, 860–861.

declaration of war made on such grounds? The problem was one of selling a war which the administration sincerely believed to be inevitable and necessary to a public which might find it hard to understand and accept.

To this end, the Tripartite Pact was an almost perfect means. It is always expedient, and in time of war almost mandatory, to identify one's enemies, if they are separate, as one in the public consciousness. To a majority of the American people, Hitler was the great enemy. This was the point of view that the administration had been advancing for some years. There could be no more direct and effective way to justify going to war with Japan over her drive southward than to show that Japan was tied to Hitler and participating in his plan for world conquest. The evidence for this contention was wonderfully simple and convenient: Japan's continued adherence to a fighting alliance with Germany. Hull could argue—just as some years later he would contend—that he had done everything possible to try to draw Japan away from her alliance, but all without success. Instead of drawing apart, the Japanese and Germans had continued to connive together, to plan every step of their drive toward world conquest, to conspire for an ultimate attack upon the United States. Thus the move by Japan which the United States anticipated, the drive southward, could be presented to the public as only a part of a vast Axis plan for world conquest which would reach America in its own good time unless she acted immediately to stop it. The sudden and violent emphasis upon the Pact in the last weeks of negotiation, in short, may be explained as part of a propaganda device. It was intended to set the stage for the employment of the Pact as a selling point for the anticipated war, as a symbol to link together, for public consumption, two enemies and two wars into one.

Some significant facts seem to bear out this interpretation. In an important White House Conference of November 25, there arose this very question of how best to present the American case versus Japan to the American public in case of a Japanese southward drive. Hull contended that a war with Japan should be justified not on the ground of Japanese aggression in Asia, but on the broad grounds of freedom of the seas and "the fact that Japan was in alliance with Hitler and was carrying out his policies of world aggression." [76] Hull was not alone in this point of view. When the actual attack on Pearl Harbor came, Secretary of War Stimson, along with Hull and other cabinet members, objected to the President's war message to Congress because it did not point out that the real enemy was Germany, who had pushed Japan into her attack.[77] As it turned out, the Japanese solved the whole problem of selling the war to the American people by their direct attack on American soil at Pearl Harbor. The blow had the effect, among other things, of raising the doctrine of close Japanese-German collaboration to the status of unchallenged dogma. The American people no longer needed to be convinced that Hitler and Japan were in close connivance. Even after the war was over, the Tripartite Pact still proved useful as a selling point for American policy. Then, when American prewar diplomacy began to be questioned, Hull and other American spokesmen rang every possible change on the theme that the Japanese attack was the result of Japanese-German conspiracy arising out of the Tripartite Pact.

Hull's testimony before the Pearl Harbor Congressional Investigation Committee shows how heavily he relied upon the Tripartite Pact as a weapon of defense for his policy. The following excerpts are only random samples of his repeated emphasis of this theme:

[76] Richard N. Current, *Secretary Stimson: A Study in Statecraft* (New Brunswick: Rutgers University Press, 1954), 156. See also the draft of a proposed war message to Congress, drawn up for President Roosevelt by the State Department, Nov. 29, 1941, with its emphasis upon the importance of the Axis Alliance and Japan's participation in "the Hitler-dominated movement of world conquest," *Foreign Relations, 1941*, IV, 693–697.

[77] Langer and Gleason, *Undeclared War*, 938; text of message, Roosevelt to Congress, Dec. 8, 1941, *Foreign Relations, Japan*, II, 793–794.

They [Hitler and Tojo] were hooked together by links of steel in their plans. . . .

Germany and Japan were linked together, operating together as any two highwaymen operate and as closely as any two could operate. . . .

I must have observed dozens of times the Japanese close military alliance with Germany. . . .

This bunch of Japanese in extreme control, knowing what kind of a savage they were in partnership with, and Tojo and the others being savages themselves when they were at war or getting into war, they hung onto the Germans with this pact. . . .

The Japanese war party in supreme control was tied in hard and fast with Hitler. . . .

All of these machinations [were] going on daily and nightly between representatives of Hitler and Tojo, planning every imaginable step. . . .

The broad question of danger to this and to all peaceful countries was Japan's military partnership with Hitler for conquest.[78]

One perceives a definite will to believe behind statements such as these. It was a theory that Hull wanted to believe, was anxious, almost frantic, to defend, for it underlay his whole concept of the war the United States fought with Japan. Nor was he the only one to defend it. Congressman Bertrand W. Gearhart of California, who had before the war strongly advocated a hard policy with Japan, shared Hull's feelings and purpose. His interrogation of Admiral Stark at the Pearl Harbor hearings shows it:

Gearhart: "Then it was the belief of the State Department, and possibly of the War Council, that Germany, Italy, and Japan had in mind belligerent action on the part of the United States at the time they entered into that agreement [the Tripartite Pact]?"
Stark: "I think so, at least a possibility of it. I might add that for a longer period our diplomatic effort was to pry Japan loose from the Axis set-up or Tri-partite agreement."

[78] Testimony, Nov. 23, 26, and 27, 1945, *Pearl Harbor Attack*, II, 456, 558–559, 609, 612; written testimony, May 16, 1946, *ibid.*, XI, 5408.

Gearhart: "Well, you were familiar with the intercepts, in one of which the Japanese . . . informed Berlin of their steadfast adherence to the Tri-Partite agreements."

Stark: "Yes, sir."

Gearhart: "So far as anything that has ever been acquired along the line through any of the discussions with the Japanese Ambassadors, no progress was made toward separating the Japanese from their Axis obligations."

Stark: "No sir; we didn't get to first base on that."

Gearhart: "Yes. And the intercepts told you, all of the time that we were negotiating with them, that the Japanese were adhering strictly to their Axis obligations?"

Stark: "I believed there was one intercept showing Germany's dissatisfaction with the fact that Japan was not doing more, at least one."

Gearhart: "Well, I won't take the time." [79]

Behind these loaded questions is the desire to uphold a theory at once popular and useful. The doctrine of close Axis cooperation, the picture of Hitler and Tojo jointly planning to attack the United States, was what people believed at the time. It helped to justify American policy, from the freezing orders to unconditional surrender. It fitted in well with the hard-and-fast, black-and-white distinctions of wartime, of fascism versus democracy the world over. It harmonized with the widespread belief in one world, indivisible peace, and indivisible democracy, important ideals behind the United States war effort and peace aims. There is nothing more natural than that this theory should, under the circumstances, be maintained and defended without too scrupulous an attention to its foundation in fact.

This is not to say that American leaders, particularly Hull, meant to deceive the American people. One may suppose that Hull really believed that the Pact was all that he said it was. It is very easy to believe the worst of one's enemies, particularly when a conflict seems inevitable or is already under way. The

[79] Testimony, Jan. 4, 1946, *ibid.*, V, 2314.

only contention here is that Hull found it easy to accept this idea and to pass by a large body of evidence making it dubious, because it fitted the requirements of the situation. Certainly there is nothing unique in an attempt to use an unreal issue for propaganda purposes. The Japanese, like the Americans, used the issue of the Pact for their own ends. After the negotiations with the United States had broken down, they tried to persuade the Germans that the break with Washington had come over the United States efforts to nullify the Pact,[80] a contention just as unfounded as Hull's thesis. For both sides, the Pact really had propaganda significance and nothing more.

There remains the question why Japan, if she actually set little store by the Pact and had no intention of honoring it, refused to agree to American demands that she accept a formula nullifying it. The Japanese had their reasons for not wishing to abandon the Pact prematurely, reasons which were not without validity within their limits. The first was the matter of Japanese national pride. The Pact had been adopted only a year before with an Imperial Rescript defining it as a measure for peace. For Japan now to abandon the Pact under heavy pressure from the United States would first of all be a sign that Japan was not faithful to her international commitments. As Frederick Moore writes, "The Government would not and could not undo the Alliance. Apart from the fact that an Imperial Sanction cannot be undone, anything like the denunciation of a treaty would bring upon Japan anew the charge that she did not keep agreements."[81] Still worse, it would be an admission that the Pact really had constituted a menace to America and hence that the Emperor had himself been deceived or had deceived the Japanese people. Even if the American charges in regard to the Pact were true, something the Japanese never conceded, the demand that

[80] See below, Chapter VI, pp. 151–152; Langer and Gleason, *Undeclared War*, 910–911.

[81] Moore, *With Japan's Leaders*, 275. The same view is espoused by Grew, *Turbulent Era*, II, 1313–1314.

Japan admit this publicly before the world would have been a bitter pill to swallow.

Closely connected with the matter of national pride was the practical problem of Japanese domestic politics and public opinion. The Pact always had friends in Japan, especially among those who in 1941 could still believe in an ultimate German victory. They could be controlled and, in the event of a turn in the war favorable to the Allies, finally subdued. To ride over them roughshod by virtually abrogating the Pact, however, was to invite political trouble in large amounts. This was particularly true in a country like Japan, where the political balance of power was always precarious and assassinations for political reasons were an all too frequent occurrence. Moreover, Japanese leaders faced the same problem as those of any other nation in presenting an international agreement to the public. They had to be able to justify the agreement, if not as a victory, at least as a reasonable diplomatic compromise. An agreement with America, however, in which Japan simply in effect dropped the Pact with an apology for ever having signed it in the first place would have constituted a gratuitous public humiliation which a Japanese government could not possibly have explained to the people.[82]

A third reason also doubtless played a part, although the Japanese, understandably enough, never talked about it. The Pact, even though inoperative as far as Japan was concerned, retained a certain amount of insurance value which made it too valuable simply to be discarded. Like the American statesmen, the Japanese could perceive that in all likelihood war was coming. In this event, the Pact might still prove useful. For while Japan had no intention of fighting for Germany, she had no objection to Germany's fighting with her; any ally was better than none.

[82] Konoye cites the above-named reasons—the internal political situation, Army pressure, and the necessity of maintaining at least a show of good faith in regard to the Alliance—as explaining why the Pact could not be denounced, even though he personally was willing to sacrifice it for the sake of better Japanese-American relations (*IMTFE*, Record, 24306–24307).

Even though she was seriously negotiating for peace, as long as there was a grave prospect of war with the West, Japan was in no position to burn her bridges behind her by abrogating the Pact and making her diplomatic isolation final and complete. It is now, of course, easy to see that it would have been better for the Japanese to have done this very thing. By remaining allied with Germany, though only nominally, they succeeded in drawing upon their own heads some of the wrath deserved by the Nazis and in making their already desperate situation infinitely worse.

V

Japan and Germany:
The Pact in the Making

THE rapid decline of the Tripartite Pact from its position of importance in late 1940 to one of merely nominal existence in late 1941 was no strange phenomenon. Although the trend was not one which could have been confidently predicted at the outset, it was always at least a strong possibility. For this was only one of a series of similar ups and downs in recent German-Japanese relations. Ever since the two nations had begun to draw closer together in the 1930's, Japan and Germany had acted toward each other not like bosom friends, but like unprincipled adventurers each out to use the other for his own purposes. The only difference between them on this score was that Germany was even more ruthless and unprincipled in the application of the politics of self-interest than was Japan.

The virtual split which took place between Germany and Japan in the latter half of 1941 was therefore the product not only of new events and circumstances, but also of the inherently unstable nature of the Axis relationship. Japan and Germany simply were not constituted for alliance with each other, or with anyone. The rift between them is naturally easier to describe fully now than it was then. However, at the very time when Japanese-German estrangement was taking place, the trend was clearly recognized in all essential features by a wide range of observers. To anyone acquainted with the story of earlier relations between the two powers, it came as no great surprise.

This account might well begin with the first concrete evidence of a German-Japanese entente, the conclusion of the Anti-Comintern Pact by the two nations on November 25, 1936. The Pact was renewed, with Italy adhering, a year later. It was supposed to be merely an agreement to exchange information and give mutual support against the subversive activities of the Comintern.[1] The Japanese contended at the time of its signature as well as later that the Pact was strictly of an ideological nature and involved no alliance with Germany.[2] Actually, this was not true, for the Pact contained secret provisions calling for joint consultation in case of an unprovoked attack by the Soviet Union against either contracting party. It also provided that neither nation should conclude a basic treaty with the Soviet Union without the other's consent, thus going considerably beyond a purely ideological agreement.[3] Japan was justified, however, in claiming that the Pact represented no decisive political alignment for her. In fact, she had been reluctant to enter into it, fearful lest it alarm and unduly alienate Russia. Particularly after the Italian adherence to the Pact, however, American diplomats feared that Japan had definitely aligned herself with the European fascist powers.[4]

[1] Agreement and Supplementary Protocol between Japan and Germany, Berlin, Nov. 25, 1936, *Foreign Relations, Japan*, II, 153–155; agreement between Italy, Germany, and Japan, Rome, Nov. 6, 1937, *ibid.*, 159–160.

[2] Statement by Japanese Foreign Office, Tokyo, Nov. 25, 1937, *ibid.*, 155–157; Seiji Hishida, *Japan among the Great Powers* (London: Longmans Green, 1940), 348–352.

[3] Jones, *Japan's New Order*, 25; "Secret Attached Agreement to the Agreement against the Communist International," *IMTFE*, Doc. no. 1561E.

[4] "The Problem of the Conclusion of a Japanese-German Political Con-

Any ideological and political affinity thus reached between Japan and Germany, however, was soon put under a severe strain when the Sino-Japanese conflict broke out. The Japanese advance into China was embarrassing to Germany for a variety of reasons. For one thing, unofficial German military advisers had been assisting Chiang Kai-shek in his fight against the Communists. For another, China had placed large military contracts in Germany. In addition, it was generally disturbing to Germany to see two nations with whom she had been improving relations at war with each other, to the detriment of their common fight against communism.[5]

For these reasons Germany, while trying to conciliate Japan in her demands that the German aid to China be cut off, worked from October 1937 to January 1938 to end the conflict. The leading German representative in the attempt at mediation was the German Ambassador to Japan, Heinrich von Dirksen. His efforts failed, however, largely because sweeping Japanese victories led the Imperial government to expand its demands on China to completely unacceptable proportions. Germany at length gave up the mediation attempt, opposed both to the Japanese terms and to her continuation of the war. The Germans had met with neither success nor gratitude through their intervention in the China Affair. "This is one of several episodes," says F. C. Jones, "which show Germany and Japan not as firm partners in policy, but as very much at cross purposes."[6]

After this failure to bring an end to the war, a serious split in opinion developed in the German Foreign Office over future policy toward Japan. The German Ambassador to China, Erich Trautmann, argued strongly against a pro-Japanese policy. Hitler and Foreign Minister Joachim von Ribbentrop, however,

---

vention," July 24, 1936, *IMTFE*, Rejected Defense Document no. 1423; "Report of the Investigations concerning the Conclusion of the Japanese-German Pact," Nov. 20, 1936, *ibid.*, Docs. no. 1105A, B, C; Grew to Hull, Tokyo, Nov. 13, 1937, *Foreign Relations, Japan,* II, 160–161.

[5] Jones, *Japan's New Order,* 41–42, 57–59. [6] *Ibid.,* 70.

counting on an early victory by Japan, decided to adhere to a pro-Japanese policy in order to secure a preferential position for Germany in a Japanese-dominated China.[7] Accordingly, Germany complied with Japanese demands for a halt to all aid and supplies to China. This conciliatory policy proved in the long run to be helpful only to Japan. Once she had secured what she wanted in the way of cancellation of Chinese war contracts with Germany and the withdrawal of German military advisers from China, she was no more anxious to favor German economic interests in China than those of any other power. Germany was quick to sense Japanese ingratitude and react to it. From July 1938 and throughout the year that followed, the story of Japanese-German relations was one of repeated German complaints against Japanese discrimination, the squeezing out of German business, confiscation of property, and similar offenses.[8] The German Ambassador to Japan, Eugen Ott, even complained that as a reward for all the German efforts in behalf of Japan, Japan was giving Germany worse treatment than she was according Great Britain.[9]

Japan had thus proved to be quite intractable over China. Her whole policy of aggression and economic domination there was a definite blow to German interests. Nevertheless, Germany was not ready to write off Japan, a potential ally, as a dead loss. At the same time, strong elements in Japan, particularly in the Army, favored a pact with the Axis which would strengthen Japan against her most dangerous and likely enemy, Soviet Russia. With these motives, the two powers conducted active negotiations from the summer of 1938 till June 1939, designed to expand the Anti-Comintern agreements into a Tripartite Pact.

[7] *Ibid.*, 88–92.

[8] *Ibid.*, 93–96; memo by Economics Ministry Director Wiehl, Berlin, July 28, 1938, *IMTFE*, Doc. no. 4041; "Account concerning the Situation of German Economic Interests in the Parts of China Occupied by Japan," Berlin, July 24, 1938, *ibid.*, Doc. no. 4041B.

[9] Ott to Foreign Office, Tokyo, Nov. 17, 1938, *IMTFE*, Rej. Def. Doc. no. 1312.

There was one major stumbling block, however, which the talks could not remove—the conflicting interests and motives of Germany and Japan. Germany and Italy wanted a strong alliance which would bind Japan to military action and would be directed primarily against the Western democracies. Japan was interested only in a pact directed against the U.S.S.R. and refused out of fear of Anglo-American naval power to be bound to any commitment for military action against the West.[10]

The kind of pact Japan wanted would have been useless to Hitler. Giving up on Japan temporarily, he turned to Russia and concluded his startling nonaggression pact with Stalin on August 23, 1939. In the process he ignored some last-minute Japanese proposals and did not bother to inform Japan of his intentions. The pact, needless to say, was a humiliating blow to Japan. Not only was it an obviously underhanded action and a direct violation of one of the secret provisions of the Anti-Comintern Pact, but it also completely upset the basis for Japanese foreign policy. Germany now would be of no use to Japan in case of a Russo-Japanese conflict, which seemed more than barely possible in 1939. The Japanese Premier, Baron Hiranuma, resigned over the issue after making a protest to Germany. Pro-Axis elements in Japan were for the moment discredited.[11]

The European war which broke out just a few days later did nothing to calm Japanese feeling. While the war conceivably might provide a golden opportunity for Japanese expansion in Asia while the Western powers were preoccupied, there was also the danger that Japan would be caught in the spread of a world conflagration. Japan's unsolicited and unwelcome advice to Germany about the European war was that Germany should mediate her conflict with Great Britain and France. The suggestion, to

[10] Jones, *Japan's New Order*, 99–121; Von Ribbentrop to Ott, Berlin, April 26, 1939, *Documents on International Affairs, 1939–1946*, edited by Arnold J. Toynbee (London: Oxford University Press, 1951), I, 157–159.

[11] Jones, *Japan's New Order*, 125–129; Ott to Von Ribbentrop, Tokyo, Aug. 25, 1939, *IMTFE*, Record, 6122–6123.

which Japan was repeatedly to recur, brought, needless to say, no response from Germany.[12]

Although the blow to Japanese pride involved in the Russo-German pact did not cause a severance of relations between Germany and Japan or an end to Axis influence in Japan, it did bring on an independent, wait-and-see policy in Tokyo during the Abe and Yonai governments from September 1939 to June 1940. The Germans continued to solicit Japanese friendship, arguing that "the idea of close cooperation between Germany, Italy, and Japan was . . . by no means dead."[13] But this invitation received little audience in the Japanese government. "Close cooperation" was hindered not only by Japanese anger at her humiliation, but also by the fact that both nations had at the moment irreconcilable political and strategic goals. Germany, anxious to use Japan to help her win in Europe, wanted the Japanese to compose their differences with the Russians and to advance in southeast Asia against the British. Japan, on the other hand, was determined to keep out of the European war and to end the China Affair. For this reason she wanted Germany to exert pressure on Russia to make her stop aiding Chiang Kai-shek.[14] The Japanese attitude toward the war in Europe, moreover, was unsatisfactory to Germany in other ways. Japan seemed to take no interest in a decisive German victory. The Japanese Ambassador to Germany, Saburo Kurusu, strongly advised Germany against invading the Lowlands, a step which he said would make an enduring German-Japanese friendship extremely difficult.[15]

[12] Ambassador Mackensen to State Secretary Weiszaecker, Rome, Sept. 4, 1939, *Documents on German Foreign Policy, 1918–1945* (Washington: Government Printing Office, 1949), Ser. D, VIII, 11.

[13] Von Ribbentrop to Ott, Berlin, Sept. 9, 1939, *ibid.*, 37.

[14] *Ibid.*, 36–38; Ott to Von Ribbentrop, Tokyo, Oct. 5, 1939, *ibid.*, 216; memo by Woermann, director of Political Division VIII, Berlin, Sept. 20, 1939, *ibid.*, 111–112.

[15] Memo, Political Director Knoll to Von Ribbentrop, Berlin, Feb. 1, 1940, *ibid.*, 728–732.

At the same time, Germany was not disposed to give Japan any further help in regard to China. Kurusu still had hopes of German mediation in the Sino-Japanese conflict, but this the Germans had no intention of providing. In late 1939, an unofficial feeler was received from a Chinese official, the Counselor of the Chinese Embassy in Berlin, who suggested that if Germany would use her good offices Chiang Kai-shek might be ready to settle the war on terms very favorable to Japan. In return for mediation, Chiang would orient his policy in a pro-German direction. The German Foreign Office, however, refused to consider mediation. Since Japan was unreliable and might even line up with the West in a long war, the Germans believed that it would be safer for Germany to leave Japan tied down in China.[16]

Economic issues likewise served to exacerbate feeling between the two nations. Germany complained sharply about Japan's "very unsatisfactory" economic policies in regard to the war. Japan, the Germans claimed, had obeyed British instructions implicitly on matters of contraband, black lists, and the routing of shipments to Germany via British ports, ignoring German wishes. She had even gone so far as to extend Great Britain credit while giving Germany none.[17] German economic policies toward Japan were not much more generous. German emissaries in Tokyo advised their home office that Germany's economic measures were defeating her efforts to woo Japan politically. Ambassador Ott urged concessions, arguing that without them Japan would be driven into the arms of England and America. The home office refused, however, again because of Japanese unreliability.[18]

All this does not mean that relations between the two nations

[16] *Ibid.*, 731; memos, Woermann to Weiszaecker, Berlin, Oct. 5 and 8, 1939, *ibid.*, 220–222, 243.

[17] Memo, Wiehl to Weiszaecker, Berlin, Dec. 5, 1939, *ibid.*, 491–493; another memo, June 20, 1940, *IMTFE*, Record, 6166–6168.

[18] Helferrich and Ott to Von Ribbentrop, Tokyo, March 1, 1940, and Ott to Von Ribbentrop, Tokyo, March 2, 1940, *Documents on German Foreign Policy*, D, VIII, 820, 835–837, 837 (note).

were hostile. Each was simply following an opportunistically independent course of action. Japan in particular, having at first secured what she wanted from Germany in China and then having met with humiliation in the Russo-German pact, saw no reason for showing the Germans any special favor.

An independent policy like this, however, would work for Japan only as long as the issue remained in doubt in Europe. If Germany emerged triumphant, she would then be too powerful to be dallied with. This fact was recognized in Japan. As early as March 1940, rumblings of opposition appeared within the Japanese government over the Yonai cabinet's hands-off policy regarding Europe. Germany was going to win the war, opponents contended, and Japan needed help from her in order to fulfill her aims in Asia against Anglo-American opposition.[19] With the crushing German victories in the Lowlands and France in May and June, the pro-Axis critics of Japan's policy appeared to be vindicated. The sweeping German conquests soon made inevitable the fall of the wait-and-see Yonai government and at the same time revived the prospect of closer Japanese-German ties. Japan, "alarmed at what a Germany, apparently victorious in Europe, might elect to do in the Far East," chose once again in June 1940 to become more friendly with Germany.[20]

The Germans, quite aware of the opportunistic nature of Japanese advances, were not ready to welcome Japan back with open arms. When Japan first tried to get help from Germany in coercing an agreement from the Vichy government for "joint protection" of French Indo-China, she met with a polite rebuff. Von Ribbentrop made it clear that Germany was interested in helping Japan only if Japan on her part began to show an interest in the European war. The Japanese attempted to meet this requirement by drafting a proposed agreement in which Japan would promise to help Germany against Great Britain, short of

[19] "Excerpts from Records of Budget Committee Meeting, Imperial Diet, March 22, 1940," Tokyo, *IMTFE*, Rej. Def. Doc. no. 3008.

[20] Jones, *Japan's New Order*, 97–98.

war, in exchange for German sanction of Japanese leadership in Asia. This was not sufficient, however, and in the end Japan received no German help at all in dealing with Vichy.[21] At the same time, all of Ambassador Kurusu's attempts to secure German recognition of the Greater East Asia Co-Prosperity Sphere were met with bland indifference by Germany.[22]

Obviously, Germany would be conciliated not by mere gestures, but by a real change in Japanese policy. Since the change in policy called for could be carried out only by new leaders, the Yonai cabinet resigned. A new cabinet was called into office in late July, headed by Prince Konoye as Premier and containing Matsuoka as Foreign Minister and Tojo as Minister of War.[23] Matsuoka immediately began to confer with Ambassador Ott about strengthening German-Japanese relations. Their conversation, though paving the way for further steps, was not without evidence of cross-purposes and duplicity on both sides. Matsuoka showed himself concerned entirely with Asia and the Co-Prosperity Sphere and insisted that he wanted co-operation with the United States as well as Germany. Ott, while taking occasion to complain of previous Japanese insults and unpleasantries, nevertheless glibly promised Germany's good offices in Japan's relations with both the United States and Russia.[24]

Following this initial talk, in August 1940 Matsuoka reorganized the Japanese diplomatic service, a step which he announced as necessary in promoting a new policy.[25] On September 4, a Four-Ministers Conference (comprising Japan's "inner cabinet" of the Prime, War, Navy, and Foreign Ministers) reached agree-

[21] *Ibid.*, 221–224; Langer and Gleason, *Undeclared War*, 24.

[22] Memos, Weiszaecker to Von Ribbentrop, Berlin, Aug. 1, 2, and 7, 1940, *IMTFE*, Doc. no. 4029A, B.

[23] See above, Chapter I, pp. 15–16.

[24] "An Outline of the Conversation between Foreign Minister Matsuoka and German Ambassador Ott," Tokyo, Aug. 2, 1940, *IMTFE*, Docs. no. 1590A, C; Ott to Von Ribbentrop, Tokyo, Aug. 2, 1940, *ibid.*, Doc. no. 4025E.

[25] Ott to Von Ribbentrop, Tokyo, Aug. 23, 1940, *ibid.*, Doc. no. 4029F.

ment on the new course Japan was to pursue, their decision subsequently being endorsed by a Liaison Conference.[26]

The economic and political aspects of the new policy have already been touched upon. Diplomatically the new course meant a bold gamble for Japan. In order to achieve her goals in Asia, she intended to strengthen her alliance with Germany and Italy and to take a firm stand against the United States and Great Britain. By concluding a Tripartite Alliance with the European Axis powers, the ministers hoped to accomplish several ends. First, Japan would secure recognition of her sphere of influence from the apparent victors in Europe. This was of primary importance. "The principal purpose of the negotiations . . ." the Japanese leaders stated, "is to obtain over-all recognition of Japan's predominance in the whole of East Asia." To gain such sweeping recognition, Japan expected to have to maneuver carefully. Anticipating that Germany would pose a problem on the matter of the Netherlands East Indies, the ministers agreed that the Japanese definition of her Co-Prosperity Sphere, which by this time had reached its widest extent, would have to be narrowed somewhat in negotiation with Germany and Italy. If either of the Axis powers showed a disposition to hedge in regard to specific areas, Japan would try to get her way by individual negotiations.

The other major purposes of the Tripartite Pact were to be the isolation of the United States, the weakening of Britain's position in the Far East, and the neutralization of Russia in Asia. Japan expected the Pact to restrain Russia, to induce her into alignment with the Axis, and to turn the Russian sphere of influence toward the Middle East. As for the United States, "while peaceful means will be adhered to as far as possible," firm pressure would have to be used in order to keep her from interfering in Asia. In the meantime, everything should be done to weaken Great Britain's position in southeast Asia. Whether this would

[26] Decisions of the Four-Ministers Conference and the Liaison Conference, Tokyo, Sept. 4 and 19, 1940, *ibid.*, Doc. no. 2137D.

include military action would be entirely subject to circumstances. In general, no military measures would be taken until the China Incident was settled or unless conditions were absolutely favorable and circumstances made a move mandatory.

The Japanese leaders knew, of course, that they would have to pay some price for German help; they were only concerned with paying as low a price as possible. "In the event that Germany and Italy propounds [*sic*] a desire for Japanese military cooperation with them against Britain," they determined, "Japan is prepared, as a matter of guiding principle, to meet the desire." A "guiding principle" for Japan, however, was anything but a firm promise. Germany and Italy, the ministers agreed, should be informed that all the Japanese restrictions on the use of armed forces would apply, that is, the China Incident would have to be settled and foreign and domestic conditions would have to be perfectly ripe for it. In fact, the Japanese leaders had no intention of committing themselves to anything. "Concerning the possible use of armed force against Britain and the United States," they resolved, "Japan will make decisions independently." [27]

After receiving, through this conference, an inner cabinet mandate to secure a Tripartite Pact with Germany and Italy, Matsuoka proceeded to negotiate for it in conversations with the special German envoy, Heinrich Stahmer, and Ambassador Ott. It was soon apparent that the German and Japanese conceptions of a desirable pact were sharply different. The German representatives still wanted a strong, automatically enforceable military treaty, insisting that without it a war between the United States and Japan was inevitable. To induce Japan to agree to it, they were free with assurances and promises. Promising all possible technical and military assistance to Japan and disclaiming any intent to call on Japan for immediate participation in the war against England, they insisted that Germany only wanted Japan

[27] *Ibid.*, Appendixes 3 and 4.

to act as a restraint against an expansion of the war. Not only would Germany help Japan achieve better relations with the U.S.S.R., but also Germany would "make use of every means in her power to prevent the clashing between the United States and Japan, and even to improve the relations between the two, if it is humanly possible." [28]

It is hard to tell whether Matsuoka was much moved by these implausible promises; he certainly used them himself to sell the Pact to his colleagues in the Japanese government. But in any case the plan he presented fell far short of German desires. In the crucial section, Article III, his draft proposal called on the contracting parties only to co-operate and consult with one another as to means for removing obstacles in the paths of their respective New Orders.[29] The Germans promptly revised this article to commit the three powers not only to co-operate and consult, but also to aid one another with all political, economic, and military assistance possible if any of them was attacked. Even this revision did not fully satisfy Von Ribbentrop, who was following the conversations closely from Berlin. He eliminated the words "co-operate and consult" entirely and added the stipulation that the Pact should be invoked if any of the three powers were attacked "either openly or in concealed form." He also added Article V to his draft, excluding Russia specifically as a target of the Pact and directing it more pointedly at the United States.[30] A later German draft couched Article III in different but equally drastic and binding terms: If another power should commit "an act of aggression" against any of the Axis partners, all three allies would "undertake to declare war on such

[28] "Some of the Salient Points in the Informal Conversations between Matsuoka and Stahmer, with the German Ambassador Assisting," Tokyo, Sept. 9 and 10, 1940, *IMTFE*, Doc. no. 1129.

[29] "Tentative Formula," *ibid.*, Rej. Def. Doc. no. 1656I; see also Rej. Def. Doc. no. 1656H.

[30] *Ibid.*, Rej. Def. Doc. no. 1656J; "Formula of the German Foreign Minister," *ibid.*, Rej. Def. Doc. no. 1656M.

power." [31] The Germans argued, of course, that such an automatic pact would be all to Japan's interests in restraining the United States:

In our opinion an explicit emphasis of the obligation to declare war would have a specially strong neutralizing effect on America. America would certainly hesitate ten times before entering the war if the pact stated in clear and impressive terms that America would then automatically be at war with three great powers.[32]

When it became apparent to Matsuoka that Germany was not remotely interested in a mere consultative pact, he then turned to the other alternative open to him. This was to agree to the German demand in principle, but secretly to reserve for Japan full independence of decision by fashioning loopholes for escape from obligations. To this end Matsuoka tried two devices. The first was to insert a provision in the protocol setting up the joint military and naval commissions provided for in the Pact, stipulating that "whether or not a Contracting Party or Parties has or have been attacked openly or covertly as stipulated in Paragraph III of the Pact shall be dtermined [*sic*] by the respective Governments." Even should the fact of an attack be established, the measure of assistance would still be decided by the respective governments.[33]

Although this device was initially unacceptable to Germany, Matsuoka's second plan was more successful. He drafted a "Personal Letter" to be sent to him by Ott, in which the German Ambassador would verify Japan's independence of decision. The letter was to read:

Conclusions of the Technical Commissions stipulated in Article 4 of the Pact shall be submitted to the respective Governments for approval in order to be put into force.

[31] "Three Powers Pact between Japan, Germany, and Italy," *ibid.*, Rej. Def. Doc. no. 1656P.
[32] *Ibid.*, Rej. Def. Doc. no. 1656Q.
[33] "Protocol," *ibid.*, Rej. Def. Doc. no. 1656N.

Furthermore:

It is needless to say that whether or not a Contracting Party has been attacked within the meaning of Article 3 of the Pact shall be determined upon consultation among the three Contracting Parties.

This letter Matsuoka did secure.[34]

The Japanese also gained a number of lesser concessions from Germany. They obtained a promise of German and Italian help in the event of Japanese involvement in war with Britain in the Far East.[35] Perhaps more important to Japan, she secured confirmation of Japanese possession of the mandated islands in the Pacific formerly owned by Germany.[36] Matsuoka also apparently got his way in substance on the procedure governing the mixed technical commissions as well. The joint memorandum setting up the commissions stipulated that their findings on whether or not an attack had occurred and on what action should be taken would be submitted to the respective governments for final approval.[37]

On the main question in dispute, the import of Article III, the Pact as concluded was clearly a compromise. Germany did not get the automatic military agreement she wanted; Japan did not get the merely consultative pact she desired. The final compromise actually concealed the divergence of views without bridging it. Germany obtained what on paper looked like an effective military alliance, something she might at least hope would impress the United States. But she could never confidently rely on Japan's honoring the Pact. Japan, on the other hand,

---

[34] Draft letter, *ibid.*, Rej. Def. Doc. no. 1656AB; actual letter, Tokyo, Sept. 27, 1940, *ibid.*, Doc. no. 940B.

[35] Ott to Matsuoka, Tokyo, Sept. 27, 1940, *ibid.*, Doc. no. 940C.

[36] Matsuoka to Ott, Tokyo, n.d., *ibid.*, Doc. no. 1214A; Ott to Matsuoka, Tokyo, Sept. 27, 1940, *ibid.*, Doc. no. 940A.

[37] Memo by Ott, Italian Ambassador Mario Indelli, and Matsuoka, Tokyo, Dec. 20, 1940, *ibid.*, Doc. no. 955. The commissions, according to Japanese testimony, never functioned prior to the outbreak of the Pacific war—another sign of the Pact's ineffectiveness (affidavit of Naokuni Nomura, *ibid.*, Def. Doc. no. 1606).

secured the loophole for independent interpretation of the Pact upon which she had insisted and upon which she later laid so much stress in talks with the United States. As Langer and Gleason point out, the effect of this secret proviso was substantially to lessen the Pact's value for Germany: "Of course the whole purpose of the treaty, to deter the United States from intervening against Germany, would have been destroyed if the proviso attached to Article 3 had become known." [38]

Having reached their agreement with Germany, Japan's ministers now had to sell the pact to the rest of the Japanese government. This proved to be no easy task, for there was grave opposition to it, especially among the leaders in the Navy. One of the Pact's opponents, incidentally, was Admiral Isoroku Yamamoto, Commander in Chief of the Fleet and architect of the plan to attack Pearl Harbor.[39] Upon Matsuoka and Tojo in particular fell the task of making a determined defense of the Pact in order finally to gain the approval of the Privy Council, a special Investigation Committee, and an Imperial Conference. In each case the great questions raised were the same. Would not the Pact bring grave danger of a war with England and the United States? Would it not also be likely to evoke extreme economic pressure from the United States? [40] Were Japan's oil supplies adequate to meet an emergency? Would not the Pact increase the likelihood of American alignment with Soviet Russia? Could Germany be trusted? [41]

The Pact's defenders gave answers to these questions which were sometimes evasive and at other times either deliberately deceitful or amazingly naïve. Matsuoka in particular relied upon

[38] Langer and Gleason, *Undeclared War*, 32.
[39] Jones, *Japan's New Order*, 199 (note).
[40] "Salient Points of Questions (Privy Council)," Tokyo, Sept. 16, 1940, *IMTFE*, Doc. no. 1259.
[41] "Conclusion of the Tripartite Pact between Japan, Germany, and Italy," Minutes of the Investigation Committee, Tokyo, Sept. 26, 1940, *ibid.*, Doc. no. 1461.

German promises and arguments. The Pact, he claimed, would help bring America's twenty million Germans to Japan's side. Moreover, the Pact would bring Germany to Japan's aid if the United States Fleet entered Singapore. In reply to the objection that, since the United States seemed determined to go to war with Germany, Japan was bearing the whole burden and danger of the Pact, the Foreign Minister answered that, for one thing, Stahmer had assured him that the United States would not enter the war; for another, America's German population would keep the United States out of the European conflict, while a Japanese-American war was a real danger.[42]

These reckless assurances probably made little impression on Matsuoka's audiences. Much more convincing were his arguments that Japan's commitments under the Pact were strictly limited and that she could expect great benefits from it. The Foreign Minister placed strong emphasis on Japan's complete independence of decision under the Pact and insisted manfully that he had negotiated it solely with an eye to her national interests.[43] Never, he maintained, would he agree to a treaty tying Japan to Germany's coattails. Tojo argued, along with others, that the Pact would restrain the United States from aiding China, thus helping to settle the China Affair.[44] All the proponents of the Pact urged that it would help solve the problem of relations with Russia.[45] The most weighty argument of all, however, was the contention that Japan had no alternative, that the Pact was her only way out of an increasingly dangerous position. Japan simply could not go on as she was, isolated in world politics, bogged down in China, surrounded by hostile nations, and under increasing economic pressure from the United States. The inevitable

[42] *Ibid.*
[43] "Regarding Conclusion of the Tripartite Pact," Tokyo, *ibid.*, Doc. no. 1202.
[44] "Salient Points," *ibid.*, Doc. no. 1259.
[45] Minutes of the Investigation Committee, *ibid.*, Doc. no. 1461.

end to a policy of drifting would be a disastrous war. Japan's only hope was to take what Tojo conceded to be a strong measure: to join with Germany and Italy in restraining the United States.[46]

Although the various councils and conferences finally agreed to the Pact on the basis of this reasoning, they did so with grave misgivings and strict conditions. The Investigation Committee based its acceptance of the Pact on the ground that without the Pact war was inevitable. But it insisted at the same time that the anti–Anglo-American movements in Japan must be controlled and that the United States and Great Britain should not be antagonized.[47] The Privy Council, sitting with the Emperor present, endorsed the Pact only with reluctance. Council Vice-President Suzuki accepted the Pact as a last resort, calling it "truly unavoidable." But, he urged, Japan must immediately take steps to calm Great Britain and the United States and to negotiate with Russia. Councilor Ishii went even farther. Hitler and Germany, he said, were completely untrustworthy. Even though he advocated the alliance with them, he said, he did so solely because it was opportune at the present time.[48] The Emperor, in announcing the act in an Imperial Rescript, presented it entirely as a means to peace and the Japanese ideal of world unity (*Hakko Ichiu*).[49]

There was thus a considerable diversity of reasons that led the Japanese government into the Pact. The only one conspicuous by its absence was a real desire to help the Axis as such. Self-interest was supreme; Japan was gambling on a German victory only in the hope that she might gain spoils by it. Some members of the cabinet had broader aims in the Pact than did others. Matsuoka and Tojo, for example, wanted it as a means to secure a free hand for Japan in all of southeast Asia and to prevent the

[46] *Ibid.*   [47] *Ibid.*
[48] "Record of the Minutes of the Privy Council," Tokyo, Sept. 26, 1940, *ibid.*, Doc. no. 1215.
[49] Imperial Rescript, Tokyo, Sept. 27, 1940, *ibid.*, Doc. no. 2600A.

United States from interfering with Japan's plans. Konoye, who along with moderates generally was always worried about the Pact, hoped only that it might help settle the China Affair and improve relations with Russia. On one point, however, all could agree: Japan was forced by her diplomatic isolation into the Pact. By providing her with powerful allies, the Pact would actually help Japan to stay out of further war, especially with the United States. On this account even Matsuoka really believed what he so often proclaimed, that the Pact was an instrument for peace. That the peace he envisioned meant a free hand for Japan in Asia goes without saying.[50]

[50] Jones, *Japan's New Order*, 200–201; Langer and Gleason, *Undeclared War*, 29–30; deposition by Yoshie Saito, Matsuoka's secretary, *IMTFE*, Rej. Def. Doc. no. 1592. In an "Outline of Japanese Foreign Policy," Sept. 28, 1940, Matsuoka indulged in the wild dream of using the Pact to mediate peace between England and Germany and with the aid of Axis pressure on Russia to coerce Chiang into peace terms with Japan, so that world-wide peace would be attained—and Japan left to enjoy her expansive Co-Prosperity Sphere (*IMTFE*, Doc. no. 837A).

VI

The Pact on the Wane

ONLY a short time after the signing of the Pact, Japanese disappointment with it set in and hints began to leak out to the world that the alliance was not the tight link that it seemed. From the outset Ambassador Grew suspected the existence of secret provisos.[1] Signs of internal discord in the Japanese government over the Pact emerged as early as November 1940. One such sign was the attempt of Prince Konoye, with Matsuoka's knowledge, to approach the United States for negotiations through two Maryknoll missionaries, Bishop Walsh and Father Drought. The good-will trip to the United States of unofficial ambassador Tetsuma Hashimoto was another.[2] The evidence, which quickly came to light, that the Pact would not produce the desired and promised results in regard to the United States, Russia, and China served to bolster the opposition in Tokyo.[3]

Matsuoka, however, had made his bed and was determined to lie in it. He used the Pact to the fullest extent in trying to force the United States to keep her hands off Asia and while proclaiming the Pact's peaceful purposes also proclaimed for both foreign

[1] Grew to Hull, Tokyo, Sept. 29, 1940, *Foreign Relations, Japan*, II, 170.
[2] Langer and Gleason, *Undeclared War*, 311–312.
[3] *Ibid.*, 291–293; Jones, *Japan's New Order*, 209.

and domestic consumption Japan's determination to enforce the Pact if necessary.[4] Moreover, as Langer and Gleason point out, he seems to have had sufficiently powerful support in Army circles which enabled him to keep his policy at least nominally in force until his fall in July 1941.[5]

The real danger, naturally, lay not in what Japan's more extreme leaders might say, but in what they might lead Japan to do. Specifically, in response to Hitler's urgings and their own plans, they might launch a southward offensive. It was this fear in the Western powers' camp that accounted for the "southern move" war scare of early 1941. When Japan intervened in a Thailand–French Indo-China border dispute in February, both Great Britain and the United States feared that the stage was being set for a plunge southward toward Singapore. On this occasion, at least, the democracies' fears proved unfounded. Hitler was indeed urging such a step, but Japan was ignoring him.[6]

There remained a real danger, however, particularly during the period of apparent solidarity in the Axis Alliance in the winter and spring of 1941, that the Tripartite Pact would become in fact a joint instrument of Japanese-German aggression. One of the charges against the Nazi leaders in the Nuremberg war trials was that they had used the Tripartite Pact to spur Japan to war against the United States and Great Britain. The charge read in part: "The Tripartite Pact of 27 September 1940 thus was a bold announcement to the world that the fascist leaders of Germany, Japan, and Italy had cemented a full military alliance to achieve world domination." [7] The Germans, it was contended,

[4] Grew to Hull, Tokyo, Oct. 5, 1940, *Foreign Relations, Japan*, II, 171–173; Address, Matsuoka to Imperial Diet, Tokyo, Jan. 21, 1941, *IMTFE*, Doc. no. 1204E.

[5] Langer and Gleason, *Undeclared War*, 315.

[6] Feis, *Road to Pearl Harbor*, 152–156.

[7] Statement, Prosecutor Alderman, Dec. 10, 1945, *Trial of the Major War Criminals at the International Military Tribunal* (Official Documents, Proceedings, and Documents in Evidence) (Nuremberg, 1948), III, 370.

not only encouraged the Japanese to attack Great Britain during the spring of 1941 and urged her to move against Russia from July 1941 on, but they also actively encouraged a Japanese attack on the United States throughout that year, a course which Japan finally followed.[8]

The last of these accusations is extremely dubious, as will be shown, and constituted one of the weakest points in the prosecution's case at Nuremberg. The first two charges, however, were entirely true and were in fact freely admitted by the accused Germans. Germany certainly used every device, including her influence through the Tripartite Pact, to persuade Japan to move against Singapore in the spring of 1941. The important question, though, is how much attention Japan paid to her ally's urgings.

By February 1941 the Germans were exerting strong pressure both in Berlin and in Tokyo for a southward move by Japan. Von Ribbentrop, for example, urged Japanese Ambassador Hiroshi Oshima to work for an immediate attack on Singapore. The United States would not dare intervene, he said, though even if she did she would be able to do nothing. Moreover, a Japanese move now would prove the solidarity of the Axis Alliance.[9] Ott was instructed to use the same arguments in Tokyo. But the German pleas, even though they fitted in well with the plans of Japan's ardent expansionists, met with a noncommittal reception in the Japanese government, Japan's leaders wanting to be much more sure of a British collapse before they moved in to gather up the Far Eastern spoils. The German naval intelligence service reported to Hitler that Japan would not attack Singapore until German troops landed in Great Britain.[10] State

---

[8] *Ibid.*, 388–399; Judgment, *ibid.*, I, 215–216. The charge of close Japanese-German-Italian conspiracy is also Count 5 in the indictment made in the war crimes trials at Tokyo—and constitutes, one might say, one of the numerous weak spots in the prosecution's case there.

[9] Circular memo by Von Ribbentrop, Berlin, March 2, 1941, *Pearl Harbor Attack*, XIX, 3644–3647.

[10] "Report of the Commander in Chief of the Navy to the Fuehrer," March 16, 1941, *IMTFE*, Doc. no. 4013.

Secretary Ernst Von Weiszaecker informed Von Ribbentrop of his conviction that only new successes against England would make Japan enter the war.[11] Even Ambassador Ott, who usually put the most favorable construction possible on everything he reported to Berlin, could say only that he still believed an attack on Singapore was possible, "if the Army's and Navy's objections could be eliminated." At that, he emphasized, it would be essential that Japan be free in the rear from the menace of Russia.[12]

In view of Japanese intractability, the Germans had to consider what course to take with Matsuoka during the Japanese Foreign Minister's forthcoming visit to the Axis capitals. Weiszaecker urged frankness. Matsuoka, he said, should be warned of the impending Russo-German conflict, so as to protect him from surprises and "in order to control Japanese policy through him after his European journey."[13] Hitler, deeply distrustful of Japan, determined to do just the opposite. His directive ordered that every effort be made to get Japan to attack Singapore, stipulating at the same time that "no hint must be given to the Japanese concerning the operation 'Barbarossa' [the attack on the Soviet Union]."[14]

Matsuoka's conferences with Axis leaders beginning in Berlin on March 27, 1941, widely hailed as a sign of Axis solidarity, thus actually began in an atmosphere of secretiveness and deception. The German objectives in the conversations—admittedly difficult ones—were to persuade Japan to attack Great Britain and to discourage the Japanese from concluding a treaty with Russia, with whom Germany would soon be at war. At the same time the Nazis wished to conceal from Japan the knowledge of the impending German attack on the Soviet Union. Matsuoka's purposes are less clear. Apparently he was

[11] Memo, Weiszaecker to Von Ribbentrop, Berlin, March 24, 1941, *ibid.*, Doc. no. 4038C.
[12] Ott to Ribbentrop, Tokyo, March 25, 1941, *ibid.*, Doc. no. 4038B.
[13] Weiszaecker's memo, *ibid.*, Doc. no. 4038C.
[14] Directive no. 24, "Concerning Collaboration with Japan," *ibid.*, Doc. no. 4003.

there to learn what he could of German plans, to secure German aid, if possible, in settling Russo-Japanese and Sino-Japanese relations,[15] and to get promises of German technical assistance. In return, he intended to placate the Germans with fair-sounding words about Japanese action, without committing himself to anything definite.

With such objectives being pursued by each side, the talks followed a predictable pattern of false assurances and deceitful urgings. Von Ribbentrop and Hitler marshaled all their arguments in favor of an immediate Japanese blow at Singapore. They promised German technical assistance for the move [16] and insisted that Japan must not let her present golden opportunity pass.[17] Above all, the fear of American intervention should not deter Japan, they urged. Hitler said that he had already taken this possibility into his calculations and claimed that the best way to stop the United States was to move now.[18] The Tripartite Pact "could best accomplish its true purpose [i.e., keeping America out of the war] . . . if at the proper time the treaty partners made joint arrangements for the final defeat of England." [19]

To all this pressure Matsuoka responded with a great show of agreement but no promises. He himself, he assured the German leaders, strongly favored an immediate move southward. Unfortunately, he was hampered by strong pro-British and pro-American circles in Japan and by others who were very hesitant about any overt action which might bring the United States

[15] Ott to Von Ribbentrop, Tokyo, Dec. 19, 1940, *IMTFE*, Doc. no. 4042C.

[16] Memo of conversation, Matsuoka and Von Ribbentrop, Berlin, March 29, 1941, *Nazi-Soviet Relations, 1939–1941*, edited by Raymond J. Sontag and James S. Beddie (Washington: Government Printing Office, 1948), 309–310.

[17] Memo of conversation, Hitler and Matsuoka, Berlin, March 27, 1941, *ibid.*, 292–293.

[18] Hitler and Matsuoka, Berlin, April 4, 1941, *ibid.*, 313–314.

[19] Von Ribbentrop and Matsuoka, March 27, 1941, *ibid.*, 288.

into the war. He likewise stood solidly behind the Tripartite Pact, but again not all Japanese leaders shared his feelings.[20] In fact, he would have to confess that his own belligerent policy was unpopular in Japan, so much so that he would not dare mention a word of the plans he had discussed with Hitler but could only say that Singapore was considered in a hypothetical way. The best he could promise the Germans was that he would use his influence to win Prince Konoye and the Emperor to his point of view. If he were unable to convince them, it would be a clear sign that his influence and power in office were not sufficient for the task.[21]

Thus Germany received no worth-while assurance on the question of a move southward. On the other hand, Matsuoka received no help on the matter of relations with Russia. Anxious to exploit Germany's promise to help improve Russo-Japanese relations, the Japanese Foreign Minister hinted that the road seemed clear for a Soviet-Japanese accord, as far as his recent conversations with Molotov and Stalin had indicated. Tactfully he sought out Von Ribbentrop's reaction to the idea of a German-Russian-Japanese alliance. But Von Ribbentrop replied that such an alliance was ideologically impossible.[22] Moreover, according to the German Foreign Minister, Russia had shown many signs of "unfriendliness" in recent months toward Germany; and although Germany had no hostile designs against the Soviet Union, she would be prepared to deal with her if necessary. Warning Matsuoka not to get too close to the Soviets, he promised that Germany would attack Russia if she menaced Japan. This assurance, he was confident, would secure Japan's rear and pave the way for a Singapore move.[23]

Just how seriously Matsuoka took these hints of German trou-

[20] Hitler and Matsuoka, March 27, April 4, 1941, *ibid.*, 294–296, 314–316.
[21] *Ibid.*, 315–316.
[22] Von Ribbentrop and Matsuoka, Berlin, March 28, 1941, *ibid.*, 301–302.
[23] *Ibid.*; also Von Ribbentrop and Matsuoka, Berlin, March 27 and 29, 1941, *ibid.*, 285, 303–305.

ble with Russia is hard to determine. He must have been aware in any case that Germany would give Japan no help in improving relations with Russia, that, as Langer and Gleason say, "Japan would have to shift for itself." [24] Matsuoka therefore left Berlin with no concrete achievements of which to boast.

The Japanese Foreign Minister was not to go home empty-handed, however. On his return journey to Tokyo he stopped at Moscow. There, in conversations with Foreign Minister Vyacheslav Molotov and Premier Josef Stalin, he succeeded with surprising suddenness in negotiating a Russo-Japanese nonaggression treaty. From the Japanese point of view, the treaty was at least better than nothing in paving the way for a possible move southward.[25] But it was also the very step against which Matsuoka had been warned in Berlin. Hitler's reaction on hearing of the pact was one of ill-concealed anger.[26] It could hardly have soothed his feelings to learn of Matsuoka's explanation that the pact was really favorable and useful to the Axis powers as a demonstration of Soviet friendliness and willingness to cooperate with them.[27] Worse yet, the Russians, despite the concessions they had made, were reported as being very happy over the treaty.[28] Though the new pact was in no way a betrayal of the Axis Alliance, Japan had again acted unilaterally and in her own interests. The general reaction to the treaty in Tokyo was also favorable, largely because the Japanese expected—wrongly, as it turned out—that the treaty would help to settle the China Affair by putting an end to Russian aid to China.[29] In the final

[24] Langer and Gleason, *Undeclared War*, 351.
[25] *Ibid.*, 356.
[26] Feis, *Road to Pearl Harbor*, 188.
[27] German Chargé Tippelskirch to Von Ribbentrop, Moscow, April 16, 1941, *Nazi-Soviet Relations*, 326–327.
[28] Memo of conversation, German Ambassador to Russia Count Von Schulenburg with Hitler, Berlin, April 28, 1941, *ibid.*, 330.
[29] Telegram, Boltze to Berlin, Tokyo, April 14, 1941, *IMTFE*, Doc. no. 4056A.

analysis, Matsuoka's journey, undertaken to demonstrate and strengthen Axis solidarity, had had quite opposite results.

The Japanese Foreign Minister's absence from Tokyo, moreover, had provided an opportunity for Konoye to press his attempts at an American-Japanese agreement. While Konoye even at home did not enjoy uniform support in this project, he succeeded in making some progress within his own government. His efforts contributed to the drawing up of the informal Japanese proposal transmitted to the American government on April 9, 1941.[30] When Hull asked Nomura to request the Japanese government to make this informal proposal official, Konoye, in order to comply with the request, met with other high officials in a Liaison Conference to consider what definite terms should be proffered to the United States. The meeting showed that Axis sentiment in the Japanese government was neither dead nor dominant. According to Konoye, the consensus was that Japan for numerous reasons needed an agreement with the United States. Foremost among these reasons was the necessity for settlement of the China Affair. The regime of the Chinese puppet Wang Ching-wei was a failure, the conferees agreed. Since Chiang was dependent on the United States, the best course was to negotiate with him through America. In addition, a Japanese-American accord would help prevent the spread of the European war to the Pacific. As for the southward advance being then contemplated in some quarters, "The Supreme Command," Prince Konoye records, "itself confessed to having neither the confidence of success nor the necessary preparation." [31]

Japan was not ready, however, to buy an agreement with the United States at any price. The Liaison Conference decided that Japan should not concede any infringement of the Tripartite Pact or sacrifice good faith with Germany. If the United States

[30] See above, Chapter II, 32.
[31] Konoye, "Memoirs," *Pearl Harbor Attack*, XX, 3986.

wanted an accord with Japan only in order to free her hands for an Atlantic war, she was trying the wrong tack. Moreover, Germany should be informed before any agreement was concluded, though not while negotiations were in progress.[32]

The conference thus showed considerably more concern for German feelings and the Axis relationship than Japan was to display later. But the spirit shown was still not at all satisfactory to Matsuoka. On his return to Tokyo on April 22, he began a strenuous effort either to make the talks with the United States conform with Japan's Axis obligations or to sabotage them entirely. In his reckless attempts to do this, he often far exceeded his authority. He delayed the transmission of the Japanese proposal to the United States and succeeded in revising and narrowing its terms considerably, the revisions showing up in the Japanese proposal of May 12. He took it upon himself to propose to the United States a simple nonaggression treaty. Furthermore, in violation of cabinet orders, he informed Rome and Berlin of the course of the talks and awaited their reaction.[33]

These tactics did nothing to strengthen Matsuoka's position in the government, which was rapidly being undermined in any case. The Foreign Minister was caught between two fires. On the one hand, his extreme and intransigent attitude on the Axis Alliance was alienating support within the cabinet. He complained bitterly to Konoye, "Although it appeared that Army and Navy leaders were trying to have the Japanese-American understanding put through, even at the cost, more or less of disloyalty to Germany and Italy,—what could be accomplished by such a weak-kneed attitude?"[34] His radical interpretation of Article III of the Pact and reports that he had promised Von Ribbentrop an attack on Singapore helped to render his position precarious.

At the same time, nothing he could do would satisfy the Germans. It was under their pressure that in May he made his

[32] *Ibid.*, 3985–3986.   [33] *Ibid.*, 3987–3989.   [34] *Ibid.*, 3991–3992.

belligerent statements to the effect that convoying activities by the United States Navy in the Atlantic might well mean war with Japan and that Japan would certainly honor the Pact if it was invoked.[35] He tried his best to kill the chances for success in the Japanese-American conversations.[36] But his efforts were not nearly sufficient to please the German leaders. Von Ribbentrop in particular protested against the talks in principle, maintaining that any Japanese-American agreement would render the Tripartite Pact meaningless. At the very least he insisted that Japan call the existing American naval actions in the Atlantic acts of war and demand not only their immediate cessation, but also a pledge by the United States not to intervene further in the European conflict. "Such," says Konoye, "were the high-handed representations of the Germans."[37] The Japanese proposal of May 12, although it was far stronger on the Tripartite Pact than any prior or succeeding Japanese draft, nevertheless aroused German anger.[38] While Von Ribbentrop continued to try to get the talks broken off, Hitler, having in all probability already concluded that Japan was quite unreliable on the Pact, began planning to draw the Japanese into the war later against their old enemy, Russia.[39] Even Matsuoka's patience at length wore thin under the barrage of German demands. In reply to Von Ribbentrop's complaints, he cabled Ambassador Oshima

[35] Jones, *Japan's New Order*, 272 (note); Feis, *Road to Pearl Harbor*, 202–203.

[36] Jones, *Japan's New Order*, 272; Langer and Gleason, *Undeclared War*, 474.

[37] Konoye, "Memoirs," *Pearl Harbor Attack*, XX, 3991.

[38] Von Ribbentrop cabled Ott on May 17, 1941, that the Japanese clause of May 12 on the Pact must be considered an absolute minimum and that any deviation from a strict interpretation of Pact obligations "would contradict the spirit and meaning of the Tri-Partite Pact, ultimately making the Pact illusory." He also demanded German participation in the negotiations (*IMTFE*, Record, 24724–24726).

[39] Konoye, "Memoirs," *Pearl Harbor Attack*, XX, 3990–3991; Jones, *Japan's New Order*, 273–276; Langer and Gleason, *Undeclared War*, 478.

that since the real purpose of the Pact was to keep America out of the war he felt it quite suitable to negotiate with the United States to this end. He affirmed his own unswerving loyalty to the Axis Alliance and promised to do his best to keep his understanding with Germany and Italy. "However," he reminded Oshima, "Japan has her own standpoint, and I don't think it necessary to meet the intention of Germany and Italy even in the matter concerning the execution of policy." [40]

It was plain even before the Nazi onslaught on Russia that Matsuoka was destined sooner or later to fall. This catastrophic turn in the war only precipitated the crisis in Japan. The Japanese had feared that a Nazi-Soviet break was coming (though probably not that it would come as suddenly or as violently as it did) and did not relish the idea—this is evident from the anxious query of the Japanese Ambassador in Berlin as to whether an "easing of tension" had occurred.[41] Japan's concern over the prospect of Soviet-German trouble stemmed from two potent factors. First was the long-standing Japanese fear of any extension of the European war which might involve Japan. The Japanese had long been suggesting to Germany that she should reach a compromise peace with Great Britain and had even made public an offer to Germany of her aid in mediation.[42] Second, and more immediately, by early June the Japanese Army was determined on a further move into southern Indo-China, to consolidate its position there and to prepare for possible expansion southward. The Japanese were already hinting for German help in coercing Vichy [43] and did not want Germany so com-

[40] Matsuoka to Oshima, Tokyo, May 24, 1941, *IMTFE*, Rej. Def. Doc. no. 1659.

[41] Memo by Weiszaecker, Berlin, May 17, 1941, *Nazi-Soviet Relations*, 342. See also Tojo's deposition, *IMTFE*, Record, 36255–36258.

[42] *New York Times*, March 6, 1941.

[43] Memo, Woermann to Von Ribbentrop, Berlin, June 10, 1941, *IMTFE*, Doc. no. 4061A; entry of June 18, 1941, Kido's Diary, *ibid.*, Doc. no. 1632W.

mitted in Europe that she could be of no assistance against possible Anglo-American opposition in the Far East. From all indications, Matsuoka shared this general Japanese viewpoint.

Nevertheless, when the Nazi legions moved into Russia and the Germans began to urge Japan to follow their example in Siberia, Matsuoka executed a sudden and complete reversal of policy. Overnight the advocate of expansion southward and architect of neutrality with the Soviet Union began to crusade for war against the Russians, even going over the head of Premier Konoye to make a direct appeal before the Emperor for war on Russia.[44]

His efforts, however, went without success. Instead, the Imperial Conference on July 2, as already noted, decided on a policy that, while ambitious enough in regard to Japan's interests, was quite different from the one which the Germans and Matsuoka were urging. According to the decision, Japan would adhere to the goal of the Co-Prosperity Sphere, make further efforts to clear up the China Affair, and carry out her plans already prepared for penetration into southern French Indo-China and Thailand, even at the risk of war with the United States and Great Britain. As far as the Soviet Union was concerned, Japan would make no move unless conditions were favorable (in other words, unless a Russian collapse was imminent). The Tripartite Pact would not be repudiated. Although every means would be used to keep the United States out of the war, if she came in Japan would honor the Pact, deciding independently, however, the time, manner, and scope of her action.[45]

This was a bold policy for Japan; it was also one that disregarded Axis desires at the time. Indeed, Japanese dispatches

[44] Konoye, "Memoirs," *Pearl Harbor Attack,* XX, 3993; Jones, *Japan's New Order,* 216–217.

[45] "Resolutions concerning the Japanese-American Negotiations Adopted through the Conferences in the Imperial Presence," *IMTFE,* Doc. no. 1652; dispatch from Tokyo, July 2, 1941, *Pearl Harbor Attack,* XII, 1.

showed that she intended to carry out her policy with Axis help if possible, but alone if necessary.[46] Not all influential Japanese, including some in high places, intended that the move into south Indo-China should be a necessary prelude to further southward expansion. Konoye, though opposing the step, agreed to it largely as a sop to Japan's militarist extremists, who wanted to go much farther.[47] Many Japanese leaders definitely considered it as a defensive measure against the joint American-British-Dutch military build-up in the southwest Pacific.[48] That this view is not entirely incredible is evident from the fact that Brigadier General Miles, acting Assistant Chief of Staff of United States Army Intelligence, interpreted the move in much the same way.[49] What is certain in any case is that the advance would only menace and arouse both Great Britain and the United States without really hurting either one of them and would at the same time tend to relieve the pressure on the Russian rear in Siberia. In other words, it was in German eyes the wrong kind of move in the wrong direction at the wrong time.[50]

[46] Dispatch, Canton to Tokyo, July 2, 1941, *Pearl Harbor Attack*, XII, 2.

[47] Konoye, "Memoirs," *ibid.*, XX, 4004; Ott to Von Ribbentrop, Tokyo, July 10, 1941, *IMTFE*, Doc. no. 11A(3); Army dispatch, Canton to Tokyo, July 14, 1941, *ibid.*, Doc. no. 2593C.

[48] "On the Formation of the Anti-Japanese Joint Encirclement by Great Britain, United States, and the Netherlands," April, 1941, *IMTFE*, Rej. Def. Doc. no. 1739; Matsuoka to Ambassador Kato in France, Tokyo, July 12, 1941, *ibid.*, Docs. no. 1383C, D.

[49] Memo, Washington, July 17, 1941, *Pearl Harbor Attack*, XIV, 1342.

[50] While the deliberations over Japan's course in the new and crucial situation were going on, Ott reported to his home office that, although the Army was pushing preparatory measures for a move either northward or southward, "according to reliable, confidential information, Premier Konoye and the majority of Cabinet Ministers . . . seem to maintain the view that nothing must be undertaken that would injure Japan's military position in China. Hence, the Cabinet seems thus far merely to have resolved on tightening their grip on Indo-China." In addition, Ott observed, "noted nationalists, who always closely work together with the [German] Embassy, have held various confidential conversations . . . in which caution towards the Soviet Union and determined

Nothing the Germans could do, however, would change the Japanese stand. On July 2, 1941, Matsuoka unwillingly informed the Soviet Ambassador that Japan at present intended to honor her nonaggression pact with Russia.[51] Further German efforts to induce Japan to take the plunge in Siberia drew more and more unsatisfactory answers, particularly after Matsuoka's fall in mid-July. Just as she had done in the conference of July 2, Japan was willing to affirm her allegiance to the spirit and objectives of the Tripartite Pact. But this spirit and these objectives as interpreted by Japan were useless to Germany. They meant, for Japan, simply keeping the United States out of the war and settling the China Affair. To German complaints of nonco-operation and urgings that Japan seize her golden opportunity in the north, Foreign Minister Toyoda replied that Germany had launched the Russian campaign at a moment most inopportune for Japan, presenting her with a challenge in the north rather than an opportunity.[52] The Japanese readily gave assurances that they were prepared to act when the time was right; but it must have quickly become clear to the Germans that the time would come only when and if Germany had already brought the Soviet Union to her knees. Evidence that the German attack was not proceeding according to plan only served to increase Japanese reluctance.[53]

---

action in the South was advocated. The danger exists that the Southern expansion desired by this group will at first be limited to French Indo-China, while their efforts could hinder Japan's activity in the North" (Ott to Berlin, Tokyo, June 28, 1941, *IMTFE*, Doc. no. 4081D). It is true, as Herbert Feis points out, that Germany gave some support—albeit reluctantly and tardily—to Japanese demands on the Vichy government. But it is also clear that Japan was going ahead with or without German help, as the Germans must have realized. The support may have been a way of accepting it as graciously as possible (Feis, *Road to Pearl Harbor*, 231).

[51] Oral Statement, Matsuoka to Smetanin, Tokyo, July 2, 1941, *Foreign Relations, Japan*, II, 504.

[52] Toyoda to Oshima, Tokyo, July 31, 1941, *Pearl Harbor Attack*, XII, 10.

[53] Oshima later testified that already in early August 1941 he had noted

Instructions to the Japanese ambassadors both in Washington and in Berlin made it plain that Japan had no intention of launching a northern campaign at the present time and would honor the neutrality pact as long as Russia did, although the chance of exploiting a Russian defeat was not ruled out.[54] All this, according to Toyoda, was in conformity with the "spirit and objectives" of the Tripartite Pact.[55] The attitude of the Tojo government on this question later on was no different. Foreign Minister Togo even put forward the suggestion, completely unpalatable to Hitler, that Japan should mediate the Russo-German war.[56]

The German onslaught on Russia had destroyed the tenuous identity of interests which had held the Axis together and left the Japanese and Germans to follow strategic plans fundamentally at variance with each other. This situation, incidentally, was not corrected throughout the war, with disastrous results for the Axis. The Nazi attack further precipitated a domestic change in Japan which left Germany on the outside looking in. With the news of the German attack, Konoye had reached the conclusion, long brewing in his mind, that Japan was heading for disaster unless she executed a strategic retreat. In a letter of policy to Matsuoka on July 4, just after the Imperial Conference had set forth the policy of continued expansion, the Japanese Premier set down his reasons for the absolute necessity of readjusting relations with the United States. It should be done, he maintained, even at the cost of abandoning the advance southward and estranging Germany. Japan's shortage of raw materials, the danger of Anglo-American encirclement, and the need for peace in China made an agreement with the United States mandatory.

the slowing of the German advance and reported it to his government (April 22, 1946, *IMTFE*, Doc. no. 4121).

[54] Toyoda to Oshima, Tokyo, Aug. 15, 1941, *Pearl Harbor Attack*, XII, 15-16; to Nomura, Tokyo, Aug. 20, 1941, *ibid.*, 18-19.

[55] Toyoda to Oshima, *ibid.*, 16.

[56] Togo to Nomura, Tokyo, Nov. 16, 1941, *ibid.*, 138; to Oshima, Tokyo, Nov. 21, 1941, *ibid.*, 165.

With the Emperor's support, he was determined to bring it about.[57]

Surprisingly enough, Matsuoka gave his consent to this program, but in the ensuing consideration of the American proposals of June 21 he showed that his acquiescence was exceedingly short-lived. Taking particular offense at Hull's censure of certain Japanese officials (meaning above all Matsuoka) allegedly under the influence of Nazi policies, he wanted the talks broken off. Japanese military leaders, too, put obstacles in the way of Konoye's conciliatory policy, insisting on the occupation of south Indo-China and the reservation of Japan's right to use armed force in the Pacific in case of necessity.[58] Their opposition could not be eliminated, but Matsuoka's obstruction could. After he once again exceeded his authority and defied instructions by trying to inform the Germans of the course of negotiations and by failing to transmit the Japanese proposal to the United States, Konoye and the other ministers decided that the time had come to rid themselves of their erratic Foreign Minister. When Matsuoka refused to resign, the cabinet resigned in a bloc and was reconstituted without him, Admiral Toyoda taking his place.[59]

With this move, the cloud which had already begun to settle over German-Japanese relations became impenetrable. During the week before Matsuoka's fall, Von Ribbentrop had devoted anxious efforts to finding out what was taking place in the Japanese government. He urgently requested news from Ott about Japanese-American relations and the negotiations then going on. Was it Ott's opinion that Japan was trying to secure agreement with the United States in order to involve America in the European war and thus gain a free hand for herself in the Far East? Had Nomura given Roosevelt assurances that Japan would not protest the seizure of Iceland? He had, Von Ribbentrop claimed, continued confidence in the Japanese government and in its

---

[57] Konoye, "Memoirs," *ibid.*, XX, 3994.
[58] *Ibid.*, 3994–3995.   [59] *Ibid.*, 3996–3997.

Foreign Minister, but Japan should at least make a statement that the United States was committing acts of aggression in the Atlantic and that Japan would carry out her obligations under the Tripartite Pact. Above all, he urged Ott to work through Matsuoka to insure that Japan did not miss her present unique opportunity to crush Russia.[60]

State Secretary Weiszaecker voiced to Ambassador Oshima the same grave suspicions of Japan's intentions. Did the United States, he demanded, consider herself as secure in the Pacific as her actions in regard to Iceland "would really lead one to believe?" [61] The Nazi diplomats, however, found no solace from any source. Oshima, though sympathetic to the German complaints, had no information to give. Further, Ott's reply to Von Ribbentrop was flatly discouraging. He cabled that he was doing his best with every means available, especially his contacts with Matsuoka and the Foreign Ministry, to promote the German policy. But he was having great difficulty persuading Japan that now was the time to strike. Moreover, "anglophile Japanese circles" were leading strong efforts to reach agreement with the United States.[62]

If any uncertainty about the Japanese attitude remained in Von Ribbentrop's mind after Ott's reply, it must have disappeared with Matsuoka's fall. True, the new Foreign Minister, Toyoda, immediately assured Germany that Japan would remain loyal to the Tripartite Pact in spirit.[63] But this was a routine Japanese promise, and the Germans were hardly to be deceived

---

[60] Von Ribbentrop to Ott, Berlin, July 10, 1941, *Nuremberg Military Tribunal*, Doc. no. 2896-PS, XXXI, 259–262.

[61] Memo, Weiszaecker to Von Ribbentrop, Berlin, July 12, 1941, *IMTFE*, Doc. no. 4025 (although this document is not numbered as such, it is included among the Rejected Defense Documents on microfilm).

[62] Ott to Von Ribbentrop, Tokyo, July 14, 1941, *Nuremberg Military Tribunal*, Doc. no. 2897-PS, XXXI, 263–265; Langer and Gleason, *Undeclared War*, 637–638.

[63] Ott to Von Ribbentrop, Tokyo, July 20, 1941, *IMTFE*, Doc. no. 4052F; Feis, *Road to Pearl Harbor*, 231.

by words when Japanese deeds spoke so much more loudly. In practical fact, Germany saw her relations with Japan quickly become as estranged as they had been during the time of the Abe and Yonai cabinets. The Japanese Foreign Office was shaken up, with results unfavorable to Germany. The inside contacts which the Axis diplomats had enjoyed were sealed off and their activities were much restricted. Tight secrecy was clamped down and maintained concerning the Japanese-American talks, so much so that even Ambassador Oshima in Berlin received no information about them from his government. Despite vigorous protests, Germany found herself excluded from official Japanese circles and coolly ignored in Japan's policy.[64]

Having no desire to burn her bridges behind her prematurely, Japan, naturally enough, did not repudiate the Tripartite Pact outright. But she took few pains to conceal from Germany her disillusionment with the Pact's actual results. In reply to Oshima's complaints on behalf of Germany, Toyoda defended Japan's independent policy in terms revealing enough to justify quotation at length. He wrote:

When we concluded the Three Power Pact, we hoped while maintaining amicable relations with America, and to tell the truth through this very means, to conclude the China trouble; to win the Soviet over to the Japanese-German-Italian camp; to have Germany use her good offices between Tokyo and Moscow (STAHMER said that Germany would be an honest go-between and would be sure to bring about the solution of our troubles with the Kremlin and OTT sent us a letter to the effect that he himself was going to work for an understanding between Japan and the Soviet); to guarantee goods from the South Seas to Germany and Italy who, in turn, were to give us mechanical and technical assistance. But since then times have changed and unexpected events have taken place. All that remains

[64] Statement by Ott, Peking, Nov. 18, 1945, *IMTFE*, Rej. Def. Doc. no. 2858; interrogation of Hiroshi Oshima, Feb. 26, 1946, *ibid.*, Doc. no. 2157D.

unchanged is Japanese-American relations, and that is about the only thing that could be patched up. . . .

At the time Germany stated that she would not spare any effort to prevent a clash between Japan and the United States and that she would even do all she could to improve relations between the two countries (this was during the MATSUOKA-STAHMER talks). Then Japan and Germany felt the need of preventing the United States from entering the war.

3. The objective of the Japan-German-Italian Three Power Pact was to prevent the expansion of the European War, to restrain the United States from participating, and to establish universal peace. Statements exchanged at the time make this perfectly clear but now the war covers the face of Europe. The only placid expanse of water on earth is the Pacific. Under these circumstances, it is felt that it is up to both nations to probe into the causes of the trouble between their respective governments and to assure the harmony of the Pacific. It is further felt that this coincides with the spirit of the Three Power Pact. . . .

It is not that we are divergent from our relations with the signatories of the Tri-Partite Pact, but we are continuing our negotiations hoping to end the China affair. (The three principles of KONOYE envision a conclusion of hostilities through a basic treaty and the use of the United States to coerce the CHIANG regime, to establish an area of co-prosperity in greater East Asia, to procure materials, to prevent the expansion of the European war, to seal peace in the Pacific area, and to prevent the United States from entering the war. Of course, however, we expect our ups and downs.) [65]

Plainly, what Toyoda meant by actions in keeping with the spirit of the Tripartite Pact were simply any moves designed to extricate Japan from her troubles and to keep her out of war with the United States.[66]

The secrecy with which the Japanese leaders conducted their

[65] Toyoda to Oshima, Tokyo, Oct. 8, 1941, *Pearl Harbor Attack*, XII, 57–58.

[66] It is surprising to find the Toyoda dispatch used by Cordell Hull in the Congressional investigation of the Pearl Harbor attack as evidence of the close German-Japanese ties. There is hardly a word in it in which

negotiations with the Washington government,[67] their refusal to warn against American naval activities in the Atlantic, as Germany had repeatedly demanded,[68] and their manifest indifference to Axis obligations—all had an inevitable effect on the German and Italian attitude toward the Japanese. The Japanese ambassadors to Germany and Italy both reported many evidences of coolness toward Japan. Oshima warned that Von Ribbentrop and the whole German Foreign Office were completely disgusted with Japan's faithlessness and that there was real danger of a break in relations between Japan and Germany should Japan reach an agreement with the United States.[69] Oshima's warning carried little weight with the home office, as can be seen from Toyoda's answer to it quoted above. Many Japanese leaders, in fact, had already reckoned with the estrangement of Germany and concluded that it did not particularly matter. Admiral Nagano, Chief of the Naval General Staff, believed that Japan should try hard for an agreement with the United States, abandoning the Tripartite Pact if need be. Tojo would not go quite so far as this; one suspects that he, along with many Japanese, was deterred by pride as much as anything else—by the stubborn determination that Japan would not bow to the humiliating demands of a hostile power in dropping the Pact. Nevertheless he agreed to the idea of a Konoye-Roosevelt meeting even though he was convinced that no matter how it was held it would hurt relations with Germany.[70] In the crucial showdown between activists and moderates which brought the fall of the Konoye

the Germans could find comfort (testimony, Nov. 23, 1945, *ibid.*, II, 456–457).

[67] Toyoda, for example, refused to divulge to Ott the content of Konoye's letter to Roosevelt (Ott to Von Ribbentrop, Tokyo, Aug. 30, 1941, *IMTFE*, Record, 24727–24729).

[68] Toyoda to Nomura, Tokyo, Oct. 16, 1941, *Pearl Harbor Attack*, XII, 71–72.

[69] Dispatches, Rome to Tokyo, Sept. 30, 1941, and Berlin to Tokyo, Oct. 1, 1941, *ibid.*, 44–45, 48–49.

[70] Kido's Diary, entry of July 31, 1941, *IMTFE*, Doc. no. 1632W; Feis, *Road to Pearl Harbor*, 253.

government in mid-October, the Tripartite Pact was not an issue. "On this," F. C. Jones comments, "there was no decisive rift between the Cabinet and the High Command." [71]

The decisive rift in the Konoye cabinet, an extension of the historic opposition within the Japanese government of the bureaucrats and the Army, was over a completely different issue—the question of whether Japan should fight or retreat in the face of the American embargo. It was this split, in which the Court party led by Konoye was pitted against the military circle represented by Tojo, and the final triumph of Tojo over Konoye, that led directly to the Pacific war. The rift was evident from the very outset in the third Konoye government. After Matsuoka's fall, the breaking-off of the negotiations by the United States and the imposition of the joint freezing orders, precipitated as they were by the Japanese move into south Indo-China, had convinced Konoye more than ever that the time had come for Japan to pull back. The same events, however, had only made the Army General Staff more opposed than ever to the talks with the United States and more firm in their belief that, since the United States would never yield an inch, Japan must prepare for war as rapidly as possible. It was their opposition that Konoye faced when he presented his plan for a Leaders' Conference. For the sake of an agreement with the United States, Konoye was ready to defer the attainment of the Greater East Asia Co-Prosperity Sphere indefinitely and to consider close German-Japanese relations expendable. "Even if Germany's attitude toward Japan becomes cool," he argued, "since there is no chance of a German conquest of the world or of a complete victory over Britain and America, there are many ways in which German-Japanese relations can be altered." [72] The Navy Minister heartily approved of the Konoye proposal, but Tojo re-

[71] Jones, *Japan's New Order*, 457; Konoye, "Memoirs," *Pearl Harbor Attack*, XX, 4026–4027.

[72] Konoye, "Memoirs," *Pearl Harbor Attack*, XX, 3999–4000.

mained unimpressed. He was not particularly concerned about the estrangement of Germany, which he considered inevitable in any case, but he was convinced that Japan could not appease America short of surrender. Predicting failure for the conference, he insisted that Konoye must agree to return and to lead the nation into war if the talks with Roosevelt failed. Konoye, ever the compromiser, acquiesced.[73]

The Japanese Premier soon discovered, however, that it was far more difficult to secure American consent to the Leaders' Conference than it had been to get his own cabinet's approval. Although Roosevelt displayed initial interest, his formal reply to the Japanese invitation on September 3 showed that Hull's theoretical diplomacy had triumphed. Japan would first have to agree with America on basic principles.[74] This evidence of uncompromising rigidity on the part of the United States served to strengthen the hand of the extremists in Japan, who in an Imperial Conference on September 6 sought and gained a definite time limit on the negotiations with America. The conference decreed that Japan would have to be ready to fight by the end of October. Until the early part of that month, she should try to obtain her demands from the United States by diplomacy. According to both Konoye and Tojo, it was at the Emperor's insistence that diplomacy was given even this much limited priority.[75] The conference also reaffirmed Japan's previous policy in regard to the Tripartite Pact and the Russo-German war.[76]

Japan's minimum demands and maximum concessions as determined by the conference of September 6 had been shown to the United States in the Japanese proposal of that same day. The proposal met no better a fate than any previous one, the key

[73] *Ibid.*, 4000.   [74] *Ibid.*, 4002–4003.
[75] *Ibid.*, 4005; Tojo's deposition, *IMTFE*, Record, 36271–36272, 36281.
[76] Resolutions of the Imperial Conference, Sept. 6, 1941, *IMTFE*, Doc. no. 1652.

problem as ever being the question of China.[77] As time wore on and the Japanese proposal of September 25 elicited only the still more doctrinaire American reply of October 2, the contention of Konoye's opponents grew irresistible that the United States had no intention of reaching an agreement with Japan and that she was simply seeking to gain time to increase her strength in the southwest Pacific.[78] By mid-October, Konoye could hang on no longer. He could not hold out any rational hope of reaching a settlement with the United States or even of having a meeting with Roosevelt unless Japan made still further concessions on the stationing of troops in China.[79] But on this point he could neither sway Tojo from his unyielding opposition nor gain the unequivocal support of the Navy Minister. With his cabinet hopelessly split, Konoye resigned on October 16,[80] a casualty in the struggle over the China problem.[81]

[77] *Ibid.*, Judgment, 49521–49522.

[78] Konoye, "Memoirs," *Pearl Harbor Attack*, XX, 4007–4008.

[79] That Konoye himself favored further concessions is seen from his letter of resignation to the Emperor, Tokyo, Oct. 16, 1941, *ibid.*, 4025–4026 (also *IMTFE*, Doc. no. 1468A). The sort of concessions he envisaged may be surmised from the document drawn up by Toyoda, Oct. 13, 1941, entitled "Opinion of the Foreign Minister concerning the Japanese-American Negotiations." Arguing that the negotiations could not possibly succeed on the basis of the terms of September 6 or 25 and that Japan must not use force except if compelled to for self-defense, Toyoda urged three steps: First, Japan should make no reinforcement of her troops in French Indo-China or any threatening move toward the south; second, Japan should agree to have her troops withdrawn from China within two years, except for a five-year occupation of the usual designated areas (parts of North China, Inner Mongolia, and Hainan); and, third, Japan should agree to a revision of the French-Japanese agreements on the stationing of troops in Indo-China (*IMTFE*, Def. Doc. no. 1891). It was on Tojo's opposition especially to the second of these concessions that the Konoye government foundered (see Kido's Diary, entry of Oct. 12, 1941, *ibid.*, Doc. no. 1632W).

[80] Konoye, "Memoirs," *Pearl Harbor Attack*, XX, 4009–4011; "Facts Pertaining to the Resignation of the 3rd Konoye Cabinet," *IMTFE*, Doc. no. 497A.

[81] *Ibid.*, Judgment, 49306–49307.

According to the decision of the Imperial Conference of September 6, Japan's time for negotiation was now just about up. The accession of Tojo to the premiership should have meant for Japan the end of conversations and the beginning of war. But as happened more than once, when faced with the final and terrible decision for war against the United States the Japanese drew back. Tojo was placed in power with the understanding that he and his cabinet would review and reconsider the policy of September 6, to see if there was any other way out.[82] This he proceeded to do. In conferences on November 1 and 2, the Supreme Command and the cabinet went over the whole ground of Japan's policy toward the United States again, only to come up with the same hard facts. Japan's oil reserves were steadily being depleted; the plan, favored by Konoye and others, to supplant imports with synthetic oil production was a hopeless chimera; the United States would never yield on her embargo; Japan must fight soon or face indefinite attrition and eventual surrender. The conferees agreed indeed upon a final try at negotiation, upon the ultimate terms to be offered to the United States, and upon the deadline of November 25 to be set for their acceptance or rejection. But they did so without much real hope of averting a war now considered inevitable. The policy, terms, and timetable set by them were approved and confirmed by an Imperial Conference of November 5.[83]

[82] Tojo's own testimony, in addition to much other evidence, shows that at the time of his accession he believed that the moment for war had arrived (Interrogation, Feb. 11, 1946, *ibid.*, Doc. no. 2501A). Nevertheless, he appears genuinely to have accepted the Imperial mandate for a new "Clean Slate" policy, even claiming in his deposition that it was his idea to review the decisions of September 6 (*ibid.*, Record, 36306–36316).

[83] Feis, *Road to Pearl Harbor*, 285–287, 291–294; deposition of Kikisaburo Okada, Chief of the Preparation Section of the Mobilization Plans Bureau of the War Ministry, *IMTFE*, Record, 24855–24866; Resolutions of the Imperial Conference, Nov. 5, 1941, *ibid.*, Doc. no. 1652. The contention here advanced that the Japanese government reviewed its decision for war after October 15 and that it made the decision for war contingent upon the final breakdown of negotiations is contradicted by an

Of the fate of this last Japanese try for agreement, embodied in the general proposal of November 7 and the *modus vivendi* proposal of November 20, we already know. The Japanese advanced their deadline for settlement with the United States once more at the very end, from November 25 to November 29. Once their final terms were rejected, however, as they were in the American note of November 26, war became inexorable.

When this happened—and only when it happened—Japan moved to revive once again her long-dormant Axis ties. In the great decisions which took Japan down the road to war, those of July 2, September 6, October 12–16, and especially November 1–5, Japan's tie with Germany and her concern with the war in Europe had not been a real factor. In the November conferences, however, Japan had made the decision—a very expedient one—that, once war became inevitable, she should make every effort to bring Germany and Italy in with her against the United States. She determined to follow this course, however, only if Germany did not set her price for entering the war too high. If Germany demanded a Japanese attack on Siberia in exchange for a German declaration of war on the United States,

---

SCAP Research Report entitled "Japan's Decision to Fight" (*IMTFE*, Exhibit no. 809), which concludes, on p. 51, "The Imperial Japanese Government had positively committed itself to the waging of war against the UNITED STATES of AMERICA, GREAT BRITAIN, and the NETHERLANDS by the end of October 1941." The report, however, deals only with military plans, which were indeed far advanced by the end of October, as, according to the decision of September 6, they were supposed to be. It says nothing concerning the reconsideration of that decision by the Tojo government. That the decision to go to war was considered contingent upon the breakdown of negotiations even by those who believed the breakdown inevitable and the negotiations largely a formality is shown by the "Liaison Conference Decision November 13th, 1941," which reads: "When the present negotiations with the United States break down and a war with her becomes unavoidable (presumed to be after November 25th), the Japanese Government shall notify Germany (and Italy), without delay, of our intention to start war against the United States of America and Britain as soon as our war preparations are ready" (*ibid.*, Doc. no. 1441).

the Japanese leaders intended to forego German help altogether.[84]

Once the final failure of the negotiations with the United States became evident, Japan began attempts to implement this policy, carefully seeking promises of German support in a war with America without letting Germany know exactly what she intended to do. As early as November 23, Ambassador Ott reported that he had received tentative requests from a Japanese general for assurances of German help in the event of a Japanese-American conflict. Ott's advice to the general was that in case of war Japan should make the American decision for war as difficult as possible by taking no action against the Philippines, confining herself to British and Dutch territory in a drive to the south.[85]

What Ott had received was only an unofficial feeler, however, anticipating any official Japanese action by some days. As late as November 29, Ambassador Oshima in Berlin still had received no word from his government on the final outcome of the negotiations. In a conversation with Von Ribbentrop, Oshima discovered to his disgust that the German Foreign Office seemed to know more about the situation from its sources than he had been told by his own superiors. The German Foreign Minister was less cautious about giving promises than the Japanese in asking for them, hinting broadly to Oshima that if Japan went to war, as now seemed probable, Germany would be at her side.[86] Germany made little progress in finding out Japan's real plans, however, for Ott's queries in Tokyo about the exact state of Japanese-American relations went unsatisfied. The Japanese wanted only an assurance that, come what might, the other Axis

[84] Langer and Gleason, *Undeclared War*, 853–854, 939; "Liaison Conference Decision November 13th, 1941," *IMTFE*, Doc. no. 1441.

[85] Ott to Von Ribbentrop, Tokyo, Nov. 23, 1941, *IMTFE*, Doc. no. 4070.

[86] Oshima to Togo, Berlin, Nov. 29, 1941, *Pearl Harbor Attack*, XII, 200; see also *Nuremberg Military Tribunal*, V, 7.

powers would stand by her.[87] It was not until December 1, when the formal decision for war was taken by the Privy Council, that Oshima was instructed to sound out the Germans on joining in the war against the United States; and on December 3 the formal request for assistance was made.[88]

For reasons best known to himself, Hitler was quite ready to grant Japan the assurance desired. Perhaps, as the German diplomatic official Erich Kordt reports, he considered that the United States was already at war with Germany to all intents and purposes; perhaps he made another of his great strategic miscalculations in overestimating the strength of Japan. In any case, it is clear that he was not informed about the plans for the attack on Pearl Harbor. As Langer and Gleason point out, "It is reasonably certain that . . . the German representatives knew nothing specific about Japan's war plans." [89] According to testimony from German war leaders, the attack of December 7 was not only a surprise but a jolt to Germany. They expected an attack on British and Dutch possessions in the Far East, which would bring America into the war only after a difficult and perhaps protracted political struggle, something very different from the actual attack on Pearl Harbor. As Von Ribbentrop testified at Nuremberg, "She [Japan] did neither of the things we wanted her to do [i.e., to move against Singapore or Siberia] but instead, she did a third." [90] The Germans, however, should not have

[87] Ott to Von Ribbentrop, Tokyo, Nov. 30, 1941, *Nuremberg Military Tribunal*, Doc. no. 2898-PS, XXXI, 266–268.

[88] Interrogation of Oshima, Feb. 26, 1946, *IMTFE*, Doc. no. 2157D; Langer and Gleason, *Undeclared War*, 910–911, 925.

[89] Langer and Gleason, *Undeclared War*, 925, 939–941; Erich Kordt, *Wahn und Wirklichkeit* (Stuttgart: Union Deutsche Verlagsgesellschaft, 1948), 333. Ernst von Weiszaecker, in his *Erinnerungen* (Munich: Paul List, 1950), 327–328, attributes Hitler's decision in declaring war on the United States to an astoundingly frivolous insistence on Germany's declaring war rather than having it declared against her.

[90] Testimony, March 30, 1946, *Nuremberg Military Tribunal*, X, 296. Cf. also testimony of Admiral Jodl, June 5, 1946, *ibid.*, XV, 395–397; of Field Marshal Keitel, April 4, 1946, *ibid.*, X, 537–538.

been surprised completely by the Japanese move. Experience should have taught them that Japan's last-minute return to the Axis and overtures to Germany would be as self-interested, opportunistic, and underhanded as the policies of Axis partners were wont to be.

VII

The Pact and the Outside World

THE whole story of Japanese-German estrangement from July to December 1941 was naturally best known to responsible officials of the two nations themselves. Neither Japan nor Germany was anxious to publicize the news that the Tripartite Pact had virtually become inoperative, this being the sort of fact which a nation does not ordinarily shout from the housetops. The true condition of Axis relations, however, far from being an inside secret to be revealed only by postwar discoveries was in reality a fact well known and widely attested by many contemporary observers. The controlled press and propaganda agencies of Germany and Japan, for example, gave clear evidence of the change of relationships. Prior to July the European Axis leaders and press put considerable stress on the importance and effectiveness of the Tripartite Pact. DNB (Deutsches Nachrichten Büro), the official Nazi propaganda agency, claimed that it would bring an "automatic declaration of war" by Japan if the United States actively intervened in the European conflict.[1] Virginio Gayda, Italian spokesman, called the Pact an "automatic war compact,"[2] to which Mussolini added boastful claims that

[1] *New York Times*, Jan. 2, 1941.   [2] *Ibid.*, May 15, 1941.

the Pact was already in operation. "Japan," he said, ". . . is in perfect line with the Tripartite Pact. The Japanese . . . would not remain indifferent in the face of American aggression against the Axis powers." In fact, Il Duce contended, "collaboration between the powers of the Tripartite Pact is under way." [3] Although this was actually typical Mussolini bombast, the Italian dictator's claim was given wider credence when Matsuoka backed it up a few days afterward.[4]

After Matsuoka's fall, however, no Axis leader was able even to keep up the pretense of expecting Japanese intervention in behalf of Germany and Italy. The attitude toward the Pact and toward Japan was one of dignified silence. The change in affairs is evident by a comparison of Mussolini's speech of June 10, quoted above, with the German announcement of November 3, immediately after Hitler had publicly charged that the United States had attacked Germany, which disclaimed any intention on the part of the German government at that time to ask Japan to honor the Pact.[5] The Nazi press mirrors the changed state of affairs equally well. Prior to July, Japan and the Tripartite Pact were prominent themes in German newspapers. The visit of Matsuoka to Berlin, for example, was the occasion for considerable publicity proclaiming Tripartite solidarity.[6] But after the German onslaught on Russia, the Pact and the Far East almost dropped out of consideration. When the anniversary of the Tripartite Pact arrived, even the Nazi press could not make much of the cool Japanese celebration. On the question of Japanese-American relations, the Far Eastern correspondent of the *Frankfurter Zeitung* conceded that the chief problem between Japan and the United States was not the Tripartite Pact,

[3] Speech before the Chamber of Fasces and Corporations, Rome, June 10, 1941, *ibid.*, June 11, 1941.

[4] *Ibid.*, June 15, 1941.

[5] See above, Chapter III, pp. 70–71.

[6] *Deutsche Allgemeine Zeitung* (Berlin), March 30, 1941, supplement; *ibid.*, April 1, 2, and 3, 1941.

but China.[7] When the Anti-Comintern Pact was renewed on
November 25, the *Zeitung*'s comment on the event barely mentioned Japan, emphasizing instead the sacrifices made by Germany and her allies in Europe against bolshevism.[8] From November 26 to December 7 the paper paid little attention to Japan
and her problems, discussing only Japan's grave economic dis-
tress in none too sympathetic a fashion, even though the crisis
in Japanese-American relations was by this time widely known.[9]
When the Pacific war finally broke out, the initial German reaction, as indicated by the release from the German Information Bureau, was to ignore Japan. The release simply recited the
long record of American aggression against Germany, claiming
that Roosevelt had deliberately provoked the war he had now
achieved. As for the Japanese-American conflict, the editors of
the *Frankfurter Zeitung* presented it as something quite separate,
the product not of Japan's Axis partnership, but of the historic
Japanese-American rivalry in the Pacific.[10]

The strained relations between Japan and Germany are even
more plainly reflected in the Japanese press.[11] The Japanese
newspapers were always, naturally enough, most concerned
about their own sphere in the world, about Asiatic issues and
Japan's particular interests. Thus even during the first half of
1941, the chief Japanese complaints against the United States
centered on American aid to China, joint American-British-
Dutch encirclement of Japan, and America's economic pressure.[12] Nonetheless, though a "Japan-first" attitude was always
implicit in the stand of the press and of Japan's leaders, there is
ample evidence that many influential spokesmen considered

[7] *Frankfurter Zeitung*, Sept. 28 and 29, 1941.   [8] *Ibid.*, Nov. 26, 1941.
[9] *Ibid.*, Nov. 28, 1941.   [10] *Ibid.*, Dec. 9, 1941.
[11] At this point I am dependent for information on the English-
language *Japan Chronicle* (Kobe) and on the press reports in the *New
York Times*.
[12] *Japan Chronicle*, April 13 and 18, June 1, 1941; *New York Times*,
May 29, 1941.

Japan's course to be bound up with the Axis and based upon the Tripartite Pact. Not only did outspoken Axis proponents like Matsuoka proclaim Japan's inflexible adherence to the Pact, but even a moderate like Konoye could call it, for public consumption, the keystone of all operations by Japan.[13] During this same period the press in Japan contained not a few belligerent statements based on the Tripartite Pact and designed to warn America away from intervention in the Atlantic. The *Tokyo Kokumin* declared in January 1941 that the United States, already involved in the war through her pro-British policies, had given Japan as well as Germany and Italy ample reasons for striking back. The *Yomiuri* of Tokyo, in support of Matsuoka's stand on the Axis Alliance, warned the United States that she was sadly mistaken if she thought that Japan would not move in the event of American intervention in the European war.[14]

Matsuoka's trip to Europe served to strengthen this theme. A common interpretation among Axis observers was that it constituted Japan's answer to the American Lend-Lease bill and an indication of Japanese determination to act.[15] Among the high expectations entertained for the Tripartite meetings in Berlin and Rome were those of the *Tokyo Asahi*. This newspaper urged that Japan, Germany, and Italy should discuss fundamental and concrete methods for political, economic, and military co-operation to keep the United States out of the war.[16] Even the *Japan Chronicle*, which tended to be more moderate, approved of Matsuoka's statement that Japan, in conjunction with Germany and Italy, would rebuild the world through their alliance.[17] Although the only positive fruit of the Foreign Minister's European trip turned out to be the Soviet nonaggression pact, the Japanese press was not discouraged. It saw the new

[13] *Japan Chronicle*, June 1, April 9, 1941.
[14] *New York Times*, Jan. 7 and 28, 1941.   [15] *Ibid.*, March 12, 1941.
[16] *Ibid.*, March 18 and 28, 1941.   [17] *Japan Chronicle*, April 10, 1941.

treaty as an Axis answer to the alignment of the ABCD powers against Japan. Since Russia had become a quasi-Axis partner, warned the *Miyako* of Kyoto, the United States should realize that now, more than ever, war against Germany would mean war against Japan.[18]

Apparently this ominous theme was softened a bit in May and June, but not abandoned. The *Manchuria Daily News* viewed Japan as a "silent partner" in the Axis, doing her part by holding down American forces in the Pacific. The *Tokyo Kokumin*, echoing Matsuoka, warned the United States that it would have to take the Japanese Navy into account if its fleet began convoying in the Atlantic. In case of actual American entry into the war, the paper continued, Japan's decision was already made. Even the relatively moderate Japanese spokesman, Koh Ishii, head of the Japanese Information Bureau, although making it clear that Japan's main concern was in East Asia, asserted on June 19 that Japan was faithfully doing her share in the Axis by deterring the United States from her almost inevitable entry into the war. Pro-Axis propaganda, in fact, was strong enough in Japan to cause concern for some Japanese. The newspaper *Hochi*, which advocated an autonomous course for Japan, charged that the widespread agitation for her entry into the war was the work of a German fifth column.[19]

The agitation which worried the *Hochi*, however, ended with the German invasion of Russia, the adoption of a new independent policy by Japan, and the fall of Matsuoka. These events brought in their wake a sharp change in the attitude of the Japanese press. The change both in policy and in public opinion was aptly described by the commentator, Yoshishighe Yomota, in his article, "The Third Konoye Cabinet," published in the *Japan Chronicle*. Although, Yomota wrote, "the advocacy of 'Axis diplomacy' as the essence of Japan's foreign policy"

[18] *New York Times*, April 21, 1941.
[19] *Ibid.*, May 11 and 20, June 20, May 15, 1941.

had been almost universal following the signing of the Tripartite Pact, no one talked about the Pact as the keystone of Japanese policy any longer since the new cabinet had taken office. Instead, the Pact was widely ignored. The meaning of the cabinet change, Yomota pointed out, was unmistakable. While Japan would keep faith by not repudiating the treaty, she would henceforth follow her own independent national policy. As Konoye had put it, " 'What we ourselves have to rely on is our own strength alone.' " [20]

A host of signs confirming Yomota's analysis of Japanese policy and public opinion soon appeared in the Japanese press. The changed climate of opinion did not, to be sure, mean a new friendliness for the United States. Here the attitude of the Japanese press was as hostile and the complaints against American action in the Pacific were as frequent and as bitter as before. The reaction to the joint freezing orders, at first relatively mild in deference to the government's desire for caution,[21] soon became intense. The charge of "encirclement" was repeatedly hurled at the United States, accompanied occasionally by the demand for action by Japan to break the chain surrounding her.[22] Every new American step in the Far East—for example, the sending of oil to Russia via Vladivostok, the proposal for American military talks with the U.S.S.R., and the dispatch of a military mission under Brigadier General John Magruder to China —aroused violent protests.[23] Notable by their absence, however, were complaints by the Japanese press on behalf of Germany. American naval actions in the Atlantic went unnoticed; the Tripartite Pact was hardly mentioned; and the prospect of American entrance into the European war, when it was discussed at all, was viewed with indifference. In fact, there was a plain

---

[20] *Japan Chronicle*, Aug. 20, 1941.
[21] *Ibid.*, July 30, Aug. 12 and 13, 1941.
[22] *Ibid.*, Aug. 21 and 26, Sept. 3, 1941.
[23] *Ibid.*, Aug. 19 and 20, 1941; *New York Times*, Aug. 27 and 29, 1941.

disposition on the part of some Japanese newspapers to dissociate Japan from Germany and the odium which attached to the Nazis in the American mind. When the Atlantic Charter was proclaimed following the Atlantic Conference between Roosevelt and Churchill, the *Japan Chronicle* remarked that since everything in it was directed against Nazism it had little to do with Japan.[24] The *Tokyo Asahi*, like other Japanese newspapers, greeted Roosevelt's militant Labor Day speech with the comment that it "merely emphasized his intention to overthrow Hitler and nazism and was of little consequence." [25] The common Japanese reaction to the *Greer* incident was dismissal of it as strictly a German-American concern. Even the militant *Tokyo Kokumin* advocated an "autonomous" attitude on the part of Japan.[26]

In spite of strenuous German propaganda efforts, the Japanese press began to reflect increasing doubts about German victory as the war went on. The *Miyako* predicted great difficulty for the Nazis in their quest for ultimate triumph, and the *Japan News Week*, often close to the Foreign Office, went even farther in claiming that the tide of war had turned against the Axis. On the Russian war, the Japanese press maintained a correct neutral attitude,[27] while it began to sound a note of "a plague on both your houses" regarding the Atlantic conflict. Mitsuru Toyama, head of the nationalistic Black Dragon Society, announced that he was opposed to all Westerners and foreigners alike in Asia, and the *Miyako* charged both the United States and Germany with seeking military supremacy in the world.[28]

Nothing was done by the Imperial authorities to discourage

[24] *Japan Chronicle*, Aug. 20, 1941.
[25] *Ibid.*, Sept. 4, 1941; *New York Times*, Sept. 3, 1941.
[26] *New York Times*, Sept. 9, 1941.
[27] *Ibid.*, Sept. 3 and 6, Oct. 11, 1941.
[28] *Ibid.*, Aug. 30, Oct. 16, 1941.

the growing coolness of the press toward Germany. Instead, it canceled and prohibited all private celebrations of the anniversary of the Tripartite Pact in September, permitting only the official celebration, a cautious and restrained one, under the auspices of the Imperial Rule Assistance Association. The whole theme of the fete, as emphasized in speeches and statements by Foreign Minister Toyoda, President of the Information Board Nobumi Ito, Koh Ishii, and Saburo Kurusu, was that of world peace. The speakers dwelt on the autonomy of Japan under the Pact, its purely defensive and pacific character, and its entire compatibility with the Japanese-American negotiations then current.[29]

While the Pact always retained some vocal defenders in Japan, even these did not advocate it any longer as an operative instrument, but rather as a statement of principle. The political commentator of the *Hochi* urged retention of the Pact as a tie with Germany in prospect of an ultimate German victory; the Great Japan and Asia Development League recommended adherence to the "guiding spirit" of the Pact.[30] No one, however, seems to have urged enforcing it either then or in the foreseeable future. The decline of the Pact in the public eye, moreover, was progressive. The tenser the Japanese-American relations became toward the end and the more violent the Japanese attacks on the United States grew, the more the Pact receded into the background. The Japanese Throne Aid League, for example, demanded in belligerent terms an end to the encirclement of Japan but made no mention of Germany in its pronouncement. Tojo, setting out Japanese demands in a strong speech before the Diet on November 17, gave the issues of Germany and the Pact only a passing nod. He was very much in earnest, however, in calling for cessation of American aid to

[29] *Ibid.*, Sept. 24, 26, 27, and 28, 1941; speech of Nobumi Ito, Tokyo, Sept. 26, 1941, *IMTFE*, Doc. no. 1204D.
[30] *New York Times*, Sept. 3 and 22, 1941.

China, an end to the economic blockade and military encirclement of Japan, and the exclusion of the war from the Pacific.[31]

The estrangement of Japan and Germany, so plainly reflected in their respective presses, was recognized by many another observer in close touch with the situation. The leading papers of both New York and London carried prompt and accurate interpretations of the turn of events which had brought it about.[32] Otto Tolischus, Tokyo correspondent for the *New York Times,* saw Japanese isolation from the Axis as an accomplished fact by mid-August. He commented, "The German-Italian-Japanese Alliance has not been heard of much since the third Konoye Cabinet was formed. Whatever practical value the alliance may have had, Japan is now completely cut off from Europe." By mid-November, according to Tolischus, the Japanese press was contending that the Axis Alliance had nothing to do with Japanese-American relations, some even arguing hopefully that a Japanese agreement with the United States might allow America to concentrate on Germany and leave Japan with a free hand. Yet, as Tolischus commented significantly, in spite of the evidences of estrangement, "Japan appears to American eyes as merely the Far Eastern wing of the German army." [33]

There were other reporters equally aware of actual conditions. Among them was Douglas Robertson, who noted by mid-August a wholesale exodus from Japan of Germans who feared the virtual abandonment of the Alliance by Japan. James Reston reported, and apparently credited, the statement of a Japanese official that Japan had given President Roosevelt advance assurance that his "shoot-on-sight" order to the United States Navy against German submarines would not bring Japanese reprisal.[34] The Far Eastern correspondent for the London *Times* reported

31 *Ibid.*, Nov. 16 and 17, 1941.
32 *Ibid.*, June 23 and 25, July 6, 11, 16, 19, and 20, 1941; *The Times* (London), July 18 and 30, 1941.
33 *New York Times*, Aug. 17 and 31, Nov. 9, 1941.
34 *Ibid.*, Aug. 18, Sept. 13, 1941.

that at the very height of Japanese-American tension German influence in Japan was weaker than ever.[35]

It is also plain that both the United States Embassy in Tokyo under Grew and the British Embassy under Craigie understood the situation. Grew, whose record for consistency of view and accuracy of perception during this period is very good, recognized, as noted previously, the change of Japanese policy under Prince Konoye. He was convinced that it reduced the Tripartite Pact to a dead letter and believed that it justified taking a chance on a meeting between Roosevelt and Konoye. Other instances of his accurate insight and information, incidentally, were his report to the State Department on the Emperor's stand for peace in the mid-October cabinet crisis and his warning that Japan, if backed to the wall, would surely fight. This warning was in sharp contrast to the belief of Secretary of War Stimson and the influential State Department Adviser on Political Relations, Stanley K. Hornbeck, that Japan would ultimately knuckle under before a strong stand.[36]

[35] *The Times* (London), Nov. 5 and 22, 1941.

[36] Grew, *Turbulent Era*, II, 1295–1296; memos, Grew to Hull, Tokyo, Oct. 25, Nov. 3, 1941, *Foreign Relations, Japan*, II, 698–699, 701–704; Current, *Secretary Stimson*, 144–147; memos by Hornbeck, Aug. 25, Nov. 27, 1941, *Foreign Relations, 1941*, IV, 414, 673. The stand taken by Hornbeck throughout the period of negotiations, incidentally, is a significant and interesting one. His position was that the United States should take no action in the Far East and make no agreement with Japan which did not conduce to a complete military defeat of Japan in China or, as he put it, "a thorough defeat and discrediting of the armed efforts of the military militaristic leadership" (memo, Aug. 27, 1941, *ibid.*, 399). Consequently, earlier in the negotiations he opposed any American agreement even to a voluntary and complete withdrawal of Japanese troops from China, because the Japanese Army would still emerge undefeated and intact; and later he advocated no relaxation of the embargo, no mediation between China and Japan, and increased military help to China, because "our interests require that we follow a course designed to defeat Japan's program in China and to immobilize (in China) Japan's military strength" (memo, Oct. 29, 1941, *ibid.*, 559; various other memos, 336, 384–387, 398–399, 412–416, 419, 425–428, 504–505). Two comments might be made: First, the Japanese charge that the whole purpose of

British Ambassador Craigie shared Grew's outlook rather closely in many ways. He, too, saw that Matsuoka's fall had gravely weakened the Axis ties; and he believed that Japan could be turned away from the Axis, since in his opinion Konoye was sincerely anxious to escape the dangers accruing to Japan from the Pact. He likewise felt that the American insistence on a sweeping agreement at a time when Japan could only reach a temporary understanding was imperiling an unprecedented opportunity for splitting the Axis.[37]

Apparently the British government itself was not unaware of the real state of Japanese-German relations. Although Prime Minister Winston Churchill was willing to leave negotiations almost entirely to the United States and favored a strong stand against Japan, he saw clearly that in the end the Tripartite Pact was no longer anything to worry about. His position on the matter and, incidentally, his secondary interest in the China question are shown in a memo to Foreign Secretary Anthony Eden:

Our major interest is: no further encroachments [by Japan] and no war, as we have already enough of this latter. The United States will not throw over the Chinese cause, and we may safely follow them in this part of the subject. . . . The formal denunciation of the Axis Pact is not, in my opinion, necessary. Their stopping [*sic*] out of the war is in itself a great disappointment and injury to the Germans.[38]

American policy in the Far East was to keep Japan bogged down in China until she was exhausted was quite simply true if applied to Hornbeck (though probably not to the State Department as a whole); second, a policy designed solely to bring about the military defeat of another power would seem to render negotiations useless from the outset.

[37] Toyoda to Nomura, Oct. 3, 1941, Tokyo, *Pearl Harbor Attack*, XII, 51; Craigie to Anthony Eden, Tokyo, Sept. 29 and 30, 1941, *IMTFE, Record*, 25848–25852.

[38] Sir Winston Churchill, *The Second World War* (Boston: Houghton Mifflin, 1948–1953), vol. III, *The Grand Alliance*, 595.

It is reasonable to believe, too, that President Roosevelt recognized the fact of the rift between Germany and Japan. The evidence presented to the President was various: an early report that Japan was disillusioned with the Pact; [39] later reports from Ambassador Grew on the significance of Matsuoka's fall and Konoye's new policy; the record of Japanese inactivity and indifference in the face of German protests over American naval activities in the Atlantic; [40] and the eloquent testimony of the intercepted Japanese messages, through which, F. C. Jones concludes, "Roosevelt and Hull knew that the Japanese were playing fast and loose with their Axis partners." [41] That this evidence was not lost on the President is suggested by the fact that Roosevelt consistently took a more flexible attitude toward Japan than did his Secretary of State or many of his other advisers. As already shown, he at first favored a meeting with Konoye. For some time he entertained the idea of mediating between Japan and China, or at least introducing the two sides for parleys. He initiated the American *modus vivendi* proposal. But most surprising of all, immediately after the fall of Prince Konoye, Roosevelt seriously intended to invite the new Japanese Premier, Tojo, to a meeting with himself and Chiang Kai-shek in the Pacific. Once again, Hull and his advisers dissuaded him from this idea.[42] It is difficult to believe that Roosevelt, with his intense hatred for all aspects of nazism, could even have contemplated a meeting with the Japanese Premier at that late date had he believed that Japan was in any more than a nominal sense still linked with Germany.

Even Hull, in the writer's opinion, knew of the estrangement, though he did not admit it. One need not infer this simply from the fact that the Secretary was fully acquainted with all the

[39] Memo, Bishop Walsh to Roosevelt, n.d., *Pearl Harbor Attack*, XX, 4291–4293.
[40] See above, pp. 68–71.   [41] Jones, *Japan's New Order*, 315 (note).
[42] Two draft letters, Roosevelt to the Emperor of Japan, Oct. 16 and 17, 1941, *Pearl Harbor Attack*, XV, 1727–1731.

evidence of it. His conduct of the negotiations during the crucial months of August, September, and October, during which time the Pact went almost unmentioned by the Americans, indicates well enough that he knew the real situation. His vigorous insistence four years later during the Congressional Pearl Harbor investigation that Japan and Germany were always linked hand in glove is best seen as the substitution of strong language and special pleading for reason and evidence in the defense of an unfortunate theory.

There was, to be sure, a large and important group in the United States who did not, or would not, recognize the rift between the European and Far Eastern Axis powers. The group consisted in the vast majority of those vocal spirits—political leaders, writers, spokesmen—who mold and largely make up public opinion. There were some exceptions to the rule, among them the political commentator Walter Lippmann, Republican Senator Arthur Vandenberg of Michigan, and, to a degree, the defeated Republican Presidential candidate of 1940, Wendell Willkie.[43] In the main, however, as will be shown, the American press, most political leaders, and the general public continued to look upon Japan as simply the Asiatic half of Hitler's New Order.

Although the later history of the Tripartite Pact during the war goes beyond our purview, it is worth while to note that the Alliance served the Axis little better in the war than it had in peace. According to Erich Kordt, co-ordination between Germany and Japan in strategy was hardly even pursued as an ideal, much less put into practice.[44] It is possible that Russia was saved because Japan persisted in her refusal to launch an attack upon Siberia.[45] The Middle East was another area of opportunity

[43] *Congressional Record*, 77th Congress, 1st Session, 1941 (Washington: Government Printing Office, 1941), LXXXVII, pt. 4, 4592; *New York Times*, Sept. 18, 1941.

[44] Kordt, *Wahn und Wirklichkeit*, 333–334.

[45] William H. McNeill, *America, Britain, and Russia—Their Co-operation and Conflict, 1941–1946*, vol. III of *Survey of International Affairs*,

lost to the Axis because Japan and Germany went their separate ways and failed to co-operate. In short, to quote F. C. Jones, Japan "had decided upon war without reference to Germany and she elected to fight it with the minimum of coordination with the strategy of that Power." [46] Not even the compelling demands of world conflict could make Japan and Germany into real partners, or change the two wars into one.

1939–1946, edited by Arnold J. Toynbee (London: Oxford University Press, 1953), 71.
[46] Jones, *Japan's New Order*, 462.

VIII

The American Policy

and Public Opinion

THE Japanese-American negotiations and the policy pursued therein by the United States have been investigated and interpreted a number of times. It is neither possible nor necessary to review those interpretations here. Only three major points in this study are to be injected into the controversy. The first of these has already been made, namely, that the Tripartite Pact was initially a major issue in dispute but soon declined in importance and was used only for propaganda purposes at the end. The other two points are more general. The first is that there was a real change in the positions and the policies of both Japan and the United States in the course of the negotiations, a change which was ultimately of decisive significance. The second point is that this change, particularly in American policy, was a development so natural as to appear inevitable and so popular as to be virtually irreversible.

The first of the two points still to be discussed is controversial. The prevailing interpretation of the Japanese-American negotiations is that no change of any importance occurred throughout the talks. In its original and most extreme form, this argument stems from the State Department. Hull and his associates have always maintained flatly that there was no change in the respective positions of the two powers throughout the negotiations. The United States never altered her fundamental policy, which was one of insisting upon Hull's Four Points, the sanctity of treaties, and the principle of being a good neighbor in international relations. "The principles set forth in our November 26 proposal," insisted Hull, "were in all important respects essentially the same principles we had been proposing to the Japanese right along." [1] Japan, on the other hand (so the argument runs), was from first to last bent on a ruthless policy of military expansion.[2] Her sole purpose in the negotiations was to persuade or compel the United States to yield to Japan control of the entire Pacific, from Hawaii to India and beyond.[3] There was nothing the United States could have done which would have deterred Japan from her course of aggression. "It was not within the power of this Government otherwise than by abject submission to Japan's terms, to halt Japan in her course," claimed Hull.[4] "Japan [in August 1941] . . . was on a steady and fixed course of conquest which would reach us in Japan's own chosen time." [5] Her aggression, moreover, was totally senseless and irrational, for the United States was offering Japan everything a peaceful nation could desire. "There was nothing in there [the Ten Points Plan]," maintained the Secretary, "that any peaceful nation pursuing a peaceful course would not have been delighted to accept." [6] Japan's incurable militarism, however, rendered of no avail all American generosity and patience. The negotiations did nothing more than to reveal the irreconcilable character of the positions of the two governments.

The clash between Japan and the United States, the argument continues, was molded by decades of history. Japan had become

[1] Testimony, May 23, 1946, *Pearl Harbor Attack*, XI, 5369.
[2] Hull's statement, Nov. 23, 1945, *ibid.*, II, 409–410.
[3] Testimony by Hull, Nov. 27, 1945, *ibid.*, 606.
[4] Testimony, May 16, 1946, *ibid.*, XI, 5384.
[5] *Ibid.*, 5395.   [6] *Ibid.*; testimony, Nov. 26, 1945, *ibid.*, II, 555.

inherently belligerent; the United States was inherently peace-loving. The policies of peace which Hull espoused embodied, as he saw it, the practices of historic Americanism. "We have," he asserted, "from over an indefinite period in the past stood for all of the doctrines that you see set out [in the Ten Points Plan]." [7] They were, in fact, universal principles, subscribed to by all peaceful men the world over. Nothing in American history resembled Japan's actions in the Pacific. In her own sphere, the Western Hemisphere, the United States had always acted solely in self-defense. The Monroe Doctrine, "as we interpret and apply it uniformly since 1823," said Hull, presumably including thereby also the Roosevelt Corollary, "only contemplates steps for our physical safety." The Japanese New Order, in contrast, was a mere cover-up for aggression.[8] In the same manner, self-defense, equal opportunity, and peace had always been the keynotes of American foreign policy in the Far East. Hull's political adviser, Stanley K. Hornbeck, who yields to no one in defense of historic American Far Eastern policy, writes:

Our people and our Government have, from the very beginning of our national life, asserted that in the commercial relations of sovereign states there should *not* be a "closed door" *anywhere*.

Again:

The intentions of the United States in regard to the Western Pacific and Eastern Asia have always been peaceful intentions. Our procedures have been procedures of peace.

The American acquisitions of Hawaii, Guam, and even of the Philippines, Mr. Hornbeck is careful to point out, are also in reality clear evidences of a peaceful, liberal attitude.[9]

[7] *Ibid.*, II, 613.
[8] Memo by Hull, April 20, 1940, *Foreign Relations, Japan*, II, 284.
[9] Stanley K. Hornbeck, *The United States and the Far East: Certain Fundamentals of Policy* (Boston: World Peace Foundation, 1942), 10, 14–16.

In contrast stood the record of Japanese aggression in the past. Japan had always intended to go to war with the United States. The negotiations in 1941 were merely a sham; Kurusu's mission was simply one of stalling the United States along until Japan was ready to attack, while Nomura served as a blind.[10] The efforts of the so-called "peace party" in Tokyo also were meaningless, the argument runs. For since 1937, according to Hull, Tojo at the head of the military was in "supreme control" of everything Japan possessed, including her Navy and the Emperor.[11] The course of Japanese aggression, moreover, had been determined long before the outbreak at the Marco Polo bridge. Following the advent of the Tanaka cabinet in 1927, Hull maintained, "Japan had consistently been pursuing only one fixed policy—that of expansion by aggression." [12] Part and parcel of this policy was an eventual attack upon the United States. Modern Japan had trained herself well in the execution of such a policy. Her whole history from 1895 to the present was one of international duplicity and military aggrandizement. The Sino-Japanese War of 1894–1895, the Russo-Japanese War of 1904–1905, the Twenty-one Demands of 1915, the Anti-Comintern Pact of 1936—these and many other events formed the pattern sinister.[13]

It is not to be supposed that this extravagant theory still finds many defenders. Most of it is plainly the product of wartime passions and postwar politics. One is tempted to remark, paraphrasing George Bernard Shaw, that even in Washington it is possible to say very foolish things about one's enemies simply

[10] Sumner Welles, *A Time for Decision* (New York: Harper, 1944), 295; testimony by Welles, Nov. 23, 1945, *Pearl Harbor Attack*, II, 471.

[11] Testimony by Hull, Nov. 26, 1945, *Pearl Harbor Attack*, II, 553; Nov. 27, 1945, *ibid.*, 612.

[12] Testimony by Hull, May 16, 1946, *ibid.*, XI, 5379.

[13] Statement by Hull, Nov. 23, 1945, *ibid.*, II, 407–410. It is ironical to note that one of the American arguments during the negotiations was that Japan, who had been so peaceful and progressive prior to 1931, should return to her old ways. See memo by Welles, Washington, Aug. 4, 1941, *Foreign Relations, Japan*, II, 541–544.

because one is at war with them. The underlying idea that no change was possible throughout the negotiations because of Japan's intransigence, however, remains current. Basil Rauch, for example, has this to say of the fixed Japanese intent:

Japan in the spring and summer of 1941 would accept no diplomatic arrangement which did not give it everything that it might win in the Far East by aggression, without the trouble and expense of military campaigns.[14]

The careful scholar Herbert Feis, who does not by any means accept the State Department's thesis uncritically, nevertheless contends that the gap between Japan and the United States never really lessened and that neither side fundamentally altered its original stand. The only two changes in their positions, Mr. Feis says, were, first, the Japanese offer to renounce further southwestern advances and to accept less than full victory in China and, second, the attempt by both governments toward the end to seek a *modus vivendi*.[15]

Other authorities could be cited with the same general intent, namely, that there was never any serious prospect of Japanese-American agreement, that the two nations' positions were fundamentally irreconcilable, and that both of them were too committed to opposite goals to change. One hesitates to disagree in the face of their more or less unanimous testimony. Yet it would seem that the basic question is not whether Japan and the United States ever approached agreement or whether they were always at odds. It is true that they never came close to a real settlement. The more important question, however, is whether Japan and the United States were at odds over the same things throughout the conversations—whether the issues that separated them were the same at the end as at the beginning.

Here, it is contended, a real change took place. That some

[14] Basil Rauch, *Roosevelt, from Munich to Pearl Harbor* (New York: Creative Age Press, 1950), 396. Italics in original.
[15] Feis, *Road to Pearl Harbor*, 171–172.

shifts in diplomatic position occurred during the negotiations no one will seriously deny. One needs only to compare the Japanese proposal of May 12 with those of November 7 and 20 and the American plan of May 16 with that of November 26 to see that there was unquestionably a change. Japan was clearly asking for less, and the United States was demanding more, in November than in May. It is also plain that there was a decisive change in regard to one of the major issues in dispute, the Tripartite Pact. These, it is here claimed, were only parts of a greater development. In the summer of 1941, the basic aims of both Japanese and American foreign policy underwent an important transformation. The result was that their basic quarrel in November was no longer the same as it had been in May.

Until approximately the middle of July 1941 the policy of Japan was unmistakably aggressive in nature. Her goals were expansionistic, although she was becoming more and more apprehensive and doubtful about attaining them. She was still committed to ending the China conflict on her own terms. She still hoped to have her puppet government headed by Wang Ching-wei coalesced into the Chinese government, with Japan preserving a very large measure of military and economic control within China. Furthermore, she had definite plans for southward expansion as far as possible—certainly into French Indo-China and Thailand and if circumstances allowed also into the Netherlands East Indies. The diplomatic methods she used to implement her program showed similarly a policy of offense. Her browbeating of the Vichy French and high-pressure negotiation with the Dutch over the East Indies testify to this. She still expected a German victory, counting on it and the Tripartite Pact to isolate the United States and persuade America not to interfere in the Pacific. The last, rather desperate expressions of this policy of offense are the resolutions of the Imperial Conference of July 2. Here Japan resolved, in spite of the danger of war with the United States and Great Britain, to press on with her previously prepared plans for expansion southward. The final overt act in the Japanese campaign was the occupation of southern Indo-China in late July, a move already determined over a month before as part of the old expansionist policy.

The American position in the Far East in this same period was definitely defensive. As has been shown, the United States policy was one of holding the line in Asia, while building up her home defenses and concentrating on aid to Great Britain in Europe. The United States had thus two essential and immediate objectives in Asia: first, stopping Japan from any further advance southward that would menace the British supply line and, second, keeping Japan out of the European war.[16] To help accomplish these objectives, a major aim of American diplomacy was to persuade Japan to withdraw from the Tripartite Pact, even if only by degrees.[17] The remaining American goal, the liberation of China, was of necessity a distinctly subsidiary and remote one. As Ambassador Grew wrote in November 1940:

We need not aim to drive Japan out of China now. That can be taken care of, perhaps, if and after Britain wins the war with Germany. But stopping Japan's proposed far-flung southward advance and driving her out of China are two different matters. We can tolerate her occupation of China for the time being, just as we have tolerated it for the past three years. I doubt if we should tolerate any great extension of the southward advance.[18]

Throughout the first half of 1941 the American position was plainly that, although she would aid China within limits to keep Japan occupied there, she did not intend to go to war for the sake of China. She would, however, go to war to defend American territory and probably also that of the British and the Dutch in Asia. Even the crucial freezing orders, strong measures though they were, were entirely consistent with the defensive nature of the American policy. They were imposed because the

[16] Grew cites Roosevelt's letter of Jan. 21, 1941, as evidence of this strategy (*Turbulent Era*, II, 1259–1260).
[17] Memo, May 19, 1942, *Foreign Relations, Japan*, II, 335.
[18] Grew, *Turbulent Era*, II, 1232–1233.

Japanese, having moved into southern Indo-China, were in a position gravely menacing all of southeastern Asia. The freezing orders were to teach Japan that she had gone far enough—indeed, too far—and that she must now begin to retreat.

The embargo produced precisely the result intended. Japan, faced with the consequences of her move, began to recoil. The struggle within Japan for the control of policy took a decided turn for the better (from the American point of view), with the initiative passing into the hands of moderates such as Konoye and Toyoda. The brave promises and boastful programs of Japanese expansionism, like those of the resolutions of July 2, were for the moment ignored or forgotten, as Japan went clearly on the defensive.[19] Her main objective now was somehow to extricate

[19] This point, that Japan went on the defensive after July 26, lies of course at the very center of the controversy over Japanese-American relations in 1941. It clashes with the opinion of Langer and Gleason, among others, who believe that the best opportunity for Japanese-American agreement existed in May and that, after the German assault on Russia, Japan was driven by her military extremists irretrievably into a course of aggression and war (*Undeclared War*, 477, 493, 625). The work just cited is an outstanding one, written by eminent scholars whose judgment must be given great weight. Nevertheless, the clear impression gained by the writer, especially from the *IMTFE* materials, is that Japan, after the freezing orders, was hesitant, worried, and in retreat, so that the final decision for war could be taken only after considerable delay and a genuine internal struggle and as a last resort. (One notes, for example, a definite progressive change in tone between the decisions of the Imperial Conferences held on July 2, September 6, and November 5 [*IMTFE*, Doc. no. 1652].)

This impression coincides with the contemporary observations of Ambassador Ott, who on this point may be more readily believed because he records facts and feelings distasteful to him and to his government. His report of Oct. 4, 1941 (*IMTFE*, Doc. no. 4065A), based, he says, on his own observations and on "a careful sounding of the Army leaders," including Tojo, paints a gloomy picture of the state of feeling in Japanese official circles. Widespread hesitancy and indecision, lack of unity in the national leadership, a recognition of the evidently hopeless stalemate in the Japanese-American negotiations and the ultimate futility of a wait-and-see policy, combined with an inability to find and decide upon any alternative course—these were the salient conditions

herself from the desperate position in which she was entangled, to get relief from the inexorable economic pressure of the embargo, and to avoid what seemed to be inevitable war. She was not concerned for the time with expanding her empire; the problem was now one of salvaging as much as she could. To gain peace or at least a breathing spell, she was willing to make what seemed to her to be two major concessions. She was ready to take a course independent of Germany and indifferent to the Tripartite Pact. She was also willing to stop her southward advance and even, at the end, to withdraw from her latest acquisition, southern Indo-China. The one thing she would not do was to evacuate China and to renounce her aims there. This in her eyes was impossible. She could modify her terms somewhat, but the retention of a considerable economic and military hold, particularly on North China, was considered by her military leaders absolutely indispensable, for political reasons if for none other. There are a number of moves in this period which indicate the defensive character of Japanese policy—the rift with Germany, Konoye's invitation to Roosevelt to attend the Leaders' Con-

---

Ott noted. Nor was opinion more hopeful in the nation as a whole. Japanese morale, Ott judged, was low. The people were oppressed by a sense of isolation and encirclement, by the futility and hopelessness of the China Affair, and by an awareness of Japan's "numerous economic and material deficiencies."

Noting a strong reluctance on the part of the Army leaders to discuss possible American participation in the war, Ott concluded that this was not simply due to the desire to preserve secrecy in the negotiations. "Even stronger," he maintained, "is the often reported atavistic fear of getting entangled in a conflict with the United States. . . . The Japanese Government . . . wants to embark on such a conflict only if worst comes to worst and wants to decide the time itself; at least help in deciding upon it."

Evidently Tojo and his associates succeeded in concealing from the German Ambassador the very considerable extent of Japanese preparation for war, and apparently Ott also underestimated the military's determination to fight if worst came to worst. Nevertheless, Ott's comments on the general climate of Japanese morale and opinion remain of interest.

ference, the postponement of the decision for war even after the fall of Konoye, and the last-minute proposals of November 20. The fall of Konoye and the accession of Tojo did not really change Japanese policy but merely presaged its ultimate failure. The real difference between Konoye and Tojo was not that the one wanted peace and the other war. It was rather that, when each was faced with a choice between war and humiliating terms, Konoye would waver indefinitely, while Tojo would choose war.

The policy of the United States, meanwhile, underwent a corresponding change: America went on the diplomatic offensive after July 1941. Her aims were no longer simply those of holding the line against Japanese advances and of inducing Japan to draw away from an alliance which the United States considered menacing. The chief objective of American policy now was to push Japan back, to compel her to withdraw from her conquests. The United States was determined to see that Japan assumed such a peaceful attitude in Asia that she could never again threaten the security of her neighbors. She was to renounce her dream of hegemony in Asia, to give up her plans for expansion, and to accept defeat in China.[20] The objective that had previously been the least important and pressing in American policy, the liberation of China, now became the crucial consideration. American diplomats made a prompt and total evacuation of Japanese troops the *sine qua non* for agreement. The weapon of severe economic pressure on Japan, which had been forged and used by the United States, up to and including the time of the freezing orders, to hold the line against Japanese expansion, now was employed to enforce the American demands for the evacuation of China. The Japanese were given to understand that there would be no relaxation of the embargo until Japan gave up her gains by aggression there.

The old defensive goals were not forgotten. They remained uppermost especially in the minds of American military planners.

[20] Feis, *Road to Pearl Harbor*, 273.

The military strategists continued to insist to the end that the primary objectives of American policy should remain the defeat of Germany and the exclusion of Japan from the war. Brigadier General Leonard T. Gerow, acting Assistant Chief of Staff, maintained that even the impending defeat of China would not warrant involvement of the United States in a war with Japan. Chief of Staff General George Marshall and Admiral Harold R. Stark agreed with Gerow.[21] The reports prepared by the Army Intelligence Service from July to December 1941 all display a single consistent point of view, along with a number of important insights. First was the belief that the European war remained uppermost and that the previous essentially defensive objectives pursued by the United States in the Far East should be maintained.[22] Second was a recognition of the estrangement between Japan and Germany and of the completely altered Japanese attitude toward the Tripartite Pact.[23] Third was a belief that the Konoye government was really trying to extricate Japan from her difficulties without war. Brigadier General Miles, in charge of Army Intelligence, believed that the United States might gain her essential objectives through the use of "strong diplomacy," provided that she made sure that Konoye could carry the Japanese Army and Navy with him in his policy.[24] Fourth and most important was the conviction that it was unnecessary, and probably even harmful, for the United States to insist on an immediate evacuation of China.

This last point, of course, touches the very heart of the whole Japanese-American controversy. The argument of the Army Intelligence Service with regard to it is important enough to be given close attention. Colonel Hayes A. Kroner, acting Assistant

[21] Memos, Gerow to Marshall, Nov. 3 and 21, 1941, *Pearl Harbor Attack*, XIV, 1066–1067, 1106–1107; memo, Marshall and Stark to Roosevelt, Nov. 27, 1941, *ibid.*, 1083.

[22] *Ibid.*, 1334–1384.

[23] Memo by Brigadier General Sherman Miles, Sept. 5, 1941, *ibid.*, 1352–1353.

[24] *Ibid.;* also memo by Miles, Aug. 16, 1941, *ibid.*, 1347.

Chief of Staff of the Service, supplies this in a memorandum of October 2. The first reason why the United States should not insist on the evacuation of China was that such a move would be impossible for Japan for political reasons:

This division is of the belief that the present Cabinet in Tokyo [Konoye's third cabinet] does not yet feel strong enough to enforce any order for withdrawal of Japanese troops from China, even though under pressure from the United States, it might be inclined to do so.

The move, Kroner maintained, would thus be disastrous for the Konoye regime. Worse, it also "would be highly detrimental to our interests." The removal of so many troops from China back to the Japanese homeland would create grave internal problems for Japan. The civilian government might well be unable to prevent a military explosion leading directly to war with the United States. In addition, with Japanese troops freed from China the threat to Siberia and the southwest Pacific would be gravely increased. "In other words," Kroner concluded, "we must cease at once our attempts to bring about the withdrawal of Japanese armed forces from China." [25]

Ironically enough, at the same time that Kroner was issuing this warning the very events which he feared were taking place. On this same day, October 2, Hull delivered to the Japanese an Oral Statement rejecting the Konoye proposals. It killed the chances for a Leaders' Conference and made certain the downfall of the Konoye government in Japan. The main reason for the American refusal to deal with Konoye, as already seen, was Japan's unwillingness to evacuate China. Thus, at this very time, the Konoye government was tottering to its fall and carrying its hope for peace in the Pacific with it because it could not budge the American diplomats from their insistence that Japanese troops had to get out of China forthwith. And all the while, American military planners were urging that the United States

[25] Memo by Kroner, Oct. 2, 1941, *ibid.*, 1357–1358.

ought by all means to let the Japanese stay. The clash between the United States strategic interests and her diplomatic policy cannot be seen more plainly.

Other men outside the military remembered the old defensive goals. Ambassador Grew, as shown, repeatedly urged that the President should make an attempt to meet Konoye halfway. His main argument was that the strong American action in the embargo had created the opportunity for the United States to gain her essential aims, if only she did not insist on getting everything at once. "History will determine," he wrote later, "whether this opportunity was missed by an attempt to achieve at once our long-range objectives, an utter impossibility under the circumstances then obtaining, at the expense of the immediately vital and essential interests of our country." [26] As for the President, his actions up to the very eve of Pearl Harbor indicate that his interest was primarily centered on Europe. He was particularly concerned with the Far East only as it affected the European war, and the China question for him was secondary.

What happened, then, was not that the original defensive goals were forgotten, but that they were submerged. As Japan began to retreat and as the United States grew steadily stronger, the original problems lost their former urgency. Once the rift between Germany and Japan became plain and the American naval activities in the Atlantic went unnoticed by Japan, there was no longer any real need to worry about the Tripartite Pact. Objectionable it might still be, but hardly dangerous. Moreover, the failure of the Japanese, after the occupation of south Indo-China, to carry farther the program of southward expansion as determined on July 2 diminished at least for the moment the imminent danger of a move to the south. At the same time, Japan's repeated pledges not to extend her advance any farther south and to withdraw from Indo-China upon reaching peace with China, backed up at the end by an offer of immediate evacuation of south Indo-China, indicated that the southward drive was not

[26] Grew, *Turbulent Era*, II, 1262.

an immutable part of Japanese policy. Any concessions the Japanese made, however, did them no good. In the wave of reaction against Japan's move into south Indo-China, the initiative in American policy had passed into the hands of those leaders who had long advocated a strong, no-compromise, no-appeasement stand against Japan. These men—Morgenthau, Knox, Stimson, and others—backed up Hull in his uncompromising principles in order to carry through a modern policy of "thorough." Japan was not merely to be contained and held back, but to be squeezed and harried until she conformed, that is, until she disgorged her gains and abandoned her evil ways.

In one way, the policy thus conceived and executed was indeed a development of historic American policy in the Far East. The United States had long upheld, at least on paper, the cause of China's integrity and independence. For an equally long period she had, for reasons of democratic idealism and commercial self-interest, stood for the Open Door in China.[27] The lively interest felt by Americans over the fate of China was always an important factor in Japanese-American relations and could easily grow, as it did, into the paramount consideration. But in another sense the change in policy was a reversal of a historic American position. For it was also a long-standing American policy, equally as traditional as the Open Door and far more consistently observed in practice, that the United States would not go to war for the sake of China. This policy was now in effect overthrown. American diplomats made it clear that the United States would accept war with Japan in preference to any settlement between Japan and China which did not restore intact China's territorial and administrative integrity. It is commonly agreed that this was the one real cause of the war. Had the China issue been solved or left to one side, the other two problems could surely have been adjusted without open conflict. In insisting that

[27] Paul H. Clyde, "Our Concern for the Integrity of China," *Annals of the American Academy of Political and Social Science*, CCXV (May 1941), 72.

the Japanese withdraw immediately and completely from China and in employing the weapon of extreme economic pressure to compel Japanese agreement, the United States was carrying out a new offensive policy which made the crucial difference between peace and war.

It would be entirely wrong to suppose that this change in policy was simply the reasoned decision of policy makers. It would be still worse to charge that it represents the underhanded maneuverings of an administration leading the nation by a back road into war. The shift in policy, decisive though it was in its effects, was a very natural development. In a sense, it was truly and tragically inevitable. For years the United States had been exerting a gradually growing pressure on Japan in an effort to hold her at bay, a pressure conceived as a countermeasure to the outward thrust of Japanese expansion and reaching its climax in the joint freezing orders. American foreign policy would have had to be extraordinarily sensitive to the changed situation and unusually flexible to have prevented the United States from going on the offensive too strongly. The moment that Japan began to draw back, the very force being exerted against her, unless relaxed, would automatically carry the United States to the offense. The measures designed to restrain Japan would serve equally well to force her back.

Moreover, even had the administration wanted to relax the pressure on Japan, this would have been very difficult to do. Chief among the reasons was public opinion. Over the course of a decade, the American people had built up a profound hatred and distrust of Japan. When the time came that the United States could put heavy pressure on the Japanese, it was the moment the public had long awaited. Virtually no one wanted the pressure relaxed. The most influential writers, politicians, and newspapers called for even more, and when at the very end there arose some concern over the probable consequences of this uncompromising policy, it was already too late.

It seems probable that never in American history has a step so momentous as the freezing orders been taken with so little public concern or dissent. If there were any fears by the administration of adverse public reaction to the move, they were groundless; the public plainly had been prepared for an embargo long before this. Agitation for the move had been going on for years in Congress, in the press, in church circles, and elsewhere. As early as February 1941, according to a Gallup poll, a majority of the American people believed that the United States was endangered by the Japanese advance southward and that the United States should take steps to stop Japan.[28] In August, after the freezing orders had been imposed, a solid majority of those interviewed in a similar poll favored "additional steps to keep Japan from becoming more powerful," even if it entailed the risk of war.[29] On the West Coast, opinion was even more positive on the subject. According to the newspapermen Richard L. Neuberger and Arthur Caylor, even the isolationists there were demanding the maintenance of a complete embargo. Few people feared Japan; most believed she could easily be handled by united ABCD action. The prevailing opinion in San Francisco was, " 'They are asking for it, let's let them have it.' "[30] Ambassador Nomura was probably correct in reporting that the American press and public were much less concerned about a war with Japan than with Germany, that in fact they were quite happy-go-lucky over the prospect.[31] As the *New Republic* commented approvingly:

Masses of people, like individuals, are always more willing to fight an enemy they think they can lick easily. . . . The average American is a little contemptuous of the Japanese. He was angered by the rape of China. He is more willing to concede the necessity for living

[28] *New York Times*, Feb. 23, 1941.
[29] *Ibid.*, Aug. 3, 1941.   [30] *Ibid.*
[31] Nomura to Tokyo, Washington, Sept. 29, Nov. 10, 1941, *Pearl Harbor Attack*, XII, 29–30, 112.

space for the least likeable Europeans than for the bad boys of the Orient. . . . It is not unlikely that the President, who thinks of such things, has taken all this into account.[32]

In part, this almost unanimous public feeling against Japan was the inevitable result of the recent Japanese record in the Far East. Her aggressions, her savage methods of warfare (or so they seemed in the pre-Hiroshima days of 1941), and her alliance with the hated Nazis all had their effect. Americans had a sentimental attachment to the Chinese as the underdogs; there were no emotional ties of national origin or common culture to mitigate the feeling against Japan. Nonetheless, this heated state of public opinion, like all such emotional fevers, did not simply arise spontaneously. It was molded and directed by the volume of denunciation emanating from high political circles, the press, and in particular the liberal journals, much of it belligerent and inflammatory in tone.

The administration, to be sure, did not take the lead in the dissemination of what may be called anti-Japanese propaganda. Colonel Frank Knox, Secretary of the Navy, laid considerable stress on the menace of Japan,[33] warning the Legion of Valor, for example, that "we are confronted in Asia by a whole continent threatened with domination by an Oriental, bloody-minded autocracy." [34] There were warnings to the public from official spokesmen, especially after November 7, of the danger of Japanese aggression and of war with Japan. Other than this, Hull, Welles, and the President maintained a certain reserve in regard to the Japanese, saving their choicest barbs for the Nazis.

Among Congressmen, however, Japan was fair game and, next to Hitler, the best target for denunciation. Before July the main argument among Congressmen was the demand for an embargo.

[32] *New Republic*, CV, no. 5 (Aug. 4, 1941), 154.
[33] For Japanese comment on Knox's speeches, see Nomura to Togo, Oct. 24, 1941, *Pearl Harbor Attack*, XII, 82–83.
[34] *New York Times*, July 29, 1941.

Most favored it on moral grounds. The sale of oil to Japan aided her in her aggression against "a great democratic people" and made the United States a partner in her crimes.[35] Others insisted that the embargo was equally necessary to stop Japan as an ally of Adolf Hitler.[36] The people, it was said, were everywhere crying for complete sanctions upon Japan, because of her partnership with Germany and her aggressions against democracy.[37]

The freezing orders were, therefore, extremely satisfying to many Congressmen as a moral step, one which cleared the United States of the taint of complicity in Japan's evil deeds and vindicated America's position as a defender of democracy. Only Senator Walter George of Georgia ventured to suggest that the embargo might possibly be relaxed and that trade on a barter basis might be resumed if Japan stopped any further advance.[38] To most others, the embargo was a just and peaceful measure to be rigorously applied until Japan came to her senses and made the necessary concessions. The concessions, it need hardly be said, meant the abandonment by Japan of her program and the adoption of peaceful (i.e., American) principles. Those who were interventionists in regard to Europe generally were equally interventionist regarding Asia. Senator Alben Barkley, Democratic majority leader from Kentucky, for example, declared that the Monroe Doctrine "now applies to Asia with equal force."[39] Such faithful supporters of the administration as Senator Claude Pepper of Florida[40] and Senator Tom Connally of Texas, head of the powerful Foreign Relations Committee, demanded the immediate evacuation of China and Indo-China as the minimum price for a settlement with Japan.[41]

It was inevitable that the question of policy toward Japan

---

[35] Radio speech by Senator Arthur Capper, March 8, 1941, *Congressional Record*, vol. LXXXVII, pt. 11, A-1636–1637. See also *ibid.*, pt. 4, 3639, 3862, 4044, 4108, 4589–4591.

[36] *Ibid.*, pt. 11, A-2189. [37] *Ibid.*, pt. 13, A-3640–3644.
[38] *New York Times*, Aug. 3, 1941. [39] *Ibid.*, Aug. 25, 1941.
[40] *Ibid.*, Nov. 20, 1941. [41] *Ibid.*, Nov. 12, 1941.

should be closely tied with the controversy over involvement in the European war. Strangely enough, in the heated debate over a proposed revision of the Neutrality Act of 1939 to permit the arming of merchant vessels, Congressmen on both sides of the question used the Japanese threat and the Axis Alliance as ammunition in their arguments. The automatic effectiveness of the Tripartite Pact, meanwhile, was assumed without question. Senator Lister Hill of Alabama argued, "If Japan moves, she moves as a partner of Hitler." Hence, he contended, a blow at Hitler through the arming of merchant ships would be equally a blow struck at Japan and in defense of democracy in Asia.[42] Senator Alexander Wiley of Wisconsin drew from the same premise an opposite conclusion: To repeal the Neutrality Act would be to invite certain reprisal from Japan under the Tripartite Pact. "Hitler," claimed the Senator, "is trying to inveigle this country into war, trying to get us to commit some overt act which will bring Japan into action against us." [43] The same argument on the same premises was repeated in the House, with Representatives agreed only on this, that Japan was completely linked with Hitler and the Axis program. According to Charles A. Eaton of New Jersey the German leader even dictated Japanese internal politics: "This [the appointment of the new Tojo cabinet] is due to the personal pressure of Mr. Hitler upon his Japanese allies, and their belief that Herr Hitler is going to take over the Ukraine." [44] What is especially striking in this debate over the Neutrality Act is not the fact that Congressmen were unaware of the signs of the times in regard to Axis solidarity. Nor is it that they failed to consider that, if convoys, patrols, and actual naval clashes between Germany and the United States in the Atlantic had failed to bring Japan into the European war, arming merchant ships would not be likely to do so. It is rather

[42] *Ibid.*
[43] *Ibid.*, Oct. 31, 1941.
[44] Speech, Oct. 16, 1941, *Congressional Record*, LXXXVII, pt. 7, 7961; see also 7997, 7999–8000.

the fact that very few of them recognized that the peaceful, moral step of embargo by the United States would be the real cause of conflict. Few, if any, seemed to realize that Japan had no intention of fighting for Hitler, but that she would certainly fight to prevent her economic strangulation at the hands of the United States and Great Britain.

There were, in fact, spokesmen in both House and Senate who believed that even the embargo was not enough. Still stronger means should be employed, and if war with Japan came as the consequence, so much the worse for the Japanese. Representative Clyde T. Ellis of Arkansas advocated giving Japan a sweeping ultimatum, to be followed by the use of force:

I am ready to give Japan 1 week to withdraw from the Axis, from China, and all Asia. Upon her failure to do that we should begin at once the process of polishing her into insignificance. [Applause] [*sic*] [45]

Senator Claude Pepper, who was quoted by an unfriendly critic, Senator Robert A. Taft of Ohio, as having called Japan "an assassin, lurking behind the door to stick a stiletto in our back," wanted the United States to supply bombers to Chiang Kai-shek and to encourage Americans to fly them against Japan. "Fifty of them, in my opinion, can make a shambles out of Tokyo," Pepper asserted.[46] When the Tojo cabinet came into office, the same Senator called for "literally—the immobilization" of Japan. Representative Karl M. LeCompte of Iowa advocated a declaration of war on Japan, "an avowed member of the aggressive Axis," if she attacked Russia.[47] A punitive attitude toward Japan is best expressed by Representative Bertrand W. Gearhart of California in a radio address of November 23, 1941. Rejecting in advance the very possibility of any settlement, Gearhart insisted that the United States had no right to bargain

[45] Speech, May 5, 1941, *ibid.*, pt. 4, 3566.
[46] Oct. 28, 1941, *ibid.*, pt. 8, 8290.
[47] Resolution introduced Oct. 30, 1941, *ibid.*, pt. 14, A-4921.

with Japan, because of the heinous Japanese crimes and the moral debt America owed to China. There could be no possible agreement, he argued, which would not make the United States a partner to Japan's foul deeds. "The question cannot be," Gearhart declared, "What should be our policy toward Japan, but rather, What is our policy toward this offending people?" A correct policy, according to the Congressman, would begin by refusing to negotiate and would embrace: first, doing nothing to help Japan; second, using every possible weapon to cripple her; and, third, extending every possible aid, military and otherwise, to the victims of Japan's aggressions. Should this policy fail to subdue Japan, the only alternative for the United States would be war.[48]

There was some scattered opposition in Congress to the administration policy vis-à-vis Japan. Unlike the isolationist opposition in regard to the European war, however, it was very much subdued and on the defensive. The chief evidence of it in Congressional sessions was the introduction into the record of editorials from isolationist newspapers like the *New York Daily News* or the *Washington Times-Herald*.[49] Senator Burton K. Wheeler of Montana accused the administration of being anxious for war in the Far East and maintained that the United States had no real reason for fighting Japan.[50] Representative William P. Lambertson of Kansas protested against the secrecy of the

[48] *Ibid.*, A-5492–5493. It was this same Congressman Gearhart who, in hearty approval of the Ten Points Plan of November 26, 1941, argued after the war that Americans should frankly state that they had given Japan the ultimatum she deserved. "I am trying to get you [Grew]," he said, "to admit that that document [the note of Nov. 26] is what every American in his heart wanted it to be. I don't think we should dodge on this ultimatum word. That, in days to come, is going to be one of the most glorious incidents in American history" (Nov. 27, 1945, *Pearl Harbor Attack*, II, 591).

[49] *Congressional Record*, vol. LXXXVII, pt. 10, A-677, A-1099; *ibid.*, pt. 12, A-2773; *ibid.*, pt. 14, A-5152, A-5451–5452.

[50] *New York Times*, Aug. 28, 1941.

last-minute negotiations, declaring that no one, not even the members of the Foreign Relations committees, knew anything about the ultimatum the United States had given Japan. Moreover, he contended, there was no reason for the United States to tell Japan she must withdraw from China or face war with America.[51] These were scattered shots, however. In general, the administration had to fear no concerted opposition in Congress to a hard policy toward Japan.

What was true of Congress was also largely true of the nation's press. As Langer and Gleason put it, "If the Administration had already decided to take a strong stand, most of the press clamored for an even stronger one. If the Japanese press was bellicose, so was the American." [52] Of course, there were isolationist newspapers such as the *Chicago Tribune*, the *New York Daily News*, and the *Washington Times-Herald* which argued that the United States was only pulling British and Dutch chestnuts out of the fire in Asia. Alongside these were papers such as the *New York Post*, the New York *PM*, and the *New York Herald-Tribune* which were jubilant over the Japanese plight and wanted only to see the noose drawn tighter around her.[53] In general, most newspapers accepted the embargo of Japan and the extension of all possible aid to China as moral policies which could not be abandoned without entailing appeasement and the sacrifice of principle. Any peace at the expense of China would be immoral and might only increase the ultimate danger to the United States.[54] They further believed, to quote typical editorial opinion, that the conflict between the United States and Japan was the result of America's "refusal to sanction new aggressions" and the fact that "Japan is unwilling to stop its murderous assault on China, and will make no pledge to stop its expansion program

[51] Speeches, Dec. 1 and 4, 1941, *Congressional Record*, LXXXVII, pt. 9, 9255, 9448–9449.
[52] Langer and Gleason, *Undeclared War*, 708.   [53] *Ibid.*, 652.
[54] *New York Times*, editorial, Sept. 23, 1941; *Dallas Morning News*, July 28, 1941.

at its already attained ends." [55] Japan, according to prevailing opinion, was simply playing Hitler's game in Asia. There was general confidence, however, that the United States and her allies could take care of Japan without weakening their effort against the Nazis.[56] Some papers sounded a punitive note. "No subscriber to Axis theories can be permitted in the future to survive as a strong nation," said the *Dallas Morning News*. The *New York Herald-Tribune* was even more outspoken:

The American people have ideas about Japan's war guilt in China and about the price she should pay for the cruel damage already done, which the Administration dare not ignore if it would.

Again:

The body of China's American well-wishers . . . expect their Government to be satisfied in the long run with nothing short of the complete restoration of China's administrative integrity, and with nothing less than Japan's complete discomfiture.[57]

The demand for a "get-tough" policy with Japan found its strongest voice in the liberal journals of opinion. It is not unreasonable to suppose that these journals exercised an influence far out of proportion to the size of their circulation. Many of their contributors, such as Owen Lattimore, Thomas A. Bisson, and Nathaniel Peffer, were recognized experts in the Far Eastern field. Moreover, all of the journals ardently supported the administration's policy in Europe. When they spoke on the Far Eastern question, as they did often and vehemently, it was with a unanimity and conviction that bore considerable weight.

The argument common to almost all of them is presented by Thomas A. Bisson. The policy of "appeasement" of Japan, attempted hitherto by the United States, he contended, had proved

[55] *Dallas Morning News*, Nov. 28, 1941.

[56] *New York Times*, Sept. 23, Nov. 28, Dec. 2, 1941. Even the isolationist *Chicago Tribune* pictured Japan in cartoons as a partner to Axis thugs, Dec. 5, 1941.

[57] Quoted in Grew, *Turbulent Era*, II, 1365.

bankrupt. It was no use attempting to appeal to so-called "moderates" in Japan. For one thing, there were none; for another, negotiation itself was meaningless when carried on with an aggressor state. The only solution to Far Eastern problems, Bisson maintained, was an airtight embargo of Japan, coupled with all-out aid to China and the forging of tight links between the United States and the Soviet Union. The joint aim would be that "the cordon around Japan is to be drawn so tight that a Japanese stroke is rendered helpless in advance." There was no need to conceal this intention from the Japanese.[58]

Nathaniel Peffer argued that America should flourish the big stick as conspicuously as possible, precisely for the purpose of threatening Japan. Japan, he asserted, was now (August 1941) in a position of desperate weakness. There could be no better time than the present to paralyze her and to render her helpless through a complete embargo and "ostentatious" reinforcements in the Far East. "There is only one chance of doing this [i.e., rendering Japan inactive]," argued Peffer, "—by frightening Japan. . . . America must penalize Japan at once." The Japanese, he observed, had been blackmailing the free world; "now Great Britain and America can blackmail Japan."[59]

There was thus, as has been noted, grave doubt entertained as to whether the United States should negotiate with Japan at all. If she did, America ought to wring the maximum concessions from Japan. As the *Nation* editorialized:

Before any negotiations begin, the United States might well ask Japan to show its good faith by evacuating Indo-China. And the least that should be accepted as the basis for a permanent settlement is withdrawal from China and the restoration of Manchuria to its rightful owner.

[58] Thomas A. Bisson, "Towards Winning Far Eastern Security," *Amerasia*, V, no. 8 (Oct. 1941), 344–349.

[59] Nathaniel Peffer, "Squeeze Japan Now!" *Nation*, CLIII, no. 5 (Aug. 2, 1941), 87–89.

Any policy less drastic, said the *Nation,* deserved the epithet "appeasement." [60]

But would not the uncompromising policy with Japan lead to war? Some writers doubted it, believing that there was an excellent chance that Japan could be forced out of China without either concessions by the United States or the use of American arms. Owen Lattimore contended, "To carry out this policy, the American Navy would not need to fire a gun nor the American Army a rifle." Economic pressure could do the whole job alone.[61] James R. Young agreed fully, saying, "Japan can be forced to withdraw from China and other occupied areas" without the use of American arms.[62] There were others who were not so confident of the effectiveness of economic pressure alone. All, however, could agree that Japan must be forced by whatever means necessary to give up her ill-gotten gains. Japan's moral guilt and China's suffering demanded no less. As Young put it, forty million Chinese had been forced from their homes; "they have been crucified, raped, assaulted, doped, slapped, beaten." [63]

Even those observers who felt that in the end Japan would fight rather than yield insisted that this was no reason for wavering or for anxiety on the part of the United States. Ever since the conclusion of the Tripartite Pact some Americans had argued that a Japanese-American war would be in the best interests of American strategy. As the *Nation* had put it, "Japan is unquestionably the weakest link in the new totalitarian alliance. And it is the essence of good strategy . . . to strike at the enemy's weakest link." [64] The weakening of the Tripartite Pact was so plain by the autumn of 1941 that even the *Nation* conceded that

[60] *Nation,* CLIII, no. 10 (Sept. 6, 1941), 192–193.

[61] Owen Lattimore, "American Responsibilities in the Far East," *Virginia Quarterly Review,* XVI, no. 2 (Spring 1940), 174.

[62] James R. Young, "Japan's Dilemma," *Amerasia,* V, no. 6 (Aug. 1941), 249.

[63] *Ibid.*

[64] "Japan's Choice," *Nation,* CLI, no. 14 (Oct. 5, 1940), 290.

there was little chance of a war by Japan on the United States for the sake of Germany.[65] But others continued to insist on the menace of this link between Japan and Hitler and to urge that, if war with Japan should not precisely be sought, at least it should not be unnecessarily avoided. There was no ground at all, William Brandt contended, "for the assumption that Japan is not going to join the war as a full-fledged belligerent ally of Hitler." Japan would surely do so, he argued, "at a time that is best-suited to Japan's and Hitler's strategic exigencies and requirements." [66] Thomas A. Bisson was in perfect accord with this contention, maintaining that "Japan's ties with the Axis are not adventitious." He could see no hope of weaning Japan away from the Axis so long as the issue in Europe was still in doubt. Even Japan's schemes for a Co-Prosperity Sphere in Asia bound her to Hitler, for "only in thorough co-operation with German aggression in Europe can this objective be achieved." The existence of the Axis Alliance raised for Bisson the question, "Should war be avoided?" His answer plainly was in the negative. The United States should "force a showdown" with the purpose of securing either a complete immobilization of Japan or war. In case the latter eventuated, Bisson argued, "A rapid victory in the Far East [within six months, in his estimate] would free the manpower and material required to turn the scales against Hitler in Europe." [67]

The *New Republic* concurred heartily with Bisson's view. It raised the question, "Must we fight Japan?" and answered it with complete confidence in an easy victory. Whether or not the United States came to actual war with Japan, said the journal, America was sure to gain a quick and relatively painless triumph.

[65] *Ibid.*, CLIII, no. 10 (Sept. 6, 1941), 192.

[66] William Brandt, "Hitler's Doom and Japan's Destiny," *Amerasia*, V, no. 9 (Nov. 1941), 380.

[67] Thomas A. Bisson, "Call Japan's Bluff!" *New Republic*, CV, no. 18 (Nov. 3, 1941), 579–581.

There was no reason for compromise; Japan was acting in Germany's interest to divert American attention from the Atlantic and represented "an essential part of the nearly-victorious Nazi threat to world order and democracy." There was also, however, no reason to fear what Japan might do in the face of a stiff American attitude. "A strict embargo would bring Japan to her knees in a matter of months," the journal confidently predicted. Even if she chose to fight, "Japan could not blockade us or take the aggressive in any decisive way." In fact, the United States Navy alone "could probably destroy Japanese naval power in short order." [68]

As seriously as most of the writers took the Tripartite Pact and as grave as they counted its menace to the United States, their fundamental reason for wanting America to oppose Japan, even if necessary to the point of war, was not that Japan was linked to Germany in a military pact. Rather it was that Japan was like Germany—this was reason and condemnation enough. As Philip Jaffe expressed it, "Both Germany and Japan are fascist aggressor nations, having no other purpose in their aggression than to loot, destroy, enslave, and impoverish." [69] It was the moral, and not the strategic, affinity between Germany and Japan which afforded the best justification for an iron-hard anti-Japanese policy.

Convinced as they were of the overwhelmingly obvious reasons, both moral and strategic, for such a policy against Japan and of the utter folly of so-called "appeasement," liberals found it significant that the United States even under a Democratic administration should have delayed so long before really taking a firm stand with the Japanese. George E. Taylor saw the reason for the policy of appeasement in the innate selfishness of Western capitalism. He noted that some persons were contending that the United States was morally bound to go to war, if necessary,

[68] *New Republic*, CV, no. 5 (Aug. 4, 1941), 135–137.

[69] Philip J. Jaffe, "Can Tokyo Follow Berlin's Lead?" *Amerasia*, V, no. 5 (July 1941), 192.

to force Japan out of China. "The lack of realism in this view," he commented, "lies in the plea that liberation of the Chinese people should be an end of American policy." As a capitalist and imperialist power, Taylor contended, the United States could not and did not follow such a moral and disinterested course of action.[70]

To others, less inclined to cynical detachment, the "soft" policy was cause for righteous indignation. William Stuart Howe found President Roosevelt's explanation of the freezing orders in July "terrible" because it confessed that the United States had hitherto considered China and the American obligation to her as unimportant in comparison to the American stake in the South Seas. Howe could explain such moral cowardice infecting even the White House only as the result of the machinations of "a small group of Americans who seem to control policy" and who managed to influence the President in spite of the opposition of the vast majority of the American people and of virtually all experts on the Far East.[71]

The *New Republic* went still further. The architects of America's appeasement policy, it maintained, were not only appeasers, but pro-Fascists. "There is solid evidence that some of the men in the State Department who have advised these successive disasters of appeasement . . . are by their own profound convictions pro-Nazi or pro-Fascist." In fact, there was "formidable evidence of anti-Semitism" among those who advocated more appeasement, that is, a continued delay on a complete embargo. From this denunciation the journal ascended gracefully to the plane of lofty dogma. The United States must learn, it said, that "democracy is indivisible; that to betray it anywhere is to betray it everywhere." [72]

[70] George E. Taylor, "America's Pacific Policy: The Role and the Record," *Pacific Affairs*, XIV, no. 4 (Dec. 1941), 434.

[71] William Stuart Howe, "Japan Awaits Her Cue," *Current Events* (n.s.), I, no. 1 (Sept. 1941), 74–75.

[72] Editoral, "Don't Appease Japan!" *New Republic*, CIV, no. 25 (June 23, 1941), 843–844.

The few men who opposed the hard policy toward Japan found no effective answer to such moral arguments and dogmas. They could argue the realities of the situation, it is true. A. Whitney Griswold, for example, contended that an American policy of attempting to drive Japan out of China then and there was highly unrealistic. The Allies, including the United States, had enough power in the Far East to hold off Japan, Griswold maintained, but would not possess sufficient power to force the Japanese to evacuate China or to restore a balance of power in the Far East until the European war was over.[73]

Kenneth Scott Latourette, the noted missionary and church historian, argued against an embargo in early 1940, adducing reasons of both expediency and morality. An embargo would not stop Japan, he contended, but would only involve the United States in a useless and disastrous war. In addition, it would lead to America's policing the world and setting herself up as judge and executioner for mankind. Latourette frankly suggested that the responsibility for China's salvation lay chiefly with China herself, that in the long run the best the United States could do for her was to help her gain a truce on as favorable terms as possible. As he put it, "Politically the Chinese must save themselves. All that another government can do is to assure them a breathing-space in which to do so." America's role between Japan and China should be that of the Good Samaritan. She should try to promote a truce; she should try to aid China in the relief of her suffering; and she should co-operate with both China and Japan in establishing good relations in the Far East once the European war was over.[74]

Even in February 1940, however, this proposal was highly unpalatable to Americans; the reader reaction to it was one of

[73] A. Whitney Griswold, "European Factors in Far Eastern Diplomacy," *Foreign Affairs*, XIX, no. 2 (Jan. 1941), 297–309.

[74] Kenneth Scott Latourette, "A Church-made War with Japan?" *Christian Century*, LVII, no. 5 (Jan. 31, 1940), 140–142.

violent dissent.[75] The *Christian Century*, though it opposed an embargo, admitted that a majority of church people in the United States favored one.[76] By the autumn of 1941, one and a half years later, the pressure of events and of public opinion had caused even this most conciliatory of journals to recede considerably from its earlier stand. It still argued that the United States ought to go easy on Japan, but it conceded that the embargo should now be used to liberate China: "The American people do not want this pressure relaxed, now that it has finally been exerted, until the independence of China has been assured." [77]

By the end of 1941, therefore, virtually no one, aside from a few now discredited isolationist editors, would openly urge that the United States purchase peace with Japan without giving full satisfaction to the Chinese. In the field of public opinion, the moral argument had carried the day. Strategic and military considerations were for the most part ignored or forgotten in the debate. Occasionally someone suggested that China was militarily vital to the Allied cause,[78] but this was plainly not the main argument in behalf of a pro-Chinese policy. In the blithe atmosphere of overconfidence toward Japan in 1941, few persons would have contended that China was essential to an American victory in the Pacific, much less to America's defense of the continental United States. It was because of China's moral significance, not her military power, that the American people demanded her liberation.

As has been noted, one important group, America's military strategists, continued to the end to oppose this policy based on moral principles and aimed at the liberation of China. Neverthe-

[75] *Ibid.*, no. 7 (Feb. 14, 1940), 220–222.

[76] "Shall We Embargo Japan?" *ibid.*, no. 9 (Feb. 28, 1940), 270–272.

[77] Editorial, "An Appeal from Japan," *ibid.*, LVIII, no. 38 (Sept. 17, 1941), 1136.

[78] For example, William Bullitt, quoted in the *New York Times*, April 28, 1941, and Freda Utley, "The Far East in World Trends," *Asia*, XLI, no. 10 (Oct. 1941), 572.

less, the exception they took to the China-first policy of the State Department still merely proves a general rule. The military planners were no different from the diplomats in the way they wanted to see Japan treated; the Army Intelligence Service consistently advocated a hard, squeeze-Japan-now policy and "the exercise of increasingly strong 'power diplomacy'" by the United States.[79] The only distinction was in their objectives, which might have had a much better chance of attainment than those held by the State Department. The demands contemplated by the military strategists—withdrawal by Japan from the Axis and guarantees against Japanese moves to the north or to the south—were demands which Japan could meet in substance, if not to the letter, while the major demand of the State Department, the evacuation of China, was one to which the Japanese had no intention of yielding.

This is not to contend that the United States played the role of an international bully toward Japan in 1941, much less that a few sinister figures in the administration or propagandists in the press led a peace-loving nation into war. Whatever swagger, muscle-flexing, or even bellicose propaganda was current in the United States was only what must be expected in any powerful nation and from any uncontrolled press at a time of crisis. Furthermore, if one may define "wanting war" as preferring war to any compromise or limitation of the nation's aims, then it was the majority of the American people, and not just a few leaders, who wanted war in 1941. The main point intended here is simply that public opinion was a very strong factor in accounting for America's persistence in following a hard, offensive policy toward Japan. It made any change in that policy, once it was finally adopted, extremely difficult, if not impossible. President Roosevelt may have seriously intended to go easier on Japan, to relax the economic pressure on her somewhat, and to postpone or to mediate the China problem. But in order to carry through

[79] Memos by Miles, July 25, 1941, and by Kroner, Oct. 2, 1941, *Pearl Harbor Attack*, XIV, 1345, 1358.

such a policy, he would have had to contend against the very elements in public life which had most strongly supported his interventionist policy toward Europe. It would have meant inviting still more violent attacks from his enemies and opening himself to the charges of inconsistency and appeasement. As F. C. Jones puts it, *"Realpolitik* in Asia would have undermined the whole basis of Rooseveltian policy." [80] Whether the decisions made in 1941 regarding Japan were wise or foolish, it is completely unrealistic to treat them as if they were made in a vacuum and not in an atmosphere of tension and uncertainty in world developments and enormous pressures at home.

[80] Jones, *Japan's New Order*, 458.

IX

An Appraisal of the

American Policy

IN JUDGING American policy toward Japan in 1941, it might
be well to separate what is still controversial from what is not.
There is no longer any real doubt that the war came about over
China. Even an administration stalwart like Henry L. Stimson
and a sympathetic critic like Herbert Feis concur in this.[1] Nor is
it necessary to speculate any longer as to what could have induced Japan to launch such an incredible attack upon the United
States and Great Britain as occurred at Pearl Harbor and in
the south Pacific. One need not, as Winston Churchill did in
wartime, characterize it as "an irrational act" incompatible "with
prudence or even with sanity."[2] The Japanese were realistic

---

[1] "If at any time the United States had been willing to concede Japan
a free hand in China, there would have been no war in the Pacific"
(Stimson and Bundy, On Active Service, 256). "Our full induction into
this last World War followed our refusal to let China fend for itself.
We had rejected all proposals which would have allowed Japan to remain in China and Manchuria. . . . Japan had struck—rather than accept frustration" (Herbert Feis, The China Tangle [Princeton: Princeton University Press, 1953], 3).

[2] Speech to U.S. Congress, Washington, Dec. 26, 1941, War Speeches
of Churchill, II, 150.

about their position throughout; they did not suddenly go insane. The attack was an act of desperation, not madness. Japan fought only when she had her back to the wall as a result of America's diplomatic and economic offensive.

The main point still at issue is whether the United States was wise in maintaining a "hard" program of diplomatic and economic pressure on Japan from July 1941 on. Along with this issue go two subsidiary questions: the first, whether it was wise to make the liberation of China the central aim of American policy and the immediate evacuation of Japanese troops a requirement for agreement; the second, whether it was wise to decline Premier Konoye's invitation to a meeting of leaders in the Pacific. On all these points, the policy which the United States carried out still has distinguished defenders. The paramount issue between Japan and the United States, they contend, always was the China problem. In her China policy, Japan showed that she was determined to secure domination over a large area of East Asia by force. Apart from the legitimate American commercial interests which would be ruined or excluded by this Japanese action, the United States, for reasons of her own security and of world peace, had sufficient stake in Far Eastern questions to oppose such aggression. Finally, after ten years of Japanese expansion, it was only sensible and prudent for the United States to demand that it come to an end and that Japan retreat. In order to meet the Japanese threat, the United States had a perfect right to use the economic power she possessed in order to compel the Japanese to evacuate their conquered territory. If Japan chose to make this a cause for war, the United States could not be held responsible.

A similar defense is offered on the decision to turn down Konoye's Leaders' Conference. Historians may concede, as do Langer and Gleason, that Konoye was probably sincere in wanting peace and that he "envisaged making additional concessions to Washington, including concessions on the crucial issue of the withdrawal of Japanese troops from China." But, they point out, Konoye could never have carried the Army with him on any such concession.[3] If the United States was right in requiring Japan to abandon the Co-Prosperity Sphere, then her leaders were equally right in declining to meet with a Japanese Premier who, however conciliatory he might have been personally, was bound by his own promises and the exigencies of Japanese politics to maintain this national aim. In addition, there was the serious possibility that much could be lost from such a meeting —the confidence of China, the cohesiveness of the coalition with Great Britain and Russia. In short, there was not enough prospect of gain to merit taking the chance.

This is a point of view which must be taken seriously. Any judgment on the wisdom or folly of the American policy, in fact, must be made with caution—there are no grounds for dogmatic certainty. The opinion here to be developed, nonetheless, is that the American policy from the end of July to December was a grave mistake. It should not be necessary to add that this does not make it treason. There is a "back door to war" theory, espoused in various forms by Charles A. Beard, George Morgenstern, Charles C. Tansill, and, most recently, Rear Admiral Robert A. Theobald, which holds that the President chose the Far East as a rear entrance to the war in Europe and to that end deliberately goaded the Japanese into an attack.[4] This theory is quite different and quite incredible. It is as impossible to accept as the idea that Japan attacked the United States in a spirit of overconfidence or that Hitler pushed the Japanese into war. Roosevelt's fault, if any, was not that of deliberately provoking the Japanese to attack, but of allowing Hull and others to talk him out of impulses and ideas which, had he pursued them,

---

[3] Langer and Gleason, *Undeclared War*, 706–707.

[4] Charles A. Beard, *President Roosevelt and the Coming of the War, 1941* (New Haven: Yale University Press, 1948); George E. Morgenstern, *Pearl Harbor: The Story of the Secret War* (New York: Devin-Adair, 1947); Charles C. Tansill, *Back Door to War* (Chicago: Regnery, 1952); Rear Admiral Robert A. Theobald, *The Final Secret of Pearl Harbor* (New York: Devin-Adair, 1954).

might have averted the conflict. Moreover, the mistake (assuming that it was a mistake) of a too hard and rigid policy with Japan was, as has been pointed out, a mistake shared by the whole nation, with causes that were deeply organic. Behind it was not sinister design or warlike intent, but a sincere and uncompromising adherence to moral principles and liberal doctrines.

This is going ahead too fast, however; one needs first of all to define the mistake with which American policy is charged. Briefly, it was this. In the attempt to gain everything at once, the United States lost her opportunity to secure immediately her essential requirements in the Far East and to continue to work toward her long-range goals. She succeeded instead only in making inevitable an unnecessary and avoidable war—an outcome which constitutes the ultimate failure of diplomacy. Until July 1941, as already demonstrated, the United States consistently sought to attain two limited objectives in the Far East, those of splitting the Axis and of stopping Japan's advance southward. Both aims were in accordance with America's broad strategic interests; both were reasonable, attainable goals. Through a combination of favorable circumstance and forceful American action, the United States reached the position where the achievement of these two goals was within sight. At this very moment, on the verge of a major diplomatic victory, the United States abandoned her original goals and concentrated on a third, the liberation of China. This last aim was not in accord with American strategic interests, was not a limited objective, and, most important, was completely incapable of being achieved by peaceful means and doubtful of attainment even by war. Through her single-minded pursuit of this unattainable goal, the United States forfeited the diplomatic victory which she had already virtually won. The unrelenting application of extreme economic pressure on Japan, instead of compelling the evacuation of China, rendered war inevitable, drove Japan back into the arms of Germany for better or for worse, and precipitated the wholesale plunge by Japan into the South Seas. As it ultimately turned out, the United States succeeded in liberating China only at great cost and when it was too late to do the cause of the Nationalist Chinese much real good.

This is not, of course, a new viewpoint. It is in the main simply that of Ambassador Grew, who has held and defended it since 1941. The arguments he advances seem cogent and sensible in the light of present knowledge. Briefly summarized, they are the following: First is his insistence on the necessity of distinguishing between long-range and immediate goals in foreign policy and on the folly of demanding the immediate realization of both.[5] Second is his contention that governments are brought to abandon aggressive policies not by sudden conversion through moral lectures, but by the gradual recognition that the policy of aggression will not succeed. According to Grew, enough awareness of failure existed in the government of Japan in late 1941 to enable it to make a beginning in the process of reversal of policy—but not nearly enough to force Japan to a wholesale surrender of her conquests and aims.[6] Third was his conviction that what was needed on both sides was time—time in which the United States could grow stronger and in which the tide of war in Europe could be turned definitely against Germany, time in which the sense of failure could grow in Japan and in which moderates could gain better control of the situation. A victory in Europe, Grew observed, would either automatically solve the problem of Japan or make that problem, if necessary, much easier to solve by force.[7] Fourth was his belief that Japan would fight if backed to the wall (a view vindicated by events) [8]

[5] Grew, *Turbulent Era*, II, 1255.
[6] *Ibid.*, 1290.　　　　　　　　　　[7] *Ibid.*, 1268–1269, 1286.
[8] The opposite belief, that Japan would give way, not only was inconsonant with the best available political and military intelligence, but was also a bad estimate of Japanese national psychology and of expansionist psychology in general. F. C. Jones rightly criticizes it as "the folly of supposing that the rulers of a powerful nation, having committed them-

and that a war at this time with Japan could not possibly serve the interests of the United States. Even if one considered war as the only final answer to Japanese militarism, still, Grew would answer, the United States stood to gain nothing by seeking a decision in 1941. The time factor was entirely in America's favor. Japan could not hope to gain as much from a limited relaxation of the embargo as the United States could from time gained for mobilization; Roosevelt and the military strategists were in fact anxious to gain time by a *modus vivendi*.[9]

There is one real weakness in Grew's argument upon which his critics have always seized. This is his contention that Konoye, faced after July 26 with the two clear alternatives of war or a genuine peace move, which would of necessity include a settlement with China, had chosen the latter course and could have carried through a policy of peace had he been given the time. "We believed," he writes, "that Prince Konoye was in a position to carry the country with him in a program of peace" and to make commitments to the United States which would "eventually, if not immediately" meet the conditions of Hull's Four Points.[10] The answer of critics is that, even if one credits Konoye's sincerity and takes his assurances at face value, there is still no reason to believe that he could have carried even his own cabinet, much less the whole nation, with him on any program approximating that of Hull. In particular, as events show, he could not have persuaded the Army to evacuate China.[11]

The objection is well taken; Grew was undoubtedly over-optimistic about Konoye's capacity to carry through a peaceful

---

selves to an expansionist policy, will abandon or reverse that policy when confronted by the threat of war. So long as they see, or think they see, any possibility of success, they will elect to fight rather than face the humiliation and probable internal revolt which submission to the demands of their opponents would entail" (*Japan's New Order*, 461).

[9] Grew, *Turbulent Era*, II, 1276–1277.   [10] *Ibid.*, 1263–1264.

[11] Feis, *Road to Pearl Harbor*, 275–277; Jones, *Japan's New Order*, 457–458.

policy. This one objection, however, does not ruin Grew's case. He countered it later with the argument that a settlement with Japan which allowed Japanese garrisons to remain in China on a temporary basis would not have been a bad idea. Although far from an ideal solution, it would have been better, for China as well, than the policy the United States actually followed. It would have brought China what was all-important—a cessation of fighting—without involving the United States, as many contended, in either a sacrifice of principle or a betrayal of China. The United States, Grew points out, had never committed herself to guaranteeing China's integrity. Further, it would not have been necessary to agree to anything other than temporary garrisons in North China which, in more favorable times, the United States could work to have removed. The great mistake was to allow American policy to be guided by a sentimental attitude toward China which in the long run could do neither the United States nor China any good. As Grew puts it:

Japan's advance to the south, including her occupation of portions of China, constituted for us a real danger, and it was definitely in our national interest that it be stopped, by peaceful means if possible, by force of arms if necessary. American aid to China should have been regarded, as we believe it was regarded by our Government, as an indirect means to this end, and not from a sentimental viewpoint. The President's letter of January 21, 1941, shows that he then sensed the important issues in the Far East, and that he did not include China, purely for China's sake, among them. . . . The failure of the Washington Administration to seize the opportunity presented in August and September, 1941, to halt the southward advance by peaceful means, together with the paramount importance attached to the China question during the conversations in Washington, gives rise to the belief that not our Government but millions of quite understandably sympathetic but almost totally uninformed American citizens had assumed control of our Far Eastern policy.[12]

[12] Grew, *Turbulent Era*, II, 1367–1368.

There remains the obvious objection that Grew's solution, however plausible it may now seem, was politically impracticable in 1941. No American government could then have treated China as expendable, just as no Japanese government could have written off the China Affair as a dead loss. This is in good measure true and goes a long way to explain, if not to justify, the hard American policy. Yet it is not entirely certain that no solution could have been found which would both have averted war and have been accepted by the American people, had a determined effort been made to find one. As F. C. Jones points out, the United States and Japan were not faced in July 1941 with an absolute dilemma of peace or war, of complete settlement or open conflict. Hull believed that they were, of course; but his all-or-nothing attitude constituted one of his major shortcomings as a diplomat. Between the two extremes existed the possibility of a *modus vivendi*, an agreement settling some issues and leaving others in abeyance. Had Roosevelt and Konoye met, Jones argues, they might have been able to agree on a relaxation of the embargo in exchange for satisfactory assurances on the Tripartite Pact and southward expansion, with the China issue laid aside. The United States would not have had to cease aid, nor Japan to remove her troops. The final settlement of the Far Eastern question, Jones concludes,

would then have depended upon the issue of the struggle in Europe. If Germany prevailed, then the United States would be in no position to oppose Japanese ambitions in Asia; if Germany were defeated, Japan would be in no position to persist in those ambitions in the face of the United States, the USSR, and the British Commonwealth.[13]

Such an agreement, limited and temporary in nature, would have involved no sacrifice of principle for either nation, yet would have removed the immediate danger of war. As a temporary expedient and as an alternative to otherwise inevitable and useless

[13] Jones, *Japan's New Order*, 459.

conflict, it could have been sold by determined effort to the public on both sides. Nor would it have been impossible, in the writer's opinion, to have accompanied or followed such an agreement with a simple truce or standstill in the China conflict through American mediation.

This appraisal, to be sure, is one based on realism. Grew's criticism of Hull's policy and the alternative he offers to it are both characterized by fundamental attention to what is practical and expedient at a given time and to limited objectives within the scope of the national interest. In general, the writer agrees with this point of view, believing that, as William A. Orton points out, it is foolish and disastrous to treat nations as morally responsible persons, "because their nature falls far short of personality," and that, as George F. Kennan contends, the right role for moral considerations in foreign affairs is not to determine policy, but rather to soften and ameliorate actions necessarily based on the realities of world politics.[14]

From this realistic standpoint, the policy of the State Department would seem to be open to other criticisms besides those of Grew. The criticisms, which may be briefly mentioned here, are those of inconsistency, blindness to reality, and futility. A notable example of the first would be the inconsistency of a strong no-compromise stand against Japan with the policy of broad accommodation to America's allies, especially Russia, both before and after the American entrance into the war.[15] The

[14] William A. Orton, *The Liberal Tradition* (New Haven: Yale University Press, 1944), 239; George F. Kennan, *American Diplomacy, 1900–1950* (Chicago: University of Chicago Press, 1951), 95–103.

[15] One notes with interest, for example, a pre-Pearl Harbor statement by Senator Lister Hill of Alabama, a strong proponent of a radical anti-Japanese policy, as to America's attitude toward the Soviet Union: "It is not the business of this government to ask or to receive any assurance from Stalin about what he will do with regard to Finland after the war. . . . It is the business of this government to look out for and defend the vital interests of the United States" (*New York Times*, Nov. 5, 1941). If in the above quotation one reads "Tojo" for "Stalin" and "China" for

inconsistency may perhaps best be seen by comparing the American stand in 1941 on such questions as free trade, the Open Door in China, the territorial and administrative integrity of China, the maintenance of the prewar *status quo* in the Far East, and the sanctity of international agreements with the position taken on the same questions at the Yalta Conference in 1945.[16]

"Finland," the result is a statement of the extreme isolationist position on the Far East which Hill and other supporters of the administration found so detestable.

[16] The writer has no desire to enter here into the controversy over the merits of the Yalta decisions, but only to draw a certain parallel. The standard defense for the Yalta policy on the Far East has been the contention that the United States conceded to Soviet Russia only what the U.S.S.R. could and would have seized without American leave, that the only alternative to agreement would have been war with Russia, and that securing Russian entrance into the Far Eastern war was considered militarily necessary (George F. Lensen, "Yalta and the Far East," in John L. Snell, Forrest C. Pogue, Charles F. Delzell, and George F. Lensen, *The Meaning of Yalta: Big Three Diplomacy and the New Balance of Power* [Baton Rouge: Louisiana State University Press, 1956], 163–164). The argument may be quite sound, but surely it would serve equally well—indeed, much better, *mutatis mutandis*—to justify a policy of conciliation toward Japan in 1941. Applied to Japan, the argument would then read as follows: The United States would have conceded to Japan only the temporary possession of a part of what Japan had already seized without American leave; the only alternative to agreement would have been war with Japan; and preventing Japanese entrance into the European war was considered militarily necessary. The great difference between the two situations would seem to be that the concessions envisioned by Japan in 1941 were temporary and reversible; those gained by Russia in 1945 were not. The very necessity of pursuing the Yalta policy in 1945 casts doubt on the wisdom of the hard-and-fast stand of 1941. Felix Morley has put the parallel neatly: "To assert that the sudden and complete reversal of the long-established Far Eastern policy was justified was also to say, by implication, that the policy reversed was fundamentally faulty, that to fight a war with Japan in behalf of Chinese nationalism had been a dreadful mistake" (*The Foreign Policy of the United States* [New York: Alfred A. Knopf, 1951], 87–88). One may, as Morley does, reject both the above premise and the conclusion, or one may accept both; but it is difficult to see how one may affirm the premise and deny the

The blindness to reality may be seen in the apparent inability of American policy makers to take seriously into account the gravity of Japan's economic plight or the real exigencies of her military and strategic position, particularly as these factors would affect the United States over the long run.[17] Equally unrealistic and more fateful was the lack of appreciation on the part of many influential people and of wide sections of the public of the almost certain consequences to be expected from the pressure exerted on Japan—namely, American involvement in a war her military strategists considered highly undesirable. The attitude has been well termed by Robert Osgood, "this blind indifference toward the military and political consequences of a morally-inspired position."[18]

The charge of futility, finally, could be laid to the practice of insisting on a literal subscription to principles which, however noble, had no chance of general acceptance or practical application. The best example is the persistent demand that the Japanese

---

conclusion. For those who believe that a vital moral difference existed between the two cases, the problem would seem to be how to show that it is morally unjustifiable to violate principle in order to keep a potential enemy out of a war, yet morally justifiable to sacrifice principle in order to get a potential ally into it. The dilemma appears insoluble.

[17] In his very interesting book, *America's Strategy in World Politics* (New York: Harcourt, Brace, 1942), Nicholas Spykman displays some of the insights which seem to have been lacking in the American policy of the time. He points out, for example, that Japan's economic and geographic position was essentially the same as that of Great Britain; that her position vis-à-vis the United States was also roughly equivalent to England's; that therefore it made little sense for America to aid Great Britain in maintaining a European balance of power, while at the same time trying to force Japan to give up all her buffer states in Asia; that the Japanese war potential could not compare to that of a revivified and unified China; and that one day (a striking prediction in 1942!) the United States would have to undertake to protect Japan from Soviet Russia and China (pp. 135–137, 469–470). Spykman saw then what is today so painfully evident—that without a Japanese foothold on the Asiatic mainland no real balance of power is possible in Asia.

[18] Robert E. Osgood, *Ideals and Self-Interest in America's Foreign Relations* (Chicago: University of Chicago Press, 1953), 361.

pledge themselves to carrying out nineteenth-century principles of free trade and equal access to raw materials in a twentieth-century world where economic nationalism and autarchy, trade barriers and restrictions were everywhere the order of the day, and not the least in the United States under the New Deal. Not one of America's major allies would have subscribed whole-heartedly to Hull's free-trade formula; what good it could have done to pin the Japanese down to it is hard to determine.[19]

But these are all criticisms based on a realistic point of view, and to judge the American policy solely from this point of view is to judge it unfairly and by a standard inappropriate to it. The policy of the United States was avowedly not one of realism, but of principle. If then it is to be understood on its own grounds and judged by its own standards, the main question will be whether the policy was morally right—that is, in accord with principles of peace and international justice. Here, according to its defenders, the American policy stands vindicated. For any other policy, any settlement with Japan at the expense of China, would have meant a betrayal not only of China, but also of vital principles and of America's moral task in the world.

This, as we know, was the position of Hull and his co-workers. It has been stated more recently by Basil Rauch, who writes:

No one but an absolute pacifist would argue that the danger of war is a greater evil than violation of principle. . . . The isolationist believes that appeasement of Japan without China's consent violated no principle worth a risk of war. The internationalist must believe that the principle did justify a risk of war.[20]

This is not an argument to be dismissed lightly. The contention that the United States had a duty to fulfill in 1941, and

[19] A memorandum by the Chief of the State Department Division of Commercial Policy and Agreements (Hawkins) to Ballantine, Washington, Nov. 10, 1941, offers interesting comments on the extent and nature of the trade discriminations then being practiced against Japan by nations throughout the world, including the United States (*Foreign Relations, 1941*, IV, 576–577).

[20] Rauch, *Roosevelt*, 472.

that this duty consisted in holding to justice and morality in a world given to international lawlessness and barbarism and in standing on principle against an unprincipled and ruthless aggressor, commands respect. It is not answered by dismissing it as unrealistic or by proscribing all moral considerations in foreign policy. An answer may be found, however, in a closer definition of America's moral duty in 1941. According to Hull, and apparently also Rauch, the task was primarily one of upholding principle. This is not the only possible definition. It may well be contended that the moral duty was rather one of doing the most practical good possible in a chaotic world situation and, further, that this was the main task President Roosevelt and the administration had in mind at least till the end of July 1941.

If the moral task of the United States in the Far East was to uphold a principle of absolute moral value, the principle of non-appeasement of aggressors, then the American policy was entirely successful in fulfilling it. The American diplomats proved that the United States was capable of holding to its position in disregard and even in defiance of national interests narrowly conceived. If, however, the task was one of doing concrete good and giving practical help where needed, especially to China, then the American policy falls fatally short. For it can easily be seen not only that the policy followed did not in practice help China, but also that it could not have been expected to. Although it was a pro-China and even a China-first policy in principle, it was not in practical fact designed to give China the kind of help needed.

What China required above all by late 1941 was clearly an end to the fighting, a chance to recoup her strength. Her chaotic financial condition, a disastrous inflation, civil strife with the Communists, severe hunger and privation, and falling morale all enfeebled and endangered her further resistance. Chiang Kai-shek, who knew this, could hope only for an end to the war through the massive intervention of American forces and the consequent liberation of China. It was in this hope that he pleaded so strongly for a hard American policy toward Japan. Chiang's hopes, however, were wholly unrealistic. For though the United States was willing to risk war for China's sake, and finally did incur it over the China issue, the Washington government never intended in case of war to throw America's full weight against Japan in order to liberate China. The American strategy always was to concentrate on Europe first, fighting a defensive naval war in the Far East and aiding China, as before, in order to keep the Japanese bogged down. The possibility was faced and accepted that the Chinese might have to go on fighting for some years before eventual liberation through the defeat of Japan. The vehement Chinese protests over this policy were unavailing, and the bitter disillusionment suffered by the Chinese only helped to bring on in 1942 the virtual collapse of the Chinese war effort during the latter years of the war.[21]

As a realistic appraisal of America's military capabilities and of her world-wide strategic interests, the Europe-first policy has a great deal to recommend it. But the combination of this realistic strategy with a moralistic diplomacy led to the noteworthy paradox of a war incurred for the sake of China which could not then be fought for the sake of China and whose practical value for China at the time was, to say the least, dubious. The plain fact is that the United States in 1941 was not capable of forcing Japan out of China by means short of war and was neither willing nor, under existing circumstances, able to throw the Japanese out by war. The American government could conceivably have told the Chinese this and tried to work out the best possible program of help for China under these limitations. Instead, it yielded to Chinese importunities and followed a policy almost sure to eventuate in war, knowing that if the Japanese did attack, China and her deliverance would have to

[21] Levi, *Modern China's Foreign Policy*, 229–237. On the danger of internal collapse in China as early as 1940, see U.S. Department of State, *Foreign Relations of the United States: 1940*, vol. IV, *The Far East* (Washington: Government Printing Office, 1955), 672–677.

take a back seat. It is difficult to conceive of such a policy as a program of practical aid to China.

The main, though not the only, reason why this policy was followed is clearly the overwhelming importance of principle in American diplomacy, particularly the principle of nonappeasement of aggressors. Once most leaders in the administration and wide sections of the public became convinced that it was America's prime moral duty to stand hard and fast against aggressors, whatever the consequences, and once this conviction became decisive in the formulation of policy, the end result was almost inevitable: a policy designed to uphold principle and to punish the aggressor, but not to save the victim.[22]

It is this conviction as to America's moral duty, however sincere and understandable, which the writer believes constitutes a fundamental misreading of America's moral task. The policy it

[22] It is Secretary of War Henry L. Stimson who gives evidence on how strong was the role of avenging justice in the prevailing picture of America's moral duty. He displays a striking anxiety to acquit the administration of the charge of being "soft" on Japan and to prove that the administration was always fully aware of the Japanese crimes and morally aroused by them. The nation's leaders, he insists in one place, were "as well aware as their critics of the wickedness of the Japanese." Avenging justice, too, plays an important role in the defense he makes of the postwar Nuremberg and Tokyo war crimes trials. These trials, he claims, fulfilled a vital moral task. The main trouble with the Kellogg Pact and the policy of nonrecognition and moral sanctions, according to Stimson, was that they named the international lawbreakers but failed to capture and punish them. The United States, along with other nations in the prewar world, had neglected "a duty to catch the criminal. . . . Our offense was thus that of the man who passed by on the other side." Now, this is a curious revision of the parable of the Good Samaritan, to which the Secretary here alludes. According to the Stimson version, the Good Samaritan should not have stopped to bind up the victim's wounds, put him on his beast of burden, and arrange for his care. Had he been cognizant of his real moral duty, he would rather have mounted his steed and rode off in hot pursuit of the robbers, to bring them to justice. This is only an illustration, but an apt one, of the prevailing concept of America's moral duty, with its emphasis on meting out justice rather than doing good (Stimson and Bundy, *On Active Service*, 384, 262).

gave rise to was bad not simply because it was moralistic but because it was obsessed with the wrong kind of morality—with that abstract "Let justice be done though the heavens fall" kind which so often, when relentlessly pursued, does more harm than good. It would be interesting to investigate the role which this conception of America's moral task played in the formulation of the American war aims in the Far East, with their twin goals of unconditional surrender and the destruction of Japan as a major power, especially after the desire to vindicate American principles and to punish the aggressor was intensified a hundredfold by the attack on Pearl Harbor.[23] To pursue the later implications of this kind of morality in foreign policy, with its attendant legalistic and vindictive overtones, would, however, be a task for another volume.

In contrast, the different kind of policy which Grew advocated and toward which Roosevelt so long inclined need not really be considered immoral or unprincipled, however much it undoubtedly would have been denounced as such. A limited *modus vivendi* agreement would not have required the United States in any way to sanction Japanese aggression or to abandon her stand on Chinese integrity and independence. It would have constituted only a recognition that the American government was not then in a position to enforce its principles, reserving for America full freedom of action at some later, more favorable time. Nor would it have meant the abandonment and betrayal of China. Rather it would have involved the frank recognition that the kind of help the Chinese wanted was impossible for the United States to give at that time. It would in no way have precluded giving China the best kind of help then possible—in the author's opinion, the offer of American mediation for a truce in the war and the grant of fuller economic aid to try to

[23] Admiral William D. Leahy (*I Was There* [New York: McGraw-Hill, 1950], 81) expresses his view of America's war aims in dubious Latin but with admirable forthrightness: "*Delenda est Japanico.*" He was, of course, not the only American leader to want to emulate Cato.

help the Chinese recover—and promising China greater assistance once the crucial European situation was settled. Only that kind of morality which sees every sort of dealing with an aggressor, every instance of accommodation or conciliation, as appeasement and therefore criminal would find the policy immoral.[24]

What the practical results of such a policy, if attempted, would have been is of course a matter for conjecture. It would be rash to claim that it would have saved China, either from her wartime collapse or from the final victory of communism. It may well be that already in 1941 the situation in China was out of control. Nor can one assert with confidence that, had this policy enabled her to keep out of war with Japan, the United States would have been able to bring greater forces to bear in Europe much earlier, thus shortening the war and saving more of Europe from communism. Since the major part of the American armed forces were always concentrated in Europe and since in any case a certain proportion would have had to stand guard in the Pacific, it is possible that the avoidance of war with Japan, however desirable in itself, would not have made a decisive difference in the duration of the European conflict. The writer does, however, permit himself the modest conclusions that the kind of policy advocated by Grew presented real possibilities of success entirely closed to the policy actually followed and that it was by no means so immoral and unprincipled that it could not have been pursued by the United States with decency and honor.

[24] See the introductory remarks on the possibilities of appeasement, under certain circumstances, as a useful diplomatic tool, along with an excellent case study in the wrong use of it, in J. W. Wheeler-Bennett, *Munich: Prologue to Tragedy* (London: Macmillan, 1948), 3–8.

X

Epilogue: The Axis Alliance and the Tokyo War Crimes Trials

IN CONTRAST to their Nuremberg counterparts, the war crimes trials held in Tokyo from 1946 to 1948 have received relatively little attention from historians and from the general public. Although the proceedings and exhibits of the International Military Tribunal for the Far East have been recognized and used as an important historical source, they have never been published, unlike those from Nuremberg, and remain accessible only at certain large libraries. (This is partly due, perhaps, to the great length and prolixity of the proceedings.) Moreover, to the writer's knowledge, no definitive account exists of the story of the trials themselves, which constituted an important chapter in the history of the postwar occupation of Japan.[1] If these comments serve no other purpose, they may possibly stimulate such a study.

[1] Valuable information on the trials is given by Solis Horwitz, *The Tokyo Trial* (International Conciliation series, no. 465; New York: Carnegie Endowment for International Peace, 1950). Mr. Horwitz was assistant counsel for the prosecution from the United States. The work needs to be supplemented, however, because of its brevity.

This is not the place to discuss the difficult questions of the legal and juridical bases for the trials. For the pro and con on these questions, one can best see the majority judgment of the Tribunal (which has also been issued separately) and the dissenting judgment of Mr. Justice Radhabinod Pal of India.[2] Nor is it possible here to take up the question of the Tribunal's rules of evidence and procedure and whether, as Justice Pal contended, they were irregular, inconsistent, and applied in a manner prejudicial to the defense.[3] Finally, one can do no more than to mention what Justice Pal evidently considers (along with the writer) to be the fundamental fallacy in the prosecution case and the majority judgment, namely, the attempt to force great impersonal events, often representing parts of world-wide trends

[2] *Judgment of the International Military Tribunal for the Far East* (Tokyo, 1948); *International Military Tribunal for the Far East*, Judgment and Opinions: India. Justice Pal has also published his dissent under the title *International Military Tribunal for the Far East: Dissentient Judgment* (Calcutta: Sanyal, 1953). In the present writer's opinion, this lengthy work, with its dispassionate tone and searching analysis, constitutes a devastating critique of the prosecution case and majority judgment.

[3] *IMTFE*, Judgment: India, 280–348. Without being a lawyer, the present writer finds what Justice Pal has to say on these points very convincing and in line with his own impressions gained through reading the trial record. He would cite the following as illustration: One of the major prosecution contentions was that the course of Japanese industrialization, especially after 1931, was evidence of a conspiracy to wage aggressive warfare against China, the United States, Great Britain, and several other countries. The defense reply was that Japanese industrialization was necessitated by Japanese economic conditions and the international situation and implied no aggressive designs. In remarking on this defense argument and rejecting certain defense testimony pertaining thereto, Sir William Flood Webb of Australia, President of the Tribunal, commented: "Japan's industrialization was notorious, a matter of common knowledge. . . . The purpose of it may have been, of course, innocent to some extent. You can only judge the purpose by the use to which it is put eventually" (*IMTFE*, Record, 25419–25420). One might dismiss this as an offhand remark without significance, did not the prosecution case on this point seem to rest precisely on such an astounding rule of inference.

(e.g., the industrialization of Japan, her total mobilization, her efforts for economic autarchy, and her successive steps for economic and territorial expansion), into the narrow confines of a legalistic-moralistic concept of a seventeen-year collective conspiracy with individual criminal responsibility.[4]

It will be worth while, however, to consider in some detail the conclusions of the Tribunal on the two main points dealt with in this study, the Axis Alliance and the course of the Japanese-American negotiations. It might be noted, first of all, that the position of the Tribunal in judging these issues was much different from that of the administration in Washington in 1941. In the latter case, the uncertainty of the evidence, the pressure of events, and the climate of opinion combined to make policy making extremely difficult. If the policy pursued in the latter half of 1941 was a mistake, it was certainly only that and, in view of the conditions, an entirely understandable and almost inevitable one. On the other hand, a judicial tribunal, presumably impartial, having a wealth of evidence at hand, under no pressure of time, and dealing with events lying some distance in the past, would clearly be in a better position to judge the issues at stake. In the writer's opinion, the Tribunal's decisions of 1948 turned out to be as one-sided and as untenable as those of 1941, and with less excuse.

The conclusion reached by the Tribunal on the Tripartite Pact is simple and straightforward: "In summary, the Tripartite Pact was a compact made between aggressor nations for the furtherance of their aggressive purposes."[5] To support this conclusion, the majority judgment gives an account of the negotiation of the Pact, the aims and purposes of Japanese leaders, and its implementation by Japan and Germany, which the writer regards as wholly misleading. The account of the negotiation of the Pact, for instance, completely denies any material difference between the aims and desires of Germany and of

[4] *IMTFE*, Judgment: India, 694–741, 873–876, 980–984, *et passim*.
[5] *IMTFE*, Judgment, 49005.

Japan.[6] Yet the evidence summarized in Chapter V of this study (much of which evidence was rejected by the Tribunal for technical legal reasons) clearly shows a very substantial difference both in the kind of pact Germany and Japan each wanted and in what each hoped to achieve through it.

The section of the judgment entitled "The Intentions of Japanese Leaders in Concluding the Tripartite Alliance" proceeds with the argument:

The Tripartite Alliance was concluded as a necessary step in Japanese preparations for a military advance into South-East Asia and the South Seas. At the numerous discussions and conferences of September 1940 it was clearly recognized by all who took part that the conclusion of the alliance would commit Japan to waging war against France, the Netherlands, and the countries of the British Commonwealth; and that it implied also Japan's willingness to wage war against the United States, should that country seek to stand between Japan and the attainment of her aggressive aims.[7]

As a summary of the intentions of Japanese leaders, the first sentence quoted above is one-sided; the second is false. Some Japanese leaders envisioned the Pact as a means for advancing Japan's drive southward; others did not. None of those, however, who took part in the conferences on the Pact ever recognized or believed that the Pact would commit Japan to waging war against anyone, particularly the United States. As has been shown, Japan's strongest diplomatic efforts were directed precisely toward retaining as much freedom of decision and action as possible under the Pact. Those who spoke of war with the United States or Great Britain spoke of it as a danger to be guarded against or an eventuality to be prepared for, but not as a goal to which the Pact would commit them. Those who defended the Pact maintained that it would prevent war, not bring it on.

Furthermore, the Tribunal's account is significant as much for

---

[6] *Ibid.*, 48994–48996. [7] *Ibid.*, 49002–49003.

what it does not say as for what it does. All the emphasis is laid upon Japan's alleged aggressive motives in concluding the Pact; no mention is made of several others—the desire of Japan to escape from her diplomatic isolation, the hope of using German good offices to end the China Incident, the further hope of using Germany to coerce Soviet Russia into ceasing aid to China, and the hope that the diplomatic isolation of the United States would cause her to stop her aid to China and also prevent the spread of the European war to the Pacific. Yet it is exactly these hopes and desires, however illusory, which appear most frequently and prominently in the various discussions and conferences referred to.

The Tribunal judgment then goes on to consider the Pact in action. Conceding that the Alliance was defensive in form, it nevertheless contends that "the three powers were determined to support one another in aggressive action whenever such action was considered necessary to the furtherance of their schemes."[8] That such mutual support in aggression actually took place is maintained in the section entitled "Cooperation under Tripartite Pact," where the judgment states: "Active cooperation with Germany and Italy under the Pact began shortly after it was signed." This charge of "active cooperation" is then supported only by the flimsiest evidence—that is, the appointment of mixed technical commissions (which never functioned), the sending of Ambassador Oshima to Berlin, and the visit of Foreign Minister Matsuoka to the Axis capitals.[9] Similarly, in the section entitled "Preparations for Move to South," the judgment alleges, "Action [by Japan] was to be coordinated with German military plans."[10] Again, no evidence of any consequence is cited.

Most interesting are the sections of the judgment dealing with the Tripartite Pact and Soviet Russia. Despite the existence of Article V specifically exempting Russia from its provisions, the Pact, according to the Tribunal, was also directed against

[8] *Ibid.*, 49003–49004. [9] *Ibid.*, 49424. [10] *Ibid.*, 49426–49427.

Russia.[11] Indeed, according to the Tribunal, the Pact was planned and consummated with aggressive war against the Soviet Union in mind. After a long section purporting to show that Japan had disregarded and violated her nonaggression pact with Russia following the German attack (a charge based largely on the testimony of Ambassador Ott, who on this point clearly reflects the wishful thinking and urgings of the German Foreign Office), the Tribunal concludes:

The Tribunal is of the opinion that a war of aggression against the U.S.S.R. was contemplated and planned throughout the period under consideration, that it was one of the principal elements of Japan's national policy, and that its object was the seizure of territories of the U.S.S.R. in the Far East.[12]

The conclusion by Japan of a nonaggression pact with Russia presents no problem to the Tribunal's argument:

It would appear that Japan was not sincere in concluding the Neutrality Pact with the U.S.S.R., but considering her agreements with Germany more advantageous she signed the Neutrality Pact to facilitate her plans for an attack upon the U.S.S.R.[13]

That this conclusion flies directly in the face of Japan's notorious refusal throughout the war to attack the Soviet Union, despite repeated German pleas that she do so, seems not to have disturbed the Tribunal judges.[14]

The judgment portrays in much the same fashion the policy of Japan and the course of Japanese-American relations in 1941.

[11] *Ibid.*, 49004.   [12] *Ibid.*, 49360.   [13] *Ibid.*, 49382–49383.

[14] This charge of Japanese aggression against Russia gains in irony when one remembers that, however opportunistic Japan's attitude toward the U.S.S.R. undoubtedly was, she did in fact honor the nonaggression pact throughout the period of Russia's great crisis, whereas the Soviet Union, abetted and encouraged by the United States and Great Britain, chose the moment of Japan's defeat to repudiate the pact and attack her in the interest of gaining Far Eastern spoils.

It traces, for example, a firm decision on the part of Japan to attack Pearl Harbor back to April 1941, on the grounds that by this time certain plans and preparations were under way.[15] In so doing, it seems to ignore the repeated review of the basic question of war and peace on September 6, October 12–15, and November 1–5, as well as the fundamental fact that plans for the attack were always contingent on the failure of negotiations.

The split of opinion in Japan over which policy to follow after the German attack on Russia is depicted simply as indecision over which direction Japanese aggression should take. Matsuoka pressed for an attack on Siberia, while "there were others, including Konoye and Kido, who argued that the original plan of September–October to prosecute the advance to the South should not be abandoned." [16] This is certainly a distortion of the position of Konoye, who held then and later that it was time for Japan to concentrate on settling the China Incident and improving relations with the United States, even at the cost of postponing the southward program. The Imperial Conference decision of July 2, meanwhile, is summed up as follows:

Necessary diplomatic negotiations were to be continued while final preparations for the attack upon Singapore and Pearl Harbor were being completed and the Japanese forces were moving into position in southern French Indo-China and Thailand for the attack.[17]

Ambitious and aggressive though the decision of July 2 was, it did not say or mean, as the above quotation implies, that negotiations were to be used by Japan as a blind to gain time to prepare for the attack.

As would be expected, the Japanese move into southern Indo-China is interpreted as being carried out solely to secure bases for a drive southward. Moreover, any promise Japan made to

[15] *Ibid.*, 49498.   [16] *Ibid.*, 49500.   [17] *Ibid.*, 49502.

withdraw from this position, including that of November 20, was false and insincere.[18]

As for the Tripartite Pact, there was no weakening of Japanese allegiance to it during the third Konoye cabinet, but rather a policy of steadfast adherence.[19]

The Tribunal's portrayal of the split between Konoye and Tojo, which led to the fall of Konoye's government in mid-October, is particularly illuminating. In discussing the difference of opinion between the two leaders, the judgment says, "He [Konoye] tried to persuade Tojo to agree to an abandonment of the plans for the advance to the South and to concentration of Japan's efforts on settlement of the China war."[20] Inasmuch as the whole issue between Konoye and Tojo was not at all the prosecution of the southern advance versus concentration on the China Incident, but rather the question of withdrawal of troops from China, the passage quoted evades the issue and misrepresents the situation. Still worse is the Tribunal's summary of Konoye's letter of resignation to the Emperor, which, the judgment says, gives "a vivid explanation of the situation." The letter is summarized by the Tribunal as follows:

He [Konoye] explained that, when he organized the Third Konoye Cabinet to prosecute the expansion to the South, it was his firm conviction that his Cabinet's objective would be obtained through negotiations with the United States Government, and that although his expectations had not been realized to date he still believed that "If we take the attitude of yielding to her in appearance but keeping for us the substance and casting away the name," those objectives might be obtained through the negotiations.[21]

A more complete perversion of the Konoye letter and of his entire position can hardly be imagined. The whole letter is actually an explanation to the Emperor of Konoye's efforts to reach a negotiated settlement with the United States and thus

[18] *Ibid.*, 49515–49516.   [19] *Ibid.*, 49526–49527.
[20] *Ibid.*, 49532–49533.   [21] *Ibid.*, 49534.

avoid war—efforts which, Konoye claimed, had shattered on the refusal of the High Command to agree to further concessions on withdrawal of troops from China. The sentence quoted above, concerning yielding to the United States in form but retaining for Japan the substance, does not at all refer, as the Tribunal says, to the objective of prosecuting the southern advance, but simply and solely to the question of withdrawal of troops. The implication thus made by the Tribunal, that Tojo and Konoye were united in their determination to prosecute the southward advance and that they differed only on whether that advance was to be effected openly by war or in concealed fashion by diplomacy, is totally untrue. In the October crisis, the question of a southern advance was not at issue.

With such an interpretation of documents and issues, it is not surprising that the Tribunal should conclude that the whole process of Japanese negotiation was designed solely to deceive. A statement such as the one assented to by Tojo, conceding that Imperial policy "was on the one hand to negotiate for peace and on the other to prepare for war," [22] is interpreted as evidence that Japan throughout was prosecuting the plans of aggression conceived in September and October, 1940. The plain meaning and intent of Tojo's words, that Japan, while negotiating for peace, would also prepare for other eventualities (a self-evident policy for any government), is apparently ignored. Similarly, the Tribunal seems to concur in the American judgment that "Proposal B (the Japanese modus vivendi of November 20, 1941) was not sincere," because the Japanese troops removed from southern Indo-China could be moved back in again.[23]

Finally, for the argument that Japan was driven to fight by Allied economic pressure the Tribunal has only contempt. The argument, the judgment maintains, "is indeed merely a repetition of Japanese propaganda issued at the time she was preparing for her wars of aggression." The economic measures were

[22] *Ibid.*, 49538. [23] *Ibid.*, 49555.

entirely peaceful and legitimate measures of persuasion and self-defense; they were, to quote the Tribunal's words,

imposed in an attempt to induce Japan to depart from the aggressive policy on which she had determined, and in order that the Powers might no longer supply Japan with the materials to wage war upon them. In some cases, as for example the embargo on the export of oil . . . those measures were also taken in order to build up the supplies which were needed by the nations who were resisting the aggressors.[24]

It was inevitable that this view of the policies and events leading up to the Pacific war should also condition the judgment of the Tribunal on the war guilt of individual defendants. The unfortunate results may be seen best, though not alone, in the case of Shigenori Togo. In the writer's opinion, there can be no good reason for implicating Togo in a conspiracy to wage aggressive warfare against the United States, Great Britain, and other nations, even if one concedes (what is very doubtful) that such a conspiracy existed. He was a member of the peace party from first to last. Throughout his diplomatic career he opposed any course of militant expansionism for Japan. He was an opponent of the Tripartite Pact and on bad terms with Matsuoka. When he came into the Tojo cabinet as Foreign Minister in October 1941, he did so on the express condition that the decision of September 6 be reviewed and that every effort be made to reach an agreement with the United States, even at the cost of further concessions. He devoted his full energy and political influence as Foreign Minister to wresting the maximum possible concessions from the High Command on the question of troops in China. Though Proposal B was the best that he could gain, he personally would have been willing to go much farther in meeting the American demands. When the negotiations broke down, he accepted the decision for war very reluctantly and only because he could promise no hope of success in further negotia-

[24] *Ibid.*, 49582.

tions and could propose no way out of the alternative put by the military, that of Japan's fighting now or facing eventual economic strangulation. He did not resign, according to his own testimony, because to do so would have been a sign of disloyalty and an indication of disunity within the country at a time of great crisis. But his purpose in remaining as Foreign Minister was to work, if possible, for ending the war by diplomacy. He resigned in September 1942 in protest over Tojo's policy toward subject peoples in the Greater East Asia Co-Prosperity Sphere, returning to politics only in April 1945, when as Foreign Minister in Premier Suzuki's cabinet he worked strongly for peace.[25]

Most of the facts alleged by Togo in his defense were conceded or were not seriously challenged by the Tribunal. The judgment against him, however, reads as follows:

From the date of his first appointment (October 1941) until the outbreak of the Pacific War he participated in the planning and the preparing for the war. He attended Cabinet meetings and conferences and concurred in all decisions adopted.

As Foreign Minister he played a leading role in the negotiations with the United States immediately preceding the outbreak of the war and lent himself to the plans of the proponents of war. The duplicity employed in those negotiations has been dealt with earlier.

After the outbreak of the Pacific War he collaborated with other members of the Cabinet in its conduct as well as in the waging of the war in China.

To Togo's defense that he had worked steadfastly before the war to prevent it and after the war had begun to end it by di-

[25] Togo's case, which is supported by much other testimony and refuted by no evidence of which the writer is aware, is given in his deposition in the *IMTFE*, Record (see especially 35685–35694) and in his memoirs, entitled *The Cause of Japan*, translated and edited by Togo Fumihiko and Ben Bruce Blakeney (New York: Simon and Schuster, 1956). Needless to say, one can be convinced of Togo's innocence without agreeing with him on his interpretations, which seem to the writer to be marred at times by errors of fact and judgment.

plomacy, the Tribunal replied that he was insincere. Had he been sincere, the Tribunal said, he would have resigned in 1941, as he later did in 1942.[26] The sentence imposed upon Togo: imprisonment for twenty years.[27]

These comments on the International Military Tribunal for the Far East have not been written to suggest a general exoneration of Japan and the Japanese. There was doubtless war guilt enough, particularly in regard to China, and conventional war crimes committed during the course of the war in sufficient quantity. They do, however, suggest that the constitution of the Tribunal, the political situation, and the climate of opinion in the early postwar era combined to render a calm, balanced judgment of the issues impossible and, further, that the processes of history are too complex to be subjected to the adjudication of a military tribunal. The historian may find no difficulty in understanding why the war crimes trials were demanded and why, given the conditions of its existence and operation, the Tribunal reached the conclusions it did. He may, however, doubt that the conclusions represent any great advance in the development of international law and justice.

[26] *IMTFE*, Judgment, 49840–49841.

[27] *Ibid.*, 49857. Of the twenty-five defendants tried, all were found guilty. Of these, Mamoru Shigemitsu was given a seven-year term; the others (excluding Togo) were imprisoned for life or hanged. Justice Pal and Justice Henri Bernard of France voted for the acquittal of all defendants, while Justice Roling of the Netherlands would have acquitted Togo, Shigemitsu, Kido, Hirota, and General Shunroku Hata (*IMTFE*, Judgment and Opinions: Netherlands, 178–249; Horwitz, *Tokyo Trial*, 565–566).

Bibliography

PRIMARY SOURCES

Documents

Documents on German Foreign Policy, 1918–1945: From the Archives of the German Foreign Ministry. Ser. D, 9 vols. Washington: Government Printing Office, 1949–1956.

Fuehrer Conferences on Matters Dealing with the German Navy, 1939–1945. 7 vols. in 9. Washington: U.S. Navy Department, 1947.

Goodrich, Leland M., ed. *Documents on American Foreign Relations*. Vol. IV, 1941–1942. Boston: World Peace Foundation, 1942.

Hansard. *Parliamentary Debates, House of Commons*. 5th ser., vols. CCCLXXII–CCCLXXVI. London: H. M. Stationery Office, 1941.

International Military Tribunal for the Far East (Proceedings, Exhibits, Rejected Defense Documents, and Judgments and Opinions). Unpublished material, on microfilm and in mimeographed form, in the Library of Congress, Washington, D.C. The Proceedings were referred to as "Record" at the trial.

Jones, S. Shepard, and Denys P. Myers, eds. *Documents on American Foreign Relations*. Vol. III, 1940–1941. Boston: World Peace Foundation, 1941.

Judgment of the International Military Tribunal for the Far East. Tokyo, 1948.

Sontag, Raymond James, and James Stuart Beddie, eds. *Nazi-Soviet Relations, 1939–1941: Documents from the Archives of the German Foreign Office.* U.S. Department of State Pub. 3023. Washington: Government Printing Office, 1948.

Toynbee, Arnold J., ed. *Documents on International Affairs, 1939–1946.* 3 vols. London: Oxford University Press, 1951.

Trial of the Major War Criminals at the International Military Tribunal (Official Documents, Proceedings, and Documents in Evidence). 42 vols. Nuremberg, 1948.

United States Congress. *The Congressional Record.* 77th Congress, 1st Session, Jan.–Dec., 1941, vol. LXXXVII, pts. 1–14. Washington: Government Printing Office, 1941.

——. *Hearings of the Joint Committee on the Investigation of the Pearl Harbor Attack.* 39 vols. Washington: Government Printing Office, 1946.

——. *Report of the Joint Committee on the Investigation of the Pearl Harbor Attack.* Senate Document no. 244, 79th Congress, 2d Session. Washington: Government Printing Office, 1946.

United States Department of State. *Bulletin,* vol. V, no. 129 (Dec. 13, 1941).

——. *Foreign Relations of the United States, Diplomatic Papers: 1939.* Vol. IV, *The Far East, the Near East, and Africa.* Washington: Government Printing Office, 1955.

——. *Foreign Relations of the United States, Diplomatic Papers: 1940.* Vol. IV, *The Far East.* Washington: Government Printing Office, 1955.

——. *Foreign Relations of the United States, Diplomatic Papers: 1941.* Vol. IV, *The Far East.* Washington: Government Printing Office, 1956.

——. *Papers Relating to the Foreign Relations of the United States, Japan: 1931–1941.* 2 vols. Washington: Government Printing Office, 1943.

——. *Peace and War: United States Foreign Policy, 1931–1941.* Washington: Government Printing Office, 1943.

——. *United States Relations with China, with Special Reference to the Period 1944–1949.* Washington: Government Printing Office, 1949.

Books and Articles

Bisson, Thomas Arthur. "Call Japan's Bluff!" *New Republic*, CV, no. 18 (Nov. 3, 1941), 579–581.

——. "Facing Facts about a Far Eastern Peace Settlement," *Asia*, XL, no. 1 (Jan. 1940), 40–45.

——. "Towards Winning Far Eastern Security," *Amerasia*, V, no. 8 (Oct. 1941), 344–348.

Brandt, William. "Hitler's Doom and Japan's Destiny," *Amerasia*, V, no. 9 (Nov. 1941), 377–80.

Churchill, Sir Winston L. S. *The Second World War*. 6 vols. Boston: Houghton Mifflin Co., 1948–1953. Vol. III, *The Grand Alliance;* vol. IV, *The Hinge of Fate*.

——. *The War Speeches of Winston S. Churchill, 1939–1945*. Compiled by Charles Eade. 3 vols. London: Cassell and Co., 1952.

Clyde, Paul H. "Our Concern for the Integrity of China," *Annals of the American Academy of Political and Social Science*, CCXV (May 1941), 66–73.

Colegrove, Kenneth. "The New Order in East Asia," *Far Eastern Quarterly*, I, no. 1 (Nov. 1941), 5–24.

Craigie, Sir Robert. *Behind the Japanese Mask*. London: Hutchinson and Co., 1946.

Cripps, Sir Stafford. "To Save Democracy in China," *Asia*, XL, no. 9 (Sept. 1940), 459–463.

Dirksen, Herbert von. *Moscow, Tokyo, London: Twenty Years of German Foreign Policy*. London: Hutchinson and Co., 1951.

Fisher, Galen M. "Main Drive behind Japanese National Policies," *Pacific Affairs*, XIII, no. 3 (Sept. 1940), 381–392.

Go, Toshi. "Japanese Attitudes toward America," *Annals of the American Academy of Political and Social Science*, CCXV (May 1941), 166–170.

Green, O. M. "Japan's Sixth War Cabinet," *Great Britain and the Far East*, LVII, no. 1574 (July 24, 1941), 52.

Grew, Joseph C. *Ten Years in Japan: A Contemporary Record Drawn from the Diaries and Private and Official Papers of Joseph C. Grew, United States Ambassador to Japan, 1932–1942*. New York: Simon and Schuster, 1944.

Grew, Joseph C. *Turbulent Era: A Diplomatic Record of Forty Years, 1904–1945.* Edited by Walter Johnson. 2 vols. Boston: Houghton Mifflin Co., 1952.

Griswold, A. Whitney. "European Factors in Far Eastern Diplomacy," *Foreign Affairs,* XIV, no. 2 (Jan. 1941), 297–309.

——. "Should Japan Be Embargoed?" *Asia,* XL, no. 2 (Feb. 1940), 91–96.

Howard, Harry Paxton. "Japan as an Ally," *Amerasia,* V, no. 2 (April 1941), 66–78.

Howe, William Stuart. "Japan Awaits Her Cue," *Current Events,* n.s., I, no. 1 (Sept. 1941), 66–75.

Hull, Cordell. *Memoirs.* 2 vols. New York: Macmillan Co., 1948.

——. "The United States and the World Situation," *U.S. Department of State Bulletin,* IV, no. 96 (April 26, 1941), 491–494.

Jaffe, Philip J. "Can Tokyo Follow Berlin's Lead?" *Amerasia,* V, no. 5 (July 1941), 191–197.

"Japan on the Verge," *Spectator,* CLXVII, no. 5917 (Nov. 21, 1941), 1179–1180.

Kase, Toshikazu. *Journey to the "Missouri."* Edited by David Nelson Rowe. New Haven: Yale University Press, 1950.

Kuh, Frederick. "America Talks to Japan," *New Statesman and Nation,* XXII, no. 552 (Sept. 20, 1941), 272–273.

Latourette, Kenneth Scott. "A Church-made War with Japan?" *Christian Century,* LVII, no. 5 (Jan. 31, 1940), 140–142.

Lattimore, Owen. "After Four Years," *Pacific Affairs,* XIV, no. 2 (June 1941), 141–153.

——. "American Responsibilities in the Far East," *Virginia Quarterly Review,* XVI, no. 2 (spring 1940), 161–175.

Leahy, Admiral William D. *I Was There: The Personal Story of the Chief of Staff to Presidents Roosevelt and Truman.* New York: McGraw-Hill Book Co., 1950.

Masland, John W. "American Attitudes toward Japan," *Annals of the American Academy of Political and Social Science,* CCXV (May 1941), 160–165.

Peffer, Nathaniel. "Squeeze Japan Now!" *Nation,* CLIII, no. 5 (Aug. 2, 1941), 87–89.

Roosevelt, Elliott. *As He Saw It.* New York: Duell, Sloan, and Pearce, 1946.

Roosevelt, Franklin Delano. *F.D.R.: His Personal Letters, 1928–1945.* Edited by Elliott Roosevelt. 4 vols. New York: Duell, Sloan, and Pearce, 1947–1950.

——. *The Public Papers and Addresses of Franklin D. Roosevelt.* Compiled by Samuel I. Rosenman. 13 vols. New York: Random House, 1938–1950.

Smith, Robert Aura. "The Triple-Axis Pact and American Reactions," *Annals of the American Academy of Political and Social Science*, CCXV (May 1941), 127–132.

Staley, Eugene. "Let Japan Choose," *Foreign Affairs*, XX, no. 1 (Oct. 1941), 61–72.

Sternberg, Fritz. "Japan's Weakness in Nazi Eyes," *Asia*, XL, no. 2 (Feb. 1940), 100–103.

Stimson, Henry L. *The Far Eastern Crisis: Recollections and Observations.* 3d ed. New York: Harper and Bros., 1938.

Stimson, Henry L., and McGeorge Bundy. *On Active Service in Peace and War.* New York: Harper and Bros., 1948.

Taylor, George E. "America's Pacific Policy: The Role and the Record," *Pacific Affairs*, XIV, no. 4 (Dec. 1941), 430–447.

Togo, Shigenori. *The Cause of Japan.* Translated and edited by Togo Fumihiko and Ben Bruce Blakeney. New York: Simon and Schuster, 1956.

Utley, Freda. "The Far East in World Trends," *Asia*, XLI, no. 10 (Oct. 1941), 569–572.

——. "Japan's Great Bluff," *Nation*, CLI, no. 15 (Oct. 12, 1940), 320–322.

Van Mook, Hubertus J. *The Netherlands Indies and Japan: Battle on Paper.* New York: W. W. Norton and Co., 1944.

Weiszaecker, Ernst von. *Erinnerungen.* Munich: Paul List, 1950.

Welles, Sumner. *The Time for Decision.* New York: Harper and Bros., 1944.

White, Theodore H. "Party Friction in Chungking," *Asia*, XL, no. 8 (Aug. 1940), 409–414.

Young, James R. "Japan's Dilemma," *Amerasia*, V, no. 6 (Aug. 1941), 245–249.

Newspapers

Chicago Tribune, 1941.   Japan Chronicle (Kobe), 1941.
Christian Science Monitor, 1941.   New York Herald-Tribune,
Dallas Morning News, 1940–1941.   1941.
Deutsche Allgemeine Zeitung   New York Times, 1939–1942.
  (Berlin), 1941.   St. Louis Post-Dispatch, 1941.
Frankfurter Zeitung, 1941.   The Times (London), 1941.

SECONDARY WORKS [1]

Bailey, Thomas A. *A Diplomatic History of the American People.*
4th ed. New York: Appleton-Century-Crofts, 1950.
——. *The Man in the Street: The Impact of American Public Opin-
ion on Foreign Policy.* New York: Macmillan Co., 1948.
Ballantine, Joseph W. "Mukden to Pearl Harbor," *Foreign Affairs,*
XXVII, no. 4 (July 1949), 651–654.
Beard, Charles A. *American Foreign Policy in the Making, 1932–
1940: A Study in Responsibilities.* New Haven: Yale University
Press, 1946.
——. *President Roosevelt and the Coming of the War, 1941: A Study
in Appearances and Realities.* New Haven: Yale University Press,
1948.
Bemis, Samuel F. *The United States as a World Power: A Diplo-
matic History, 1900–1950.* New York: Henry Holt & Co., 1951.
Bisson, Thomas Arthur. *Shadow over Asia: The Rise of Militant
Japan.* New York: Foreign Policy Association, 1941.
Chamberlin, William Henry. *Japan in China.* London: Gerald Duck-
worth & Co., 1940.
Christopher, James W. *Conflict in the Far East: American Diplo-
macy in China from 1928–1933.* Leiden: E. J. Brill, 1950.
Clyde, Paul H. *The Far East: A History of the Impact of the West
on Eastern Asia.* 2d ed. New York: Prentice-Hall, Inc., 1952.
Current, Richard N. *Secretary Stimson: A Study in Statecraft.* New
Brunswick: Rutgers University Press, 1954.

[1] Frank W. Iklé's study, *German-Japanese Relations, 1936–1940* (New
York: Bookman Associates, 1956), was unfortunately encountered too
late to be used in the preparation of the present book.

Davis, Forrest, and Ernest K. Lindley. *How War Came: An American White Paper, from the Fall of France to Pearl Harbor.* New York: Simon and Schuster, 1942.

Feis, Herbert. *The China Tangle: The American Effort in China from Pearl Harbor to the Marshall Mission.* Princeton: Princeton University Press, 1953.

——. *The Road to Pearl Harbor: The Coming of the War between the United States and Japan.* Princeton: Princeton University Press, 1950.

Griswold, A. Whitney. *The Far Eastern Policy of the United States.* New York: Harcourt, Brace and Co., 1938.

Haushofer, Karl. *Japan baut sein Reich.* Berlin: Zeitgeschichteverlag, 1941.

Hill, Norman L. "Was There an Ultimatum before Pearl Harbor?" *American Journal of International Law,* XLII (April 1948), 355–367.

Hishida, Seiji. *Japan among the Great Powers: A Survey of Her International Relations.* London: Longmans, Green & Co., 1940.

Hornbeck, Stanley K. *The United States and the Far East: Certain Fundamentals of Policy.* Boston: World Peace Foundation, 1942.

Horwitz, Solis. *The Tokyo Trial.* International Conciliation series, no. 465. New York: Carnegie Endowment for International Peace, 1950.

Johnstone, William Crane. *The United States and Japan's New Order.* London: Oxford University Press, 1941.

Jones, F. C. *Japan's New Order in East Asia: Its Rise and Fall, 1937–1945.* London: Oxford University Press, 1954.

Kawai, Tatsuo. *The Goal of Japanese Expansion.* Tokyo: Hokuseido Press, 1938.

Kennan, George F. *American Diplomacy, 1900–1950.* Chicago: University of Chicago Press, 1951.

Kordt, Erich. *Wahn und Wirklichkeit: Die Aussenpolitik des Dritten Reiches; Versuch einer Darstellung.* Stuttgart: Union Deutsche Verlagsgesellschaft, 1948.

Langer, William L., and S. Everett Gleason. *The Undeclared War, 1940–1941.* New York: Harper and Bros., 1953.

Levi, Werner. *Modern China's Foreign Policy.* Minneapolis: University of Minnesota Press, 1953.

MacNair, Harley Farnsworth, and Donald F. Lach. *Modern Far Eastern International Relations*. New York: D. Van Nostrand Co., 1950.

McNeill, William Hardy. *America, Britain, and Russia—Their Co-operation and Conflict, 1941–1946*. Vol. III of *Survey of International Affairs, 1939–1946*. Edited by Arnold J. Toynbee. 3 vols. London: Oxford University Press, 1953.

Matsuo, Kinoaki. *How Japan Plans to Win*. Translated by Kilsoo K. Haan. Boston: Little, Brown, and Co., 1942.

Miles, Sherman. "Pearl Harbor in Retrospect," *Atlantic Monthly*, CLXXXII, no. 1 (July 1948), 65–72.

Millis, Walter. *This Is Pearl! The United States and Japan—1941*. New York: William Morrow and Co., 1947.

Moore, Frederick. *With Japan's Leaders: An Intimate Record of Fourteen Years as Counsellor to the Japanese Government, Ending December 7, 1941*. New York: Charles Scribner's Sons, 1942.

Moore, Harriet L. *Soviet Far Eastern Policy, 1931–1945*. Princeton: Princeton University Press, 1945.

Morgenstern, George E. *Pearl Harbor: The Story of the Secret War*. New York: Devin-Adair Co., 1947.

Morgenthau, Hans J. *In Defense of the National Interest: A Critical Examination of American Foreign Policy*. New York: Alfred A. Knopf, 1951.

Orton, William Aylett. *The Liberal Tradition: A Study of the Social and Spiritual Conditions of Freedom*. New Haven: Yale University Press, 1945.

Osgood, Robert E. *Ideals and Self-Interest in America's Foreign Relations: The Great Transformation of the Twentieth Century*. Chicago: University of Chicago Press, 1953.

Pal, Radhabinod. *International Military Tribunal for the Far East: Dissentient Judgment*. Calcutta: Sanyal and Co., 1953.

Quigley, Harold S. *Far Eastern War, 1937–1941*. Boston: World Peace Foundation, 1942.

Rauch, Basil. *Roosevelt, from Munich to Pearl Harbor: A Study in the Creation of a Foreign Policy*. New York: Creative Age Press, 1950.

Reischauer, Edwin O. *The United States and Japan*. Cambridge, Mass.: Harvard University Press, 1950.

Reynolds, Quentin. *Only the Stars Are Neutral.* New York: Random House, 1942.

Sherwood, Robert E. *Roosevelt and Hopkins: An Intimate History.* New York: Harper and Bros., 1948.

Snell, John L., Forrest C. Pogue, Charles F. Delzell, and George F. Lensen. *The Meaning of Yalta: Big Three Diplomacy and the New Balance of Power.* Baton Rouge: Louisiana State University Press, 1956.

Spykman, Nicholas J. *America's Strategy in World Politics: The United States and the Balance of Power.* New York: Harcourt, Brace and Co., 1942.

Swearingen, Rodger, and Paul Langer. *Red Flag in Japan: International Communism in Action, 1919–1951.* Cambridge, Mass.: Harvard University Press, 1952.

Tansill, Charles Callan. *Back Door to War: The Roosevelt Foreign Policy, 1933–1941.* Chicago: Henry Regnery Co., 1952.

Theobald, Rear Admiral Robert A. *The Final Secret of Pearl Harbor: The Washington Contribution to the Japanese Attack.* New York: Devin-Adair Co., 1954.

Tolischus, Otto D. *Through Japanese Eyes.* New York: Reynal and Hitchcock, 1945.

Trefousse, Hans L. *Germany and American Neutrality, 1939–1941.* New York: Bookman Associates, 1951.

Willoughby, Westel W. *Japan's Case Examined.* Baltimore: Johns Hopkins University Press, 1940.

Wiskemann, Elizabeth. *The Rome-Berlin Axis: A History of the Relations between Hitler and Mussolini.* London: Oxford University Press, 1949.

Yanaga, Chitoshi. *Japan since Perry.* New York: McGraw-Hill Book Co., 1949.

Index

238

*Recent books published for the American Historical Association
from the income of the Albert J. Beveridge Memorial Fund*

THE AGRICULTURAL HISTORY OF THE GENESEE VALLEY.
By Neil A. McNall.

STEAM POWER ON THE AMERICAN FARM. *By Reynold M. Wik.*

HORACE GREELEY: NINETEENTH-CENTURY CRUSADER.
By Glyndon G. Van Deusen.

ERA OF THE OATH: NORTHERN LOYALTY TESTS DURING THE
CIVIL WAR AND RECONSTRUCTION. *By Harold M. Hyman.*

HISTORY OF MARSHALL FIELD & Co. *By Robert W. Twyman.*

ROBERT MORRIS: REVOLUTIONARY FINANCIER.
By Clarence L. Ver Steeg.

A HISTORY OF THE FREEDMEN'S BUREAU. *By George R. Bentley.*

THE FIRST RAPPROCHEMENT: ENGLAND AND THE
UNITED STATES, 1795–1805. *By Bradford Perkins.*

MIDDLE-CLASS DEMOCRACY AND THE REVOLUTION IN MASSACHUSETTS,
1691–1780. *By Robert E. Brown.*

THE DEVELOPMENT OF THE AMERICAN PETROLEUM PIPELINES:
A STUDY IN PRIVATE ENTERPRISE AND PUBLIC POLICY, 1862–1906.
By Arthur Menzies Johnson.

COLONISTS FROM SCOTLAND: EMIGRATION TO NORTH AMERICA,
1707–1783. *By Ian Charles Cargill Graham.*

PROFESSORS AND PUBLIC ETHICS: STUDIES OF NORTHERN MORAL
PHILOSOPHERS BEFORE THE CIVIL WAR. *By Wilson Smith.*

THE AXIS ALLIANCE AND JAPANESE-AMERICAN RELATIONS, 1941.
By Paul W. Schroeder.